The Catholic Church Through the Ages

A History

John Vidmar, OP

Paulist Press
New York/Mahwah, N.J.

Photo Credits:

St. Peter called by Christ to be fisher of people; Damascus with Roman city wall; Emperor Constantine; St. Augustine of Hippo; The Baptism of Clovis; San Vitale Church, Ravenna; Iona, where St. Columba built his monastery; Christ with Pepin the Short, Charlemagne and his sons; Mohammad's tomb; Cover of the Hildesheim Gospels; St. Dominic; Christ leading a crusade; façade of the mosque in Cordova; Francis of Assisi; Frontispiece of Bartolomé de las Casas, *Narratio Regionum Indicarum*; Martyrdom of St. Isaac Jogues, SJ, and companions; Pope Leo XIII; Vatican II are from Anton Freitag, SVD, *The Twentieth Century Atlas of the Christian World* (New York: Hawthorn Books, Inc., 1963).

Map of Jerusalem in the time of Jesus; Roman ship of the type St. Paul journeyed in are from Harry T. Frank, *Discovering the Biblical World* (Maplewood, NJ: Hammond, 1975).

Sts. Ignatius of Antioch; Perpetua and Felicity; Athanasius; Ignatius Loyola are from Vincent Cronin, *A Calendar of Saints* (Westminster, MD: Newman Press, 1963).

Sts. Gregory Nazianzen; Catherine of Siena; Teresa of Jesus; Thomas More; John Fisher; Frances Xavier Cabrini are from Wilhelm Schamoni, *The Face of the Saints* (New York: Pantheon, 1947).

The Seeress by Mother Placid Dempsey, OSB, from Hildegard of Bingen, *Scivias*, transl. Mother Columba Hart and Jane Bishop, Classics of Western Spirituality Series (Mahwah, NJ: Paulist Press, 1990).

Martin Luther from a painting in Rydboholms Kyrka, Sweden; photograph by Nancy de Flon, © 1996.

Photo of St. Katharine Drexel courtesy of the Sisters of the Blessed Sacrament, Bensalem, PA.

Photo of Dorothy Day courtesy of the Marquette University Archives.

Photo of Henriette Delille courtesy of Sisters of the Holy Family, New Orleans, LA.

Maps of Eastern Monasticism and Western Monasticism from Jean Daniélou and Henri Marrou, trans. Vincent Cronin, *The Christian Centuries*, vol. 1, *The First Six Hundred Years* (London: Darton, Longman and Todd; New York and Paramus: Paulist Press), 1964.

The Scripture quotations contained herein are from the New Revised Standard Version: Catholic Edition Copyright © 1989 and 1993, by the Division of Christian Education of the National Council of the Churches of Christ in the United States of America. Used by permission. All rights reserved.

Cover design by Sharyn Banks
Book design by Lynn Else

Library of Congress Cataloging-in-Publication Data

Vidmar, John.
    The Catholic Church through the ages : a history / John Vidmar.
       p. cm.
    Includes bibliographical references (p.   ) and index.
    ISBN 0-8091-4234-1 (alk. paper)
    1. Catholic Church—History. I. Title.

BX945.3.V53 2005
282′.09   dc22

                                                                    2005005976

Published by Paulist Press
997 Macarthur Boulevard
Mahwah, New Jersey 07430

www.paulistpress.com

Printed and bound in the United States of America

CONTENTS

Contents

Contents

To the students and staff of the
Education for Parish Service Program
in Virginia and Washington, DC,
in gratitude for your love of the Church,
and for continually asking me
when this book would get done.

INTRODUCTION

After several years of teaching adults, I have seen the need for a one-volume history of the Catholic Church that combines substance with readability. This is not an easy balance to achieve, and the majority of historians seem to err on one side or the other. One tendency is to include so much detail that the reader gives up early on. The opposite tendency is to have a breezy approach, loosely combining broad topics. Historians do not have an easy time of it, no matter how hard they try. Once, on the Fourth of July, which happened to occur on the Sunday on which I was preaching, I decided to talk about the state of the Catholic Church in the Thirteen Colonies at the time of the American Revolution, thinking I would be conveying interesting and helpful information on a topic that was both little known and important. When the Mass ended, as I stood outside to greet the congregation as they left the church, the very first person who came out was a woman in her late forties who did not take my hand, but walked past me with her nose in the air and said, "The hungry sheep were not fed today." This book, while striving to be comprehensive, will serve as an outline—an introduction—to the history of the Catholic Church. As a supplement to each chapter, I have included an annotated list of readings and audio-visuals at the end of the chapter. These readings have been carefully chosen for their readability and accuracy. I have even included historical novels, which can be an immense aid in conveying a "feeling" for an age. The readings are rated according to difficulty. Endnotes may also help the reader to peruse supplemental material.

One question that always arises is how to divide the material. I have found that the most convenient solution is to follow Christopher Dawson's division into six distinct ages. Dawson, a twentieth-century English Catholic historian, thought church history was best divided in this way because each age—a period of between three and four hundred years—shows a remarkably similar cycle of growth and decay. There is an initial period when the church is faced with a new historical situation frequently caused by crisis. Some adaptation is made to the new situation and a new apostolate is begun. A middle period sees a flourishing of this apostolate, producing new cultural forms and more developed expressions of faith. A final period finds the church in retreat, attacked by new enemies from within or without, and the achievements are either lost or lessened, and a new period begins. This pattern has been consistent for 2,000 years of Christian history.

Church history is the record of the Christian family and is one of the most vital and interesting subjects we can study. And we should study it carefully. It is, very simply, the story of our church. And our church, as the German theologian Walter Kasper tells us, is no more than Christianity taking on flesh and blood.[1] Our faith depends entirely on that story and makes no sense without it. Cardinal John Henry Newman saw the church as "a standing Apostolic Committee—to answer questions, which the Apostles are not here to answer, concerning what they received and preached."[2]

I do not intend to prove the truth of Catholicism in this book, or who was right and who was wrong. I only want to tell what happened and want the person who reads it to know the story of Catholicism a little better—why we do the things we do, why we believe the things we believe, and thereby to know and appreciate those things a little more. I hope that, after reading this book, the hungry sheep will be better fed.

Notes

1. Walter Kasper, *Jesus the Christ* (New York, 1976), p. 27.
2. John Henry Newman, Letter to R. H. Hutton, 20 October 1871, in *The Letters and Diaries of John Henry Newman*, Vol. XXV (Oxford, 1999), p. 418.

THE FIRST AGE OF THE CHURCH (30–330 AD)

The Early Church

Two things are very important to remember about the early Christian Church: a) it did not suddenly appear out of nowhere and b) it was not given to the world whole and entire. We will examine the first of these statements in this chapter and the second of them in the next. The church was born into a world that was both Jewish and Greek, and borrowed heavily from both sources even though they were highly different from one another and often violently opposed to each other. Both of these sources influenced the church so strongly that their effects can still be seen today.

Jewish Sources of Christianity

The Jewish religion was (and still is) a historical religion. This means that the God of the Jews intervened in history and had personally directed the life of the Israelite nation in recognizable and recordable ways. This is easy to tell from the writings of the Jews, which we know as the Hebrew Scriptures or, more commonly, the Old Testament. The Old Testament is not one book, but a collection of many different books, and many different kinds of books: We find history books there, as well as books of poetry, fiction, mythology, law, and prophecy. The Old Testament, in short, is a small library. But it is the history on which I wish to focus, because the emphasis on history was unique to the Jews and would give shape to the early Christian Church.

The drama of the Jewish people began with Abraham, a figure who evokes a misty past—remote and unknown—but who is

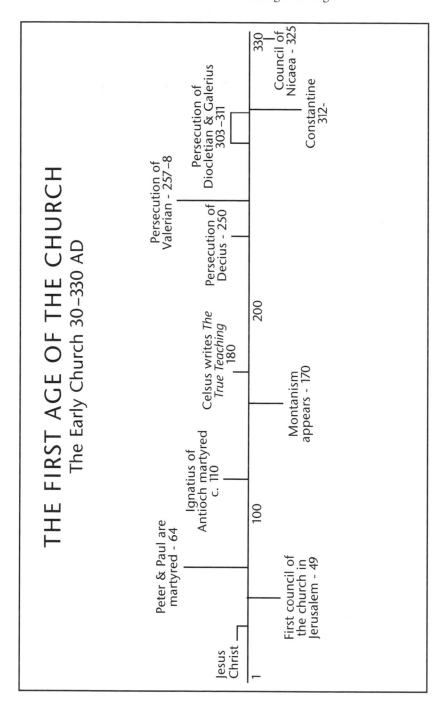

THE FIRST AGE OF THE CHURCH
The Early Church 30–330 AD

Jesus Christ

First council of the church in Jerusalem - 49

Peter & Paul are martyred - 64

1

100

Ignatius of Antioch martyred c. 110

Montanism appears - 170

Celsus writes *The True Teaching* 180

200

Persecution of Decius - 250

Persecution of Valerian - 257–8

Persecution of Diocletian & Galerius 303–311

Constantine 312-

330

Council of Nicaea - 325

closer in time to Jesus Christ than we are ourselves. It was about 1850 BC when Abraham was called by God to leave the land of Ur of the Chaldeans (modern-day Iraq) and settle in Canaan, a land later to be known as the Promised Land, or Israel. Abraham had a son Isaac, who had, in turn, a son named Jacob.[1] Jacob then had twelve sons who became the patriarchs of the twelve great families, or twelve tribes, of Israel. In the midst of a great famine (c. 1700 BC) these twelve tribes made their way to Egypt and, for the first time, began to be identified as Hebrews, or Jews. Over the centuries these Jews became a subject race. They found their condition so intolerable that they considered returning en masse to their former homeland in Canaan, a land they had heard was now flowing with milk and honey. Moses emerged as their leader (c. 1000 BC) and persistently asked the Pharaoh to "let my people go." Pharaoh's reluctance resulted in ten successive plagues, the last of which was the famous Passover, when all the firstborn males (both human and animal) were put to death—all except those of Jewish families who had eaten a prescribed meal and had sprinkled the blood of the lamb on their doorpost (Exodus 12). This meal became ritualized in succeeding years and was celebrated as a memorial of God's goodness. To this day it is the keystone of Jewish worship.

This tenth plague convinced Pharaoh to allow the Jews to leave, but he changed his mind and sent his army to bring them back. There ensued the famous "dividing of the Red Sea," which destroyed Pharaoh's army. Having disposed of one enemy, however, did not guarantee the Jews an easy trip to Canaan. It is likely that the most direct route—along the Mediterranean coast—was blocked by a settlement of hostile and powerful Philistines, so the Jews headed south into the desert and wandered there for forty years before finally reaching their goal. Once at the Jordan River, Joshua led them over and began the conquest of Palestine, beginning with the stronghold of Jericho. David became Israel's greatest king and completed the conquest.

These are the central historical events of the Jewish religion, but they are not the only things that make Judaism unique. A second trait would be the Jewish insistence on *one* God. Neither the mystery cults of the east nor the worshippers of the gods in the west had ever approached this claim, nor the claim that this God was both personal (i.e., not a thing like the sun or a statue) and transcendent (i.e., he was not of this world). As a result of God's intervention in their history and the uniqueness of their beliefs, the Jews were insistent that they were the Chosen People and the chosen interpreters of God's word. It was an elitism that would annoy various Roman administrations and result in several clashes with the authorities. What exasperated the Romans so much was not the religion as such, for the Romans were relatively tolerant of other religions, but the independence and exclusivity of the Jewish people. No people conquered by the Romans was so unwilling to compromise their religion as the Jews. Frequent rebellions drew savage reprisals from the Romans—as in the destruction of Jerusalem by the Emperor Titus in 70 AD or in the siege of Masada (73 AD).

Harassment was nothing new to the Jews, who were in many ways the doormat of the Near East—a minor nation on a major trade route, much like modern Poland in between Germany and Russia. This meant that Israel was always being eclipsed by one of the nearby powers, be it Egypt, Babylon, Assyria, Greece, or Rome. As a result of this rather constant harassment and warfare, the Jews began a slow and prolonged emigration about the year 700 BC. This is known as the *Diaspora* or Dispersion. The Babylonians hastened this Dispersion by conquering both Jewish kingdoms about 600 BC, destroying the leadership and carrying away much of the population in the process. By the time Christ was born, Jews could be found in most of the major cities in the world, a fact that was to be crucial to the spread of Christianity.

Finally, partly because of the instability of their situation, Jews were known for their adaptability, a trait in seeming contradiction to their fierce independence, but one on which their survival as a people depended. They could live in any city, in any culture, and thrive. All of these traits—insistence on history, monotheism, independence, adaptability—would be inherited by the Christian Church, as we shall later see.

Roman Sources of Christianity

The Roman Empire was at its material peak when Christ was born. This empire, which had recently flourished and expanded under Julius Caesar (d. 44 BC), was reaping a bountiful economic harvest under the *Pax Romana* (Roman Peace) of Augustus Caesar (who ruled from 27 BC to 14 AD),[2] and was about to experience further prosperity under Tiberius Caesar (14–37 AD). Rome controlled the entire Mediterranean basin, and would shortly control Europe as far north as Scotland, and Asia as far east as Persia (modern-day Iran)—all under one ruler and one (or two) languages, Greek in the east and Latin in the west.

The Roman genius was for organization—both civil and military—and for technology. A great network of roads had been constructed by the Romans, which connected all parts of the Empire and established a speed in communications previously unknown. A system of aqueducts, whose method of construction still amazes scientists today, was built in several cities to ensure the health and stability of their inhabitants.[3] What Rome did not invent, it borrowed or stole. While the Coliseum in Rome was innovative, most of Rome's architecture simply copied Greek originals. Greece, after all, had surpassed Rome in cultural achievements—literature, art, and philosophy—and Rome had the wisdom to borrow these elements wholesale. Thus Virgil's *Aeneid*, while a great literary work in its own right, Romanizes a Greek story written by Homer centuries before. Rome also had a fascination for the unusual, and this also was satisfied by the theft of valuable objects from foreign lands. These objects were brought back to Rome, often at great trouble, for the purpose of display or amusement.[4] Wild animals from Africa were used in the various arenas for combat against other animals or gladiators. Occasionally, fierce-looking barbarians, who were regarded as the equivalent of wild animals, were employed in similar combat. Obelisks and even an entire pyramid were rebuilt on Roman ground as trophies of far-reaching conquest, and can still be seen today. Triumphal arches and columns provided the details of these conquests in stone.

These two sources—Jewish and Roman—unwittingly joined together to provide a home and means of expansion for the newly

Model of the Temple in Jerusalem

founded Christian Church. Herbert Butterfield claims that Christianity could not have come along at a more opportune time:

> We may wonder whether there can ever have been so remarkable a conjunction of planets as at that point in the world's history when in the fullness of time Christianity profited from the meeting of the Jewish religion, Greek philosophy, and the Roman Empire. Not only did the virtues of those systems prove to be a benefit to the Gospel, but also their defects—Jewish legalism, the decadent state of Greek philosophy, and the frustrations and nostalgias of the imperial Roman world. Christianity emerged in the latter part of a period of many centuries which in Europe and Asia form a turning-point in the history of man's religious consciousness; and it is a remarkable fact that it made its appearance, and its implications were first developed, in a highly civilized world which had achieved an advanced form of urban life and had brought the human intellect to a refinement and subtlety never exceeded since.[5]

Influence of Jewish and Roman Sources on Christianity

The early church was thoroughly Jewish. Jesus Christ was a Jew; his apostles and first followers were all Jews. The writers of the entire New Testament (with the possible exception of Luke) were Jews. Christianity began in Jerusalem, the capital of Judaism, and spread from that city. The church regarded itself as the New Israel, and called Christ the New Law, the New Adam, the New Moses, the Son of David. Matthew's version of the Gospel cites the Old Testament forty-one times, and usually adds the statement, "that it might be fulfilled." So strong is this Christian connection to the Old Testament that Christ would make no sense without it.

The early Christians regarded everything that happened in the Old Testament as a prefigurement of what was to come in the New, a hint of what was to be fulfilled, a shadow that was to become a reality with Christ. Thus, someone like Adam is important because he makes the coming of Christ necessary. An ancient Easter hymn proclaims, "Oh Happy fault, Oh necessary sin of

Adam, which gained for us so great a Redeemer." Paintings on catacomb walls connect baptism to Noah's Flood or to the incident where Moses drew water from the rock. The Eucharistic meal has a distinctly Jewish flavor to it, from the various elements of wine and unleavened bread to the various blessings over these elements. Mary was the New Eve. And on and on it goes.

The early church, in other words, was unashamedly Jewish. So it should be no surprise that the church inherited certain Jewish qualities of exclusivity and assimilation. This was its spiritual ancestry, a heritage not lost on a twentieth-century pope, Pius XI, who announced in the face of Hitler's Aryan super race in 1936, "Spiritually, we are all Semites."

Judaism also served to house the embryonic Christian communities. It is thought that between five and six million Jews lived outside Israel, and Jewish communities existed in almost every city of any size. Some of these communities were substantial, comprising ten to fifteen percent of the population. One estimate suggests that Alexandria boasted as many as one million Jews. It was to these Jewish communities that the first Christian preachers addressed their message. Temples and synagogues seem to have been the starting point for proselytizing. Christ himself preached in the Temple in Jerusalem, and Paul is pictured by the Acts of the Apostles opening missions in several urban synagogues.[6] Every town on Paul's missionary journeys—Galatia, Thessalonika, Ephesus, Corinth, among others—had Jewish communities which became the shelter and starting point for Paul's message. These communities provided a stable environment for Christianity to grow and, by the time Judaism and Christianity went their separate ways (certainly by 70 AD, when Jerusalem was destroyed), Christianity was settled and self-sufficient.

Nor was Judaism alone in contributing to the expansion of Christianity. Rome had created an atmosphere in which missionary activity flourished. Normally, Rome was distrustful of new religions, but it was fairly tolerant of older established ones, including Judaism, and it mistook this initial Christian activity as being a peculiarly Jewish phenomenon. The Roman government did not harass the Christians in any widespread or systematic way until the year 250, which allowed the Christians a full two cen-

Roman ship of the type St. Paul journeyed in. "Three times I was ship-wrecked; for a night and a day I was adrift at sea...." (2 Corinthians 11:25)

turies to consolidate their advances. The unity of the Roman Empire also aided the missionary effort. The road system provided a safe and easy mode of transportation for missionaries, and the Greek language served as a universal vehicle for proselytization.

Even more importantly, Rome hungered for a spiritual revival. Rome, it has been said, possessed the body of the Mediterranean world, and Greece the soul. Rome's borrowing of Greek religion—in many ways simply translating the names of Greek gods into Latin—did not satisfy. Rome simply ceased to believe in these gods and they became mere ornaments. The vacuum created by this deterioration came precisely at the time Christianity was making its appearance—and it was a vacuum which Christianity was particularly anxious and well-suited to fill.

Christian Sources

Christianity did not merely borrow from existing religions and cultures; it added elements of its own that were unique and revolutionary. These elements are primary, and it is on them that the other two sources depend. Without these specifically

Christian features, the Jewish and Roman sources discussed above would be meaningless.

Jesus Christ—the Resurrection

The central message of Christianity is the resurrection—the belief that God visited this earth in the person of Jesus Christ, who had been executed by crucifixion and had risen from the dead three days later. The exact nature of the rising has always been the subject of some debate—some have called it a hoax perpetrated by the apostles to save face; others have called it an illusion, a genuine transformation, and, more recently, the effect of "resurrection language." Whatever the details of the case, it became the primary message of the early church. Everything else, from Christ's life to his words and miracles, are mere appendages by comparison. As one twentieth-century writer pointed out:

> The idea that Jesus was a great Moral Teacher, and that men afterwards came to think he had risen from the dead is simply unhistorical; you are putting the cart before the horse. The message which electrified the world of the first century was not "Love your enemies," but "He is risen."[7]

The resurrection of Christ was the central theme of every sermon reported in the Acts of the Apostles. The resurrection, in other words, *was* the Good News. C. S. Lewis, in his book *Miracles*, underlines this primacy of the resurrection:

> The Resurrection, and its consequences, were the "gospel" or good news which the Christians brought: what we call the "gospels," the narratives of our Lord's life and death, were composed later for the benefit of those who had already accepted the *Gospel*. They were in no sense the basis of Christianity; they were written for those already converted. The miracle of the Resurrection, and the theology of that miracle, come first; the biography comes later as a comment on it....The first fact in the history of Christendom is a number of people who say they have seen the Resurrection. If they had died without making anyone else believe this "gospel," no gospels would ever have been written.[8]

10

Jesus Christ—His Life and Death

When it comes to great people, no attention is paid to their early life until well after their great achievement has been accomplished. The life of Christ was no different. His resurrection had generated an interest in his background—what he had been like as a man, what had shaped him, how it had all begun. Four accounts of his life began to be written to satisfy this curiosity and to fill out the story. These accounts—by Mark, Matthew, Luke, and John—were probably first preached to specific audiences for specific purposes, and only then were recorded in writing. Thus, for example, Matthew seems to be writing for Jews; Luke for Greeks or Gentiles. The record which the evangelists give to us is unique in the history of religion because a) it is so precisely dated and b) it claims that its founder is God himself.

Christianity is historical from first to last. Luke's account reads: "In those days a decree went out from Emperor Augustus that all the world should be registered. This was the first registration and was taken while Quirinius was governor of Syria…" (Luke 2:1–2). And later, in John's account, "So the soldiers, their officer, and the Jewish police arrested Jesus and bound him. First they took him to Annas, who was the father-in-law of Caiaphas, the high priest that year" (John 18:12–13). These details can be verified against non-Christian documents, and we can conclude with confidence that Christ was born sometime between 6 BC and 1 AD, and that he died sometime between 30 and 33 AD—a lifetime of approximately thirty years.

Only Matthew and Luke discuss any details about Christ's birth.[9] Matthew attempts to show that Jesus is the fulfillment of Jewish hopes, and does this by tracing Christ's ancestry back to Abraham, the father of the Jews. But Matthew also makes the stinging comment that the Jews, precisely those people who should have recognized the Messiah, have missed him altogether. Herod the Great, a Jewish king, was alarmed at the news that a king had been born in Bethlehem, and he sought to destroy the boy by putting to death all male infants in that area.[10] It remained for the Magi or Wise Men, all of them Gentiles, to recognize Christ as the Messiah.[11]

11

Luke, on the other hand, addresses his account to the Gentiles and therefore traces Christ's ancestry back to Adam, the father of mankind. Then Luke contrasts the mighty Augustus with the low-born Christ, playing with a typically Greek irony on the themes of true kingship and true peace. Luke's point is that the child born in the stable will ultimately overcome the self-proclaimed "god" in Rome—a bold prediction indeed.

While Luke and Matthew omit details that the other includes, they both agree on the following ten points:

1) The parents-to-be are Mary and Joseph, who are legally engaged, but who have not yet begun to live together or have marital relations.

2) Joseph is from the line of David.

3) An angel announces the birth of the child.

4) Mary conceives without having intercourse with Joseph.

5) Mary conceives through the Holy Spirit.

6) The angel directs them to name the child "Jesus."

7) The angel says that Jesus is to be the Savior.

8) The birth takes place in Bethlehem.

9) The birth takes place during the reign of Herod the Great.

10) The child is raised in Nazareth.

After the return to Nazareth there is very little mention of Christ, except that he "grew and became strong" (Luke 2:40). The only incident recorded of his youth is when he is "lost" in the Temple. At the age of thirty this obscurity ends. Christ is baptized by John in the Jordan River, prepares himself in the desert, and emerges to begin his public ministry.[12] It is a ministry that is conveniently divided into words and deeds, and these we shall examine separately.

The Words of Christ

Christ needed to prepare his followers for what he was about to do, to reveal to them slowly the mysteries of his death and resurrection, so that when those things finally came to pass, those who had listened to him would understand what they meant. Much like a mathematics teacher has to build on more basic skills, so too the Lord had to bring his disciples along gradually. Even so, many things did not become clear to the disciples until after the resurrection, and sometimes long after that. Oftentimes we find the disciples puzzled by things Christ says or does, and they are frequently admonished by him for missing the point: "I have been with you all this time, and *still* you do not understand?" The words of Christ take the forms of: a) Pronouncement Stories, b) Proverbs, and c) Parables.

Pronouncement Stories

These are brief stories which can be placed anywhere in the gospels because of their independence. They do not rely on any context. Furthermore, they have a religious concern and elicit some sort of response. A good example is found in Mark 12:13–17:

> Then they sent to him some Pharisees and some Herodians to trap him in what he said. And they came and said to him, "Teacher, we know that you are sincere, and show deference to no one; for you do not regard people with partiality, but teach the way of God in accordance with truth. Is it lawful to pay taxes to the emperor, or not? Should we pay them, or should we not?" But knowing their hypocrisy, he said to them, "Why are you putting me to the test? Bring me a denarius and let me see it." And they brought one. Then he said to them, "Whose head is this, and whose title?" They answered, "The emperor's." Jesus said to them, "Give to the emperor the things that are the emperor's, and to God the things that are God's."

Proverbs

The proverb is an Old Testament form that was found throughout the Near East long before Christ ever employed it. It is a short statement about experience which is easily remembered. Current examples include "Still waters run deep" and "The early bird catches the worm." Usually its wisdom concerns the secular: hard work, punctuality, temperance, etc. But Christ brings to this secular wisdom a religious dimension—saying that the secular is no longer sufficient. The best example of Christ's use of proverb is in his famous Sermon on the Mount:

> Blessed are you who are poor,
>   for yours is the kingdom of God.
> Blessed are you who are hungry now,
>   for you will be filled.
> Blessed are you who weep now,
>   for you will laugh (Luke 6:20–23).[13]

Other examples abound, such as "Love your enemies as you love yourself." Throughout these proverbs is a startling reversal—the least will become the greatest, the leaders will serve the table, the poor will become rich—leading inexorably to Christ's climactic reversal: God himself will suffer and die.

Parables

Christ used parables to startle people into thinking about his kingdom. Thus they often provide unexpected heroes and heroines. The Prodigal Son, a good-for-nothing cad, is made a hero. The Good Samaritan—a Samaritan!—saves a man while two Jews (priests, no less) pass by. A shepherd boy looks for one sheep and leaves an entire flock behind, and a woman throws a party over finding a single coin. These stories were intended to jolt, and jolt they did. But their purpose was not to shock people for the sake of the shock, but to illustrate what God's kingdom would be like and how we might get there. God's kingdom is full of unexpected heroes and heroines and is, perhaps, the reverse of what we expect. To a nation long-accustomed to waiting for an earthly kingdom, long-accustomed to respecting the rich and successful, this was jolting news indeed.

Parables are stories usually concerned with daily life, and they frequently appear in the traditional threefold pattern: e.g., three servants were trusted with talents; the good seed falls on three kinds of ground; there were three men going up to Jericho:

> But wanting to justify himself, he asked Jesus, "And who is my neighbor?" Jesus replied, "A man was going down from Jerusalem to Jericho, and fell into the hands of robbers, who stripped him, beat him, and went away, leaving him half dead. Now by chance a priest was going down that road; and when he saw him, he passed by on the other side. So likewise a Levite, when he came to the place and saw him, passed by on the other side. But a Samaritan while traveling came near him; and when he saw him, he was moved with pity. He went to him and bandaged his wounds, having poured oil and wine on them. Then he put him on his own animal, brought him to an inn, and took care of him. The next day he took out two denarii, gave them to the innkeeper, and said, 'Take care of him; and when I come back, I will repay you whatever more you spend.' Which of these three, do you think, was a neighbor to the man who fell into the hands of the robbers?" (Luke 10:29–36).

Christ ordinarily asked his listeners to draw the necessary conclusions—"which of these three, do you think, was a neighbor to the man?" In some cases, as in this one, the answers were obvious. But other parables proved elusive and we find the apostles asking the Lord for further explanations. After the parable of the Sower and the Seed (Mark 4:3–9), Christ complains, "Do you not understand this parable? Then how will you understand all the parables?" In fact, Christ almost seems to use parables to confuse his hearers to such an extent that the word "parable" becomes synonymous with puzzle and riddle.

While all of this is difficult to unravel and has caused scholars untold difficulties, the best explanation seems to be that the parables are indicative of the listener's faith. If one believes, the parable, more often than not, is understandable. If one persists in doubt or unbelief, then the parable becomes a further stumbling-block. Hence the *purpose* of the parables is not to confuse, but rather to enlighten further the believer about the nature of the Kingdom. The *result*, however, may be confusion due to a person's unwillingness to believe.

The Deeds of Christ

When we talk about the deeds of Christ, we are essentially referring to his miracles—and here we walk over much-contested ground. Matthew Arnold summed up the argument against miracles when he said, "The great objection to miracles is that they do not occur." Rationalism and nineteenth-century science would have agreed with this statement, and indeed it is a modern tendency to deny miracles. Modern apologists, G. K. Chesterton and C. S. Lewis among them, have attempted to show the unreasonableness of such a blanket denial. They posit, first of all, that we take some gigantic miracles for granted and then balk at lesser feats. Chesterton's book *Orthodoxy* is filled with a defense of the miraculous on rational grounds—claiming that Christians are the ones who accept all the evidence and that those who reject miracles do so a priori regardless of the evidence:

> Somehow or other an extraordinary idea has arisen that the disbelievers in miracles consider them coldly and fairly, while believers in miracles accept them only in connection with some dogma. The fact is quite the other way. The believers in miracles accept them (rightly or wrongly) because they have evidence for them. The disbelievers in miracles deny them (rightly or wrongly) because they have a doctrine against them.[14]

This is in accord with John Henry Newman's dictum that if you accept the incarnation, you must accept at least the logical possibility of other miracles. And, as the formidable Pascal pointed out in the seventeenth century, "It is impossible on reasonable grounds to disbelieve in miracles." The New Testament writers took for granted the possibility of the miraculous and, even granting that they had a wider interpretation of miracles than we do today, they still attest to several miracles worked by Christ which are (if true) miracles by anyone's reckoning. In John 9 the story of the man born blind is well-documented. The man himself claims not to have seen from birth and his parents are called in to testify that he has not seen from birth, the point being that he had been certainly blind and can now just as certainly see—because of the power of Jesus. Nearly one-half of Mark's description of the public ministry of Christ is concerned with miracles. The incarnation (God becoming man) and the resurrection are both attested to as miracles. Otherwise they are worthless fictions.

Unfortunately, there is a tendency to exaggerate or misuse the New Testament miracles. They were not performed in order to prove that Jesus Christ was God. No miracle worked by Christ is an exhibition, done simply to show that he could do it—making trees walk, for example. They are not done simply to demonstrate the extraordinary. Christ, in fact, is reticent about performing or publicizing miracles. He often refuses to work miracles and castigates people who seek them. He even warns people that such signs and wonders may be deceptive (Mark 13:22–23). And it must be admitted that the gospel writers, if they were trying to convey a wonder-working Christ, could have done much more than they did. To understand miracles in the New Testament we must realize that they are always done for a purpose integrally related to Christ's mission. Almost all of them are symbolic: curing the blind man in John 9:35–41 is symbolic of the spiritual sight which comes from faith; the large catch of fish in Luke 5:1–11 is symbolic of the manner in which Christ will catch people; the raising of Lazarus a prefigurement of what will happen to Christ in rising from the dead.

This is not to say that these miracles did not happen, but rather that they must be understood as explaining Christ's message. Christ can heal the sick, but such physical healing (as he points out) is nothing compared to his ability to heal the sinner. The physical miracle is a mere shadow of the spiritual. Besides, Christ adds in a deliciously ironic passage: "If they do not listen to Moses and the prophets, neither will they be convinced even if someone rises from the dead" (Luke 16:31).

The Twelve Apostles

The role of the twelve apostles cannot be emphasized enough. Christ's words and deeds would have been ineffectual and short-lived had it not been for the witness of this small band. They are the first to sift the evidence, and whatever conviction people have had over the years about Jesus Christ lies heavily with these men. They are ordinary men ranging in occupation from fisherman to tax collector; and Christ appears to choose them for their ordinariness. He wanted normal men who were going to ask normal questions, who were not going to invent things, who were not gullible, and who were not going to believe just anything. In fact, these apostles seem to *doubt* everything. They are consistently confused by what Christ does, and often ask him to explain what he has just done or said. Many of Christ's deeds seem to take them totally by surprise—such as the multiplication of loaves and fishes (John 6:1–14) and the washing of feet (John 13:1–15). Their confusion was never higher than after Christ's death and resurrection. Thomas, when he is told by the other apostles that the Lord had risen, responds, "Unless I see the mark of the nails in his

St. Peter being called by Christ to be a fisher of people. This was and is a popular motif for Christian artists and frequently graces the walls of churches in fishing communities.

18

hands, and put my finger in the mark of the nails and my hand in his side, I will not believe" (John 20:25).

These apostles are key because, given all their confusion and doubt, they eventually come to believe in Christ. What they *say* is not so important, for anyone could have said such things, but it is what they *do* which rivets our attention: they supply a cogent witness—suffering and (if the traditions are correct) dying for the spread of the Good News. Their deaths served notice that they were either deluded or had really seen something. Violent death is not an extreme to which a common laborer will go for a hoax. These apostles also provide the first interpretation of Christ's life and message. They celebrate the first liturgies and make the first disciplinary and doctrinal decisions. Their first interpretive acts are the beginnings of Christian tradition.

The Feast of Pentecost

The first time the apostles emerge independently of Christ is on the feast of Pentecost, the Jewish Feast of Weeks occurring about fifty days after Passover, celebrating the corn harvest and the Law of Moses. On that day, according to the Acts of the Apostles (written by Luke), the Holy Spirit descended on them in the Upper Room and transformed them into courageous preachers and tireless missionaries—carrying their message that Christ had risen. Acts 2:5–11 is what might be called a "watershed" passage—before it the main work is done by Jesus Christ; after the passage the focus shifts abruptly to the church:

> Now there were devout Jews from every nation under heaven living in Jerusalem. And at this sound [of rushing wind] the crowd gathered and was bewildered, because each one heard them speaking in the native language of each. Amazed and astonished, they asked, "Are not all these who are speaking Galileans? And how is it that we hear, each of us, in our own native language? Parthians, Medes, Elamites, and residents of Mesopotamia, Judea and Cappodocia, Pontus and Asia, Phrygia and Pamphylia, Egypt and the parts of Libya belonging to Cyrene, and visitors from Rome, both Jews and

proselytes, Cretans and Arabs—in our own languages we hear them speaking about God's deeds of power."

The importance of this for Christianity is that these first Christians—Peter is reported to have converted 5,000 of them by himself—return to their various Jewish communities in northern Africa, Asia Minor, Arabia, Greece, and Rome, and begin to form Christian cells. It is these small communities that Paul worked so feverishly to keep together. His letters read like a road map of early Christianity—all because of that first Pentecost, which the church rightly observes as its foundation day.

Paul

Paul is one of the most important human figures in the Christian Church, though many critics have wondered whether that has been for good or ill. John Stuart Mill said that Paul was "the first great corruptor of Christianity," and others have accused him of being the archenemy of Christ and the one who did more than anyone else to distort the teaching of Christ. Nietzsche, of all people, called Paul "a morbid crank."

There are dissenters, of course. St. Ambrose called Paul "Christ's second eye" and Erasmus urged everyone to commit all of Paul's words to memory—and this approval has been shared by most of the Christian Church over the centuries. Regardless, Paul remains a center of controversy, and it is debated how much of his teaching was his own, and how much came from Jesus Christ.

Paul was born a Jew about the same time Christ was born. He became a highly respected rabbi under the tutelage of Gamaliel. Having been born in Tarsus in Asia Minor, Paul spoke Greek and acquired Roman citizenship through his father, who had been made a Roman citizen for reasons which are not known. Paul was an inveterate persecutor of Christians, and on his way to Damascus to arrest some Christians, he was struck down:

> Saul [Paul's Jewish name], still breathing threats and murder against the disciples of the Lord, went to the high priest and asked him for letters to the synagogues at Damascus, so that

Damascus with Roman city wall. The apostle Paul was headed to this great Roman city in Syria to persecute the followers of Jesus when he had his dramatic conversion experience ca. 34 AD.

if he found any who belonged to the Way [as Christianity was known], men or women, he might bring them bound to Jerusalem. Now as he was going along and approaching Damascus, suddenly a light from heaven flashed around him. He fell to the ground and heard a voice saying to him, "Saul, Saul, why do you persecute me?" He asked, "Who are you, Lord?" The reply came, "I am Jesus, whom you are persecuting" (Acts 9:1–5).

The ramifications of this event are twofold. First, Jesus equates himself with the church: "Saul, Saul, why are you persecuting *me*?...I am Jesus, whom you are persecuting." Secondly, something drastic happened to Paul. He changed so quickly and so completely from being a persecutor of Christians to being an eager Christian that no one who heard of it could believe it. Even the apostles in Jerusalem remained so suspicious of Paul that Barnabas, a man well-known and trusted, had to introduce him to the twelve and assure them of the authenticity of Paul's conversion. But relations between Paul and the apostles would never

_____ First Missionary Journey of Paul
.... Second Missionary Journey of Paul
- - - - - - - - Third Missionary Journey of Paul

thaw, partly because of Paul's past, but also partly because Paul began to claim to be one of the apostles.

Paul's importance is that he combined the two disparate worlds of Rome and Jerusalem. He was familiar with both worlds, with the languages, cultures, and thought-patterns. He could speak with impressive authority to either group. We might even say that Paul was the very embodiment of the church at the time, and of what the church was to become. His very person was a tension between Jew and Greek, and his final trip to Rome was symbolic of the church's eventual break from Jerusalem and inclusion in the western world.

One of Paul's tasks was to unify the scattered Christian communities, and this he did by making three missionary journeys through Asia Minor and Greece—spreading the news of Christ, instructing Christians on Christian living, passing on news from other communities, explaining points of doctrine. He made sure that each community did not become an entity unto itself, and because of his efforts the catholicity (universality) of the church was guaranteed.

Disciplinary matters were also addressed by Paul. Questions arose on how to dress, how to fast, whom to follow—and Paul plunged into these matters firmly and vigorously. He could be kind and patient, or he could be rude. In one letter he writes, "O you stupid Galatians!" and he roundly scolded them for abandoning the faith.

Another of Paul's tasks was to ease the tension between Jewish and Greek Christians. Here he undoubtedly met his greatest challenge. We have seen that the church began as an exclusively Jewish phenomenon, but after Pentecost this began to change. When the first converts returned to their homes, they brought with them a message which attracted not only fellow Jews, but pagans and Gentiles as well. A question immediately arose, "Must these Gentile converts follow the Law of Moses?" Must they, in other words, be circumcised, observe Jewish dietary restrictions, and follow Jewish regulations on cleansing? One party said yes—claiming no doubt that Christ had come to fulfill the Law and, further, that the Law had been given by God to Moses and was not optional: "Certain individuals came down

Journey of St. Paul to Rome

23

from Judea and were teaching the brothers, 'Unless you are circumcised according to the custom of Moses, you cannot be saved'" (Acts 15:1).

Against this position Paul insisted that Gentiles should not be required to obey Jewish laws and customs. The question soon became so divisive that a council was called in Jerusalem—the first council of the church—in 49 AD to settle the matter. Peter, probably torn by allegiances, spoke on behalf of the Gentiles:

> And God, who knows the human heart, testified to them by giving them the Holy Spirit, just as he did to us [Jews]; and in cleansing their hearts by faith he has made no distinction between them and us. Now therefore why are you putting God to the test by placing on the neck of the disciples a yoke that neither our ancestors nor we have been able to bear? (Acts 15:8–10)

Paul and Barnabas spoke in a similar vein and carried the day—the council decided that Gentiles did not need to become Jews in order to become Christians. The importance of the decision cannot be overestimated: It was the difference between continuing an elite local religion or making the church into something truly worldwide. The church now had a mandate to adapt disciplinary matters to the various cultures it would encounter. Little did Paul realize how far-reaching this decision would be and how many cultures would ultimately be affected. This is not to say that the church always followed the decision made at the Council of Jerusalem—unhappily the history of the church is marked by lapses from this far-sighted position—but the balance sheet is fairly impressive.

The shift from a Jewish church to a Gentile church was fortuitous in that the city of Jerusalem was destroyed by the Roman army in 70 AD. The church in Jerusalem, the mother church of Christianity, for all practical purposes ceased to exist. But, by then, the church was so well-established in Rome that it no longer depended on its Jewish support. Paul was the one mainly responsible for effecting this transition and, even though he was executed by Nero in 64 AD, he did not die before seeing his work accomplished.

Attacks on Christianity

The Jewish Persecution

Christians were persecuted almost immediately. The apostles hid in the Upper Room after Christ died "for fear of the Jews." Paul, himself an energetic hunter of Christians, suffered several times at the hands of the Jews. Just as it was by the Jews that Christ's message was so eagerly accepted, so it was also from the Jews that the initial reaction to Christianity took place. Christ was regarded as a blasphemer and his disciples as apostates and usurpers. After the deacon Stephen was stoned to death, Christians were actively persecuted: James (the brother of John) was put to death in 44, as was James (the "brother of the Lord" and head of the church in Jerusalem) in 62.

The Roman Persecution

This Jewish harassment was not to last very long. The Jews themselves came under pressure from Rome, ironically because the Christians were beginning to vex the Roman officials, who could not tell one religion from the other. Christians possessed tendencies which were thought to be subversive: they were unconcerned about the government and they were unenthusiastic about military service.[15] In addition, Christians were antisocial, avoiding public baths and spectacles. This led to a suspicion of their motives, resentment over their obvious elitism, and further distrust over their mysterious and strange religion. Often they were accused of cannibalism and infanticide. Finally, the common person was highly superstitious and was inclined to blame natural and personal calamities on the nearest scapegoat, and Christians fit the bill. They were an identifiable minority, they were defenseless, and they were suspect by reason of their secrecy.

The emperor Nero (54–68) had need of just such a scapegoat. His rule had become widely unpopular due to his brutality and corruption (in 59 he had his mother killed and, in 62, his wife), and he sought to direct the public *animus* toward somebody else. If he did not orchestrate the burning of Rome in 64, he was quick to take advantage of the destruction by beginning the building of his spectacular "Golden House" on the ruined property (which, if completed, would have covered one-third of the area of Rome) and by blaming the Christian community for the fire. The leaders of the Christian community bore the brunt of this first Roman persecution, and both Peter and Paul were executed at this time. The tradition is strong that Peter died by crucifixion in the Circus of Nero on the Vatican Hill, near the present St. Peter's Basilica, and that Paul was beheaded at Tre Fontane. Henceforward, until the year 250, persecutions focused mostly on the Christian leadership and were fortunately few and far between.

The most frequent methods of persecution were imprisonment, confiscation of property, exile to the mines in Sardinia (which was a death sentence), or execution—the last of which served not only as a penal measure but as a source of entertainment. Christians, if they were Roman citizens like Paul, were executed by beheading. If they were not Roman citizens, their deaths could be cruel—by crucifixion, by combat with animals, or by burning (which was usually done at night).

These persecutions continued sporadically until the year 250, when they took a new and ugly form. The emperor Decius wanted to restore the glory that was once Rome. It was an empire that was diminishing both in territory and in moral force. Rome itself had become little more than a welfare state and its population, according to Christopher Dawson, "existed mainly to draw their Government doles, and to attend the free spectacles with which the Government provided them."[16] Barbarians were menacing the borders, the economy was slumping badly, and mystery religions were becoming epidemic.

Decius needed to act forcefully, so he sought to reform the military, secure the borders, and unify the Roman people by means of religion—i.e., by restoring the worship of the gods, foremost of whom was the emperor. An ultimatum was made to *all* citizens to offer sacrifice to the gods or face possible death. Decius was well aware that such sacrifice was repugnant to Christians, and it put them into a terrible dilemma. Either they would submit to Decius's decree, or they would resist and face his certain wrath.

Some Christians capitulated totally to the decree by offering sacrifice, but many made lesser concessions—offering only incense or, more ingeniously, obtaining a certificate (called a *libellus* or "ticket") which said that they had offered sacrifice, even though they had not. Those who defied the decree were either imprisoned or put to death. Fabian, the bishop of Rome at the time, was among the first to die.

It seems that most of the executions took place in public theaters or arenas such as the Circus Maximus, though it is thought that the number of Christians who died in the Coliseum (built 75–80 AD) is probably exaggerated. This systematic persecution took place in three great waves—the first sponsored by Decius (who died fighting the Germans in the year 250 only a year after issuing his decree), the second by Valerian (who also enjoyed only a short anti-Christian campaign in the year 257), and the final by Diocletian and then Galerius, whose combined persecutions were by the far the worst—lasting officially from 303 until 311. Under considerable pressure, Galerius issued an edict in 311 halting the persecution. Under Constantine, who assumed control of the western half of the Empire in 313, Christianity was granted free expression and many privileges.

In a dramatic turn of events, Christianity had gone from being persecuted to being the favored religion of the Empire. The persecutions had been a defining moment in the spread of Christianity. Even though about 60,000 Christians were put to death throughout the Roman Empire between the years 250 and 311, their numbers rose in the same time period from three million to seven million believers, nearly fourteen percent of the entire population of the Empire. The persecutions had put the church on the map, and had made people take notice. Why, after all, would so many people of all social classes willingly go to their deaths?

The *Lapsi*

One problem remained: What was the church to do with the many people who had renounced the faith in one form or another, had offered some sort of homage to the pagan gods, and were now seeking readmission to the church? These people were called *lapsi* or "lapsed." This question arose immediately following the persecution of Decius in 250, when so many Christians were caught off-guard and decided to dissemble. Hard-liners, led by Novatian, who headed the Church of Rome after the death of Fabian and who fully expected to be elected the next pope (when it was safe to hold an election), argued that these *lapsi* had permanently given up the right to belong to the church, and that none of them were to be readmitted under any circumstances. Others argued that a general amnesty was the appropriate Christian response. Both extremes were fraught with difficulties, and Cornelius, the new Bishop of Rome, chosen in place of the ambitious Novatian not because of his administrative ability so much as his moderation, decided on a middle ground which allowed the *lapsi* a way back to the church, but only after serving a suitable period of time in public penance. The length and severity of this public penance would depend on the extent of the original apostasy: those who had actually sacrificed *(sacrificati)* were treated most severely, those who had offered incense *(thurificati)* less so, and those who had merely obtained certificates or tickets *(libellatici)* and had done nothing else were required merely to recite the creed. It was a solution, and probably the best one, but as we shall see in the Donatist controversy, it was by no means the end of the matter.

The Catacombs

It is impossible to discuss the persecution of the early church without mentioning the catacombs. They were underground galleries cut out of volcanic rock known as *tufa*, which was particularly suitable for burial of the dead because it was sturdy, easy to cut, and absorbent. These catacombs are found mostly outside of Rome, though lesser catacombs have been discovered in southern Italy, Germany, and France. Burials all took place outside the walls of the city for sanitary reasons—every cemetery was outside the walls of any city. Because Christians and Jews had a greater reverence for the body than did the pagans, they used cemeteries more than the pagans, who tended to cremate dead bodies. Pagan cemeteries do exist, however—in fact, St. Peter was buried in one. In Rome, at least, catacombs happened to be the most convenient way to bury the dead.

The catacombs were not secret. Everyone, including the Roman authorities, knew where the catacombs were and how to get into them—so they were not especially good hiding places. In fact, in the year 257 Pope Sixtus was caught in one of the catacombs with four of his deacons "teaching the people," and was put to death. But even so, the romantic version of the catacombs—popularized by Henry Synciewicz's *Quo Vadis* and Cardinal Wiseman's *Fabiola*—while exaggerated, is not without basis. Romans, like most people even today, were hesitant to tamper with the dead and probably left the Christian burial places alone. Secondly, large underground basilicas have been discovered in the catacombs which could house as many as two thousand people—whether they were used in times of persecution as secret gathering places is another question, but the possibility is there. Thirdly, the maze-like construction of the catacombs lends itself to possible refuge—not to mention their vast extent: ninety miles of catacombs exist in the area of Rome alone. These would have been extremely difficult to police adequately. Given the number of Christians in Rome at the time (30,000 by conservative estimates) and the severity of the persecutions, it is certainly within the realm of the possible that the catacombs were used occasionally as places for people to hide.

The name "catacomb" derives from the Greek *kata kumbas*, which means "at the place of the hidden valley." (It could also be translated as "quarry" or "pit.") Originally this referred to the area along the Appian Way, south of Rome, where we now find the catacombs of Saints Sebastian, Callistus, and Domitilla.[17] Christian burial clubs were organized to gather the bodies of the Christian dead and give them proper burial. This could be dangerous work—collecting the bodies of martyrs, for example—because it could expose the gravediggers as Christians themselves. Hence the hasty burial of St. Peter in a tomb just outside the Circus of Nero. So important was the job of gravedigger that it evolved into an *order* in the church, much along the lines of lector and acolyte. Christian women also would gather the bodies of slain infants (infanticide was not uncommon) and take them to be buried in catacombs.

The construction of the catacombs is interesting. First an underground gallery would be dug, with niches carved in either wall to hold a corpse. When the gallery was filled, the floor would be dug and a new row of tombs cut out. This process continued until the gallery was considered to be bordering on the unsafe, and a new gallery would be started. Tombs would be covered with a slab indicating the person's name, some facts of his life and death, and possibly some invocation to peace or resurrection. Sometimes ornaments were attached which were held dear by the deceased or by his family. More elaborate tombs allowed space for frescoes to be painted, and these often depicted scenes from Scripture which had to do with baptism: Moses striking the rock and watching as water flowed out, Jonah and the whale, the three men in the fiery furnace, the dove of Noah's ark.

The catacombs were abandoned in the late 300s as the barbarians neared Rome. Some important bodies (Lawrence, for example) were moved into churches within the city itself, and

Perpetua and Felicity. Perpetua, a 22-year-old noblewoman, and Felicity, a slave with an unborn child, were arrested, imprisoned, and executed in Carthage in 203 AD for defying Emperor Septimus Severus' prohibition against converting to Christianity. The account of their martyrdom, *The Passion of Perpetua and Felicity*, is one of the earliest Christian historical documents.

were reinterred within the altars of these churches. Thus began the practice of kissing the altar—not only did it represent the site of the sacrifice about to be performed, but it also contained the body of one who had given his own life in sacrifice. It also led to the practice of having the relic of a saint in an altar "stone" on every altar.

Rival Religions

Perhaps an even greater threat to the church was the assault made on it by rival religions and unbelievers. Foremost among these were mystery cults, Gnosticism, and Montanism, which attracted converts of their own.

Mystery Religions

Mystery religions, such as the cult of Mithras, were essentially nature religions with secret rites. They placed great emphasis on the seasons of the year, death and regeneration, and sex. Many of these religions had both a male and female god: Attis and Cybele in Asia Minor, Osiris and Isis in Egypt, Tammuz and Ishtar in Babylon. Believers in these religions were required to share in the experience of the gods, which tended to focus on the sensual. Thus the god, in the form of a fish or an animal, was to be eaten; blood from an animal, usually a bull or a goat, was sprinkled on the believers. At times this union with the god was accompanied by emotional experiences, often a sexual one (hence sacred prostitution). It is not difficult to see that some of this resembled Christianity's own rites, a proximity that could confuse the faithful and the authorities alike.

Gnosticism

Gnosticism was quite another matter. While it sought for a union with the unknown God, it did so in terms radically different and less physical than the mystery religions. Gnosticism could also be different depending on what part of the world it was found, and would frequently borrow elements from local religions. Thus, western Gnosticism had a Christian flavor to it. One Gnostic, Marcion, even called himself a "Christian Gnostic" and tried reconciling the two religions.

It was not to be. Gnosticism set out to answer one question: how do we explain the riddle of the world, evil, and human existence? The Gnostic answer was dualistic. Man lives in an imperfect world, controlled by an evil force, and he can escape only by gaining a knowledge of himself and the true and perfect God. Again, this sounds *almost* Christian, except that it assumes too great a divide between the human and the divine. To Marcion, it was impossible for Christ to be God since a perfect God would never lower himself to take on impure flesh.

Marcion was, in fact, a compulsive troublemaker. When he was very young he fell into conflict with the church leaders in Asia Minor and was dismissed from the congregation. In the year 140 he traveled to Rome and joined the Christian congregation there, which he quit four years later because he was unable to gain support for his ideas. Among these ideas was the view that the God of the Old Testament was a Gnostic Creator—strict, harsh, and necessarily evil because he created material things. The God of the New Testament, on the other hand, was loving, kind, forgiving. Thus it was easy for Marcion to eliminate the Old Testament entirely from his idea of a church, and to change any New Testament writings which contained Old Testament sentiments.

Montanism

Montanism was the closest of all of these rival religions to Christianity. It was both charismatic and rigorist. It began about the year 170 with Montanus, who claimed to be the mouthpiece and prophet of the Holy Spirit. His message was morally severe and was directed principally against the physical: fasting was to be continuous, poverty was to be radical, marriage to be renounced, total continence to be embraced, martyrdom to be welcomed. Tied in with this was a prediction that the Second Coming would take place very soon in Phrygia (Asia Minor). The Montanist movement underwent a change in the year 200 when Tertullian joined and tried to make it universal. His teachings—which included the notions that bishops were not needed and that the sacrament of penance was not sufficiently severe to sinners—further alienated the movement from the church.

Celsus

In addition to these rival religions, several writers attempted to disprove the claims of Christianity. Up until the middle of the second century, rather crude accusations were made that Christians were superstitious, criminal, naive, incestuous, gluttonous, and even atheistic. They were charges made by men who knew little about Christianity and who mostly repeated the popular suspicions about Christians. But about the year 180 a man named Celsus proved to be a more formidable foe. In his book, *The True Teaching*, he attacked Christianity across the board. Christianity, he wrote, victimized gullible women, children, and slaves. Furthermore it accepted the lowest forms of humanity; its talk of moral conversion was a facade; it was anti-social and unpatriotic; it was illogical. After all, why should God come to earth? To learn about it? To put it right? If so, why didn't he make it right in the first place? Why didn't God come sooner? Why did he come to Israel? Furthermore, this Jesus had all the characteristics of a maverick: he was a boaster and a liar, a magician, an imposter, and he hung around with disreputable types. No one had seen him rise from the dead. Why hadn't he shown himself to Pilate and the Sanhedrin?

For people who knew little or nothing about Christianity, the effect of Celsus's attack was significant. Seventy years later, Christianity's most important theologian, Origen, would still think it necessary to answer the charges brought by Celsus.

The Christian Response: The Apologists

There are several works still extant which show the Christian response to these attacks. The first group of responses was written by the *Post-Apostolic Writers*, men who probably knew one or more of the original apostles personally. These would include such names as Clement of Rome, Ignatius of Antioch, and Polycarp of

---

The Dating of the *Didache*

The dating of this work is crucial, because it contains very detailed directions about baptism, prayer, the Eucharistic service, as well as a description of a fairly sophisticated hierarchy. Protestants have always been anxious to prove that this is a late work (c. 150) and therefore not something known to the apostles and Scripture writers, while some Catholics have dated it as early as 60 AD.

Smyrna and such famous works as the *Didache* (or *Teaching of the Apostles*, c. 100) and the *Shepherd of Hermas* (c. 140–155).

Christians in the next generation who attempted to respond to the various attacks on the church are known today as *Apologists*, taking the name from the ancient *apology*—the speech given in defense of an accused person. This speech featured both the refutation of the charges and a counterattack against the accuser.

Like the earliest charges against the church, the apologists began clumsily, but improved greatly by the time of Celsus. Some of these apologists used Greek expressions and ideas which would have been familiar to pagan thinkers. Justin, who is also known as Justin Martyr and was martyred in Rome about the year 165, was one such—he had experimented with several religions before converting to Christianity and could, therefore, effectively counter the claims of rival religions. He knew Greek philosophy and did not hesitate to use it in defense of the church.

His pupil Tatian, however, only mocked the Greeks. Their culture, he wrote, was barbarian and the philosophy deceptive, while their theology was foolish and their entertainments sinful. Tatian's disdain for things Greek pointed out a more widespread disagreement among Christians about the use of secular thought and culture. Some felt that Greek thought and art forms should be discarded because they were pagan, while others argued that Greek philosophy often shed considerable light on the world and could be used effectively in explaining the truths of Christianity.

Some Christian authors even claimed that Plato had touched on Christian truth years before Christ was born.

Much of the apologists' literature has perished through lack of interest. What we have comes to us largely through the historian Eusebius, whose *Ecclesiastical History* (written between 300 and 325) is a goldmine of information about the early church, and has stood the test of time. The principal argument used against Gnosticism was to show its incompatibility with Christianity. The church expanded adherence to the Apostles' Creed, for example, to include mention of the birth, death, and resurrection of Christ. Other writers such as Irenaeus explained the Fall as being something which did not come about through the action of an evil God, but rather through the action of sinful man. In general the truths of Christianity were formulated more

Ignatius of Antioch was bishop of Antioch in Syria at the beginning of the second century. The author of many letters to Christian communities, he was martyred at the Colosseum in Rome around 110 AD.

precisely and more emphasis was given to them—so much so that by the year 200 Gnosticism had been pretty much defeated.[18]

One lasting result of this controversy was the formation of a *canon*, or authorized list, of books of Scripture. Since Marcion had questioned the authenticity or value of the Old Testament, the Acts of the Apostles, and the Book of Revelation, principles were established for deciding which books were to be regarded as Sacred Scripture. These principles were three:

a) the book had to go back to apostolic times, at the latest;

b) the book had to be highly esteemed from an early date;

c) the guarantors of this were the bishops who could trace their origins back to the apostles.

Thus, defenders of "scripture alone" are faced with the dilemma that the "scriptures" were defined by the bishops or by what Catholics call "tradition."

The Life of the Early Church

What kind of life did the church have at this time? How did people worship? What was the structure of church government? Despite the persecutions, the early church did not remain in a state of suspended animation. Both in organization and liturgy we can see the growth of a well-defined structure. Because Christ's message was intended for all people, and not just one particular ethnic group, several adaptations had to take place if the religion was to survive and various groups be included. Jewish law was the first casualty in this development: Circumcision could hardly be imposed on a people to whom its practice was alien, meaningless, and often abhorrent. Language also had to be adapted—the ruling principle being that the people had to understand the message. This meant translating the scriptures and the liturgy first into Greek, and then eventually into Latin.[19]

Liturgical Developments

Another factor demanding immediate attention was the rapid growth of membership in the church. No longer could the Eucharist be celebrated in private homes with small, intimate groups. Practical concerns demanded that churches be built, or temples adapted, to accommodate the growing numbers. And this had an effect on the shape of the liturgy itself. What had been an intimate meal-oriented service, characteristic of a Jewish *seder* in the home, began to take on a more sacrificial stamp, but one in which the entire community was present. Interestingly, it was not the Roman *temple* that became the model for the new Christian church building—for the typical temple was too small for anyone but the priest and his sacrificial victim[20]—but the Roman *basilica*, the large rectangular building in which the king (*basileus* in Greek) heard court cases. This, however, had the effect of emphasizing the priestly and sacrificial aspects of the liturgy rather than the memorial meal aspect, though it combined the sacrifice with the assembly of believers. With all of this attention on the sacrificial, priests and stone altars began to take on more importance. Even today the liturgy retains many of the Roman practices adopted at this time, which were originally meant to honor the king or emperor, but were adapted to honor Jesus Christ in the person of the priest: candles on either side of the priest or Gospel book, kingly vestments, genuflections, incense, etc.[21] One may safely say that the central part of the Mass today—the canon of the Mass and especially the consecration—is obviously of Jewish origin, while the "trappings" of the Mass are Roman.

The liturgy evolved in other ways as well. Much evidence has been discovered since 1870, when the catacombs were being rein-vestigated and valuable documents found in eastern libraries, about the state of the early Christian liturgy. It was composed of a two-fold service of readings and sacrifice. The latter was proba-bly more spontaneous than it is today. There is strong evidence that the different words of institution (for the Eucharist) used in Scripture are actually the words used by different traditions in the canon of the Mass.[22] Gradually the prayers of sacrifice were for-malized so that, by the early third century, Hippolytus was able to write down a Eucharistic Prayer, which he commends to those who cannot compose on their own. This prayer is now the Preface to the Second Eucharistic Prayer.

Symbolism played an important role in the early liturgy and served to instruct the faithful—often uniting Jewish and Greek parties ingeniously by using symbols which cut across both cultures. The number twelve, for example, served not only to recall the twelve tribes of Israel and the twelve apostles, but also hinted at a connection to the twelve signs of the zodiac.[23] Thus New Testament mysteries were connected both biblically and cosmically. Christ was called the New Day (twelve hours long) and the Perfect Year (twelve months long) made manifest to the world through the twelve apostles.

The Structure of the Early Church

The church also began to acquire a sophisticated structure at this time, although it is important to know that the *exact* nature of several ministries is still debated. Bishops emerged as heads of local churches and successors to the apostles. The Greek word for bishops *(episkopoi)* appears in the New Testament only five times (and in none of the Gospel accounts) and seems to be interchangeable at times with "elders" or *presbyteroi*. The word *episkopos* means "supervisor." The bishop's duties included the material oversight of a community, i.e., managing the common funds, goods, and properties. But he also oversaw the spiritual good of the community. He ensured the oneness of faith and presided at

---

Concelebration

Priests would concelebrate with the bishop at the principal Eucharist, take a portion of the host with them to their outlying communities, and celebrate the Eucharist again. This is why the priest even today breaks off a portion of the host at the Lamb of God and puts it in the chalice—as a symbol that he and his community are celebrating along with the bishop.

---

the liturgy. As time went on and the communities grew in size, priests would help him in this.

Deacons assisted the bishops and helped to supervise liturgical and temporal activities. So close were they, in fact, to the popes that several of the early popes were chosen from among the deacons, and not from the ranks of the priests.

Priests were distinct from the bishop and somewhat more independent than deacons. They celebrated the Eucharist with their bishop and served as his council. Their role was not always distinct enough from that of the deacons to prevent a rivalry which resulted in the virtual disappearance of the diaconate, though it would linger on in liturgical roles. There were deaconesses, though they disappeared with the decline of adult baptism (c. 400) and a change in the role of women in society generally.[24] Other offices, such as charismatics (also called prophets), confessors (those who suffered for the faith but did not die), widows, virgins, gravediggers—all held a certain respected position amounting to an order in the church.

Apostolic Succession

Tradition and considerable evidence has it that the apostles became heads of local churches: James the Great and James the Less in Jerusalem, John in Antioch, Mark in Alexandria, Peter and Paul in Rome. Their authority was then passed on to successors. This is referred to as "apostolic succession." Clement, in 95 AD, wrote to the Corinthians that the bishops were the successors to the apostles, who were successors to Christ. Irenaeus and Tertullian both mentioned lists of bishops who succeeded Peter and Paul in Rome, though the lists are slightly different: Linus, Cletus, Clement, Evaristus, Sixtus.

The Primacy of Peter

Related to apostolic succession were the questions surrounding the primacy of Peter: Was Peter primary over the other apostles? Was he the Bishop of Rome? Do his successors succeed him in this primacy? Both Catholic and Protestant scholars agree that Peter had an authority that superceded that of the other apostles.

Peter is their spokesman at several events, he conducts the election of Matthias, his opinion in the debate over converting Gentiles was crucial, etc.

The evidence that Peter was "bishop" of Rome is corroborated by both positive and "negative" evidence. Positively, Clement's letter to the Corinthians situates Peter in Rome by mentioning his death there. Ignatius of Antioch writes to the Romans and says, "I do not command you as Peter and Paul did." The lists of Roman bishops given by Irenaeus and Tertullian support this, as does the honor given Peter's supposed burial place on Vatican Hill. Eamon Duffy's text for a BBC production, *Saints and Sinners*, soft-pedals the position of Peter as bishop. Duffy claims that there were five Christian neighborhoods in Rome, and that Peter could not possibly have been supervisor over all of them. One argument against this is the fact that the historical letters (from Paul, Ignatius, and Clement) are all addressed to "the Romans," and not one particular community within Rome.

Historians will cite negative evidence as well, namely that there is no rival tradition. No other city claims Peter as its bishop except Antioch, and even it conceded that Peter had moved on to Rome. But there is the problem of Paul. If Paul was in Rome at the same time as Peter, who was really the bishop? Since Paul's authority depended on Peter's recognition (Gal 1:18), it would appear that Paul took second place. But the lists of Irenaeus and Tertullian, and the letter of Ignatius all mention Peter *and* Paul. Even today, the pope's name, when written out in full, bears the initials "P.P."—which stands for "Peter and Paul." The most satisfying explanation is that they were co-bishops, that Peter had supervisory authority over the Roman Church and Paul was the charismatic and preaching "celebrity." Since the Roman legal system would have favored the Petrine emphasis on administration, Paul's role was quickly eclipsed.

But the final question—did Peter's successors continue his authority?—was the cause of the rift between the Eastern and Western Churches and, later, between Reformed and Roman Catholic Churches, and is still much-debated today. Several pieces of evidence indicate that the Bishop of Rome even after Peter held some sort of preeminence among other bishops.

1) When Ignatius of Antioch was on his way to Rome to be executed in 110 AD, he wrote a letter to the Romans and spoke with unusual deference of the Roman Church: "a Church worthy of God, worthy of honor, worthy of felicitation, worthy of praise, worthy of success, worthy of sanctification, and *presiding* in love, maintaining the law of Christ, and bearer of the Father's name."

2) Eastern and Western Churches disagreed about the dating of Easter, with the East opting for 14th Nissan (no matter what the day of the week) and the West choosing the Sunday after 14th Nissan. Pope Anicetus and Polycarp, the bishop of Smyrna, had disputed the question amicably, but a crisis came about in 180, when an Asiatic group visiting Rome observed the Eastern date. Pope Victor wished to bring the East in conformity with the Western practice and was defied by the bishop of Ephesus. Victor first excommunicated the Asian group in Rome, then the dioceses of Asia—or at least he threatened to. The ensuing controversy is pertinent in that Irenaeus wrote to the pope and questioned his severity in the matter. Irenaeus did not question the pope's right to excommunicate or to intervene in the workings of another diocese.

3) Cyprian, the Bishop of Carthage, appealed to Pope Stephen when another bishop (Marcion of Arles) proved intractable in reconciling *lapsi* to the church, even on their deathbeds. The implication was that the Bishop of Rome could intervene.

4) Cyprian disagreed with the same Pope Stephen over the rebaptism of heretics. Cyprian thought they should be rebaptized and Pope Stephen held for the inviolability of one baptism. The pope won this argument and the church to this day follows his teaching, but a major schism may have been avoided when Cyprian himself was martyred and no longer able to carry on the dispute.

5) Pope Stephen featured in another appeal. When a Spanish bishop (Basilides of Emerita) was deposed by a synod for being a *libellaticus* (someone who had received a certificate of sacrifice to the gods) he appealed to the pope for reinstatement and he was reinstated. The importance of this decision is that a Spanish bishop thought Rome could overrule a Spanish synod, and it did.

6) At the Christological councils in the 300s and 400s, the pope was careful to have representatives participating. But in 431 the pope called on Cyril of Alexandria to proceed to Constantinople and demand that Nestorius, the Patriarch of Constantinople, retract his heterodox opinion within ten days.

None of these examples, taken by themselves, would be sufficient to prove the primacy of the successors of Peter and Paul. Taken together, however, they point to a Roman authority which was recognized in the early church as going beyond that of other churches.

The End of the First Age

One obvious lesson to be learned from the above is that it would be a great mistake to picture the early church as a utopian society toward which we should be striving to return. Any reading of the Acts of the Apostles and Paul's letters show plainly that the early church grew up amidst considerable division, contention, and persecution. There were problems regarding authority, discipline, membership—all sorts of problems, in fact, which were the result of circumstance, growing pains, and basic human weakness.

On top of all the difficulties, 60,000 Christians were put to death by the Roman government. The combination of internal dissension and external persecution could have been fatal to a young church, but the opposite reaction actually happened. The decline, so characteristic of the end of each age of the church, does not occur at the end of the First Age. Instead of dealing the church a crushing blow, the persecutions awoke the whole Empire to the teachings and practices of Christianity. Even the new Emperor Constantine would become a Christian. Christianity had indeed arrived.

Recommended Readings

A – Easy reading
B – Moderately difficult reading
C – Difficult reading (but rewarding
if you are interested in the topic)

(A) The Acts of the Apostles.

(B) Henry Chadwick, *The Early Church* (Grand Rapids, 1968). Probably the best one-volume history available.

(B) Jean Danielou, *The Bible and the Liturgy* (Notre Dame, 1956). An explanation of the relation between Scripture and our liturgical symbols.

(B) Jean Danielou, *Primitive Christian Symbols* (London, 1964). Short chapters cover such topics as the Number 12, the Seal or Sign of the Cross, The Vine, Living Water and Fish, the ship of the Church, the Star, etc.

(C) Josef Jungmann, *The Early Liturgy* (Notre Dame, 1959). A classic description of the Church's early liturgy to the year 500. Explains the development of the Christmas and Easter seasons, the Mass, and Baptism.

(B) Hugo Rahner, *Greek Myths and Christian Mysteries* (New York, 1963). A brilliant work detailing the Christian borrowings from (and contributions to) Greek myths.

(A) Dorothy Sayers, *The Man Born to Be King* (Grand Rapids, 1943, 1974). A series of 12 radio plays done in England during World War II to boost morale. Staging is included. Would be an interesting tool to use in schools.

(A) Henryk Sienkiewicz, *Quo Vadis* (New York, 1960). A romantic fictionalized version of the early Church, immensely popular in the 20th century, and made into a movie. See also Nicholas Wiseman's *Fabiola*.

AUDIO-VISUALS

Jesus of Nazareth. An 8-hour 'mini-series' directed by Franco Zeffirelli, based on the text by William Barclay. The last episode is superb.

The Passion of the Christ. Mel Gibson's graphic portrayal of the last twelve hours of the life of Christ.

Notes

1. Abraham also had a son named Ishmael who, it is believed, fled to the east and became the father of the Arabs. Thus, both Jews and Arabs claim Abraham as their father.

2. Augustus was also known as Octavian. He was the Roman emperor when Christ was born.

3. The main sewer in Rome, the Cloaca Maxima, was built in ancient Rome and is still in use today!

4. Some of the obelisks in Rome, for example, were brought back *in one piece*, a feat which still astonishes us today.

5. Herbert Butterfield, *Christianity and European Civilization* (London, 1951), p. 10.

6. Wayne Meeks, in his work *The First Urban Christians* (New Haven, 1983), claims that Paul's initial contacts came from social clubs common at the time (pp. 29–32).

7. Ronald Knox, *Caliban in Grub Street* (New York, 1930), p. 113.

8. C. S. Lewis, *Miracles* (New York, 1947), pp. 148–149.

9. See Raymond Brown, *The Birth of the Messiah* (Garden City, 1977).

10. The Massacre of the Innocents, as it is called, may very well be historical. While we have no other source for this incident (not even Luke mentions it), and it sounds a little too conveniently similar to the Moses story, where Moses was saved from an identical pogrom (Exodus 1:15—2:10), there is no doubt that Herod was capable of such a deed. While we do not know how many children were killed in this massacre (if any) we do know that Herod had slain not only three of his own children, but several political prisoners and some Pharisees who had been foolish enough to predict his demise.

11. A "Gentile" is simply an outsider, a foreigner. Thus anyone who was not a Jew was a Gentile.

12. Most traditions favor a three-year ministry, though an eastern tradition holds for a one-year ministry, thus drawing an interesting parallel between Christ and the year-old lamb slain at Passover, and the "Year

of the Lord" (Jean Danielou, *Primitive Christian Symbols* [London, 1964], ch. 8).

13. These are only three of the Beatitudes, so-called because the Latin word for "blessed" is *beatitudo* and began each line in the Latin version of the Bible.

14. Chesterton, *Orthodoxy* (New York, 1909), p. 278–279.

15. While the church tended to discourage military service, Christians were not necessarily pacifists. While Christians in well-protected areas like Rome could afford the luxury of pacifism, those in border areas were more likely to be found in the army.

16. Christopher Dawson, *Progress and Religion* (New York, 1938), chapter 9.

17. Most visitors to Rome today visit the Catacombs of Callistus and Sebastian, but they would do well to explore the nearby Catacombs of Domitilla and, in the northern section of the city, the two Catacombs of Priscilla and Agnes.

18. Recent attempts to resurrect the claims of Gnosticism and Gnostic writings, such as Dan Brown's *The Da Vinci Code*, are actually driven more by bigotry than by scholarship.

19. Interestingly, when Latin became more common toward the end of the second century, many Greek speakers opposed its use in the liturgy.

20. Even the Jewish sacrifice was not seen by the people. In Luke 1:21 we see the people "waiting for Zachary, wondering at his delay in the temple." This was not only because the temple area was so sacred, but also because it was too small to accommodate all the people.

21. Incense, though now spiritualized, had its practical benefits: it overcame both the odor of the slaughtered victim, in the case of sacrifice, and the odor of the public, in the case of court hearings.

22. Matt 26:26–29; Mark 14:22–25; Luke 22:19–20; 1 Cor 11:23–26.

23. See Danielou, *Primitive Christian Symbols*, chapter 8.

24. Deaconesses served in the baptismal process for other women, who would be disrobed, immersed in water, and re-robed in white. Whether these women actually served as the equal of male deacons is still a matter of debate.

THE SECOND AGE OF THE CHURCH (330–650 AD)

The Age of the Fathers

The Second Age of the Church does not begin with any real crisis, and in this it is unique. Constantine had embraced the Christian faith and had ended the persecutions directed against the Christians. Henceforward, a new and precarious alliance would exist between the church and the state, which would last for the next 1500 years. While this alliance protected the church from outside persecution, it also gave rise to internal debate. Once the church was free to become public, all sorts of troublesome issues that had lain dormant during the period of persecution suddenly rose to the surface.

The Fathers of the Church

Once the twelve apostles had died, it was left to certain people to carry on the task of spreading the good news and of interpreting Christ's message on matters about which the New Testament had nothing to say. These people are called the fathers of the church. Some of them (such as Clement of Rome and Polycarp of Smyrna) knew the apostles personally, and so are further distinguished by the title "apostolic fathers." Others lived centuries later. They all, however, share four characteristics by which they have always been identified:

1) *Orthodoxy:* Despite the fact that very few of the fathers of the church were orthodox *all* the time, they generally maintained positions which were within the accepted boundaries of

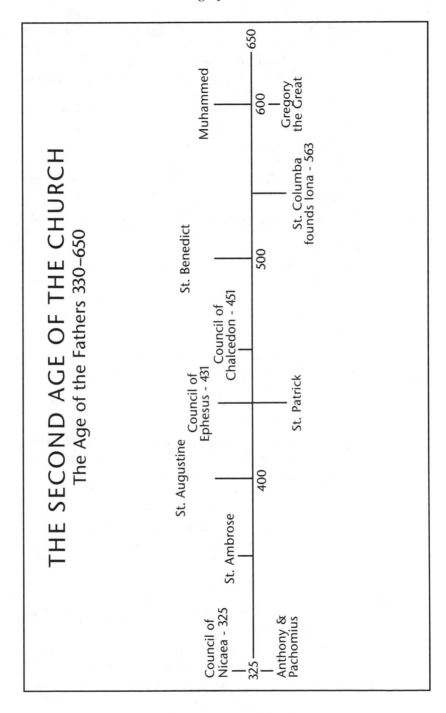

THE SECOND AGE OF THE CHURCH
The Age of the Fathers 330–650

Council of
Nicaea - 325

Anthony &
Pachomius

St. Ambrose

St. Augustine

Council of
Ephesus - 431

Council of
Chalcedon - 451

St. Patrick

St. Benedict

St. Columba
founds Iona - 563

Muhammed

Gregory
the Great

325   400   500   600   650

doctrine. In many cases, as we shall see, they helped set those boundaries. Occasionally they theorized in areas that had no boundaries, and only later would be found to be in error. Origen is the best example of this. Speculating in wholly untried opinions, he was a pioneer who would later (centuries later) be condemned for having crossed boundaries that did not even exist at the time he was living. Even those who erred significantly were not necessarily rejected. Origen and Tertullian (who became a Montanist late in life) have the nebulous honor of being regarded as fathers of the church but are not regarded as saints.

2) *Holiness of Life:* Here again, there is a wide area for interpretation. It is thought by some that Cyril of Alexandria probably committed murder. Yet most of the fathers were holy men, some of them outstandingly so. Care should be taken not to equate holiness with geniality or affability. Saints are not always nice people, nor are they always easy to live with. Jerome was famous for his sharp tongue, which he often directed at Augustine.

3) *Approval by the Church:* This is another gray area. Origen and Tertullian were both found to be in serious error, yet many of their writings have been carefully preserved and recommended by the church. With most others, the church's approval was unequivocal.

4) *Antiquity:* The fathers of the church come from a period of the church's development no later than 750 AD. John Damascene (d. 750) is generally regarded to be the last of the fathers.

Much about these men is uneven. Some of them, like Augustine, Athanasius, and Ambrose, enjoy universal reputations, while others, like Arnobius of Sica, are hardly known at all. Their literary output is also of unequal value: Certain writings are almost soaring in their insight and permanence, while others are trite and ephemeral.

The fathers should be remembered for one thing: They explained the message of the Gospel to a Greek and Roman world.[1] In translating this message they adopted a Greek, and later a Latin, vocabulary and classical forms to describe Christian ideas. Words such as *logos* and *hypostasis* were simply borrowed from

Greek philosophy and made to do service in the Christian sphere. As ingenious and necessary as this was, it also caused problems, for it entailed a complete transition of thought, and not just a mere word-for-word translation. As any translator knows, translation involves interpretation, and it was this interpretation that was a matter of considerable debate, especially in the east, where fine shades of meaning were taken very seriously. When news of the Council of Chalcedon (451) reached the people of Alexandria, they rose up and slaughtered the imperial garrison. Later on, over the same matter, they also murdered their archbishop in his cathedral.

To some of the fathers, such as Tertullian, this attempt to blend classical thought with Christian belief was a surrender. He asked, "What has Athens to do with Jerusalem?" and feared that Greek philosophy would dictate terms to the gospel.[2] But most of the fathers disagreed with this position and looked on Greek philosophy as a tool, perhaps a tool providentially placed by God, which should be used. Whatever in Greek thought was false was to be discarded, but whatever was true could be useful in explaining divine truth. Truth, after all, is truth. Thus the Greeks were looked on as having a natural revelation—given to anyone who has the gift of reason—while the Christians had an additional revelation, a particular one that was superior because it was more direct and more specific. These fathers insisted that Christianity had nothing to fear from reason. Fortunately for the integrity of the church, they carried the day.

Contributions of the Fathers

The contributions of the fathers were various. Jerome, for instance, translated the Bible into Latin about the year 400, an edition that was regarded by the Catholic Church as authoritative as late as the 1950s.[3] Tertullian (c. 200) was also a translator of sorts, famous for his invention of such Latin words as *trinitas* to describe eastern ideas. He was the first great western theologian, when the west lacked both an interest in eastern thought and a vocabulary to describe eastern abstractions. Tertullian, almost single-handedly, brought the great intellectual tradition of the east to the west.

Origen (c. 200) is another towering figure in the early church. He has been called "the greatest scholar in Christian antiquity."[4] Origen was called "The Teacher of the Church after the Apostles" by Jerome, who claimed that Origen wrote some two thousand books, though most of his literary output has been destroyed. Epiphanius, an early bishop, claimed that Origen wrote *six* thousand books. Everything Origen did was on a grand scale. One contemporary stated, "When he writes well, no one writes better; when he writes badly, no one writes worse."

Origen concentrated most of his efforts on the Bible, seeking to establish a definitive text and a method of biblical interpretation known as allegory or typology, which is now out of favor. Typology means searching out precedents in the Old Testament for New Testament events or persons. Adam, for example, is regarded as a *type* of Christ: Adam was the first man, imperfect and sinful, while Christ is the Second Adam, now perfect and sinless, correcting what Adam had made wrong. Water is another type, and whenever Origen saw water in the Old Testament, he saw a prefiguration of baptism: the rivers of creation, the deluge, the crossing of the Red Sea; the water drawn from the rock by Moses.

At times this method of interpretation was overdone and some typologists went to ridiculous lengths in drawing comparisons between the two testaments. Even Origen admitted that allegory had its limits, but he thought that, properly used, it got to the heart of the Bible. His symbolic treatment of the Old Testament gave great richness to the liturgical life of the church, a richness that is still especially evident in the liturgies of Holy Thursday, Good Friday, and the Easter Vigil. Two great schools of biblical interpretation emerged, those of Alexandria and Antioch. Generally speaking they can be identified as following the allegorical and literal interpretations of Scripture respectively, but both schools were far more nuanced than these labels suggest. The school of Alexandria was not as completely given to allegory, nor Antioch to literal interpretation, as scholars have suggested.[5]

Ambrose (339–97) was a western father and the one most responsible for giving autonomy to the church of the west. Since the days of Constantine, the emperor had gained more and more control over the workings of the church—even to the point of summoning councils and deciding when their business was over. Ambrose saw this as a danger and tried to make the church independent of this interference. Ambrose, in fact, envisioned the formation of a Christian state, in which the church would be superior to the state. So powerful was he as bishop of Milan that he humbled the Emperor Theodosius after Theodosius had perpetrated a massacre. Ambrose forbade him entry into the cathedral until he did public and humiliating penance. To Christopher Dawson, Ambrose stood at a crossroads between the classical ideal of civic responsibility and the medieval ideal of spiritual supremacy:

> He [Ambrose] has something of the Roman magistrate and something of the mediaeval pontiff. In his eyes the law of the Church...could only be administered by the magistrates of the Church—the bishops—and even the emperor himself was subject to this authority. "The emperor," he wrote, "is within the Church, not over it"; and "in matters of faith bishops are wont to be the judges of Christian emperors, not emperors of bishops."[6]

Nowhere would this ideal be more contested than over the papacy.

The Papacy

Ambrose's vision of an autonomous episcopacy was not evident to the emperor. Constantine's recognition of the Christian Church in 313 was both a blessing and a curse. The advantages were obvious: Constantine endowed the church with public security and legal recognition, he donated property and began several ambitious building projects, and he held the opposition at bay. But by recognizing the church as a public or legal body, Constantine put the church in an inferior position—under himself as the supreme lawgiver, the *pontifex maximus*. Hence he convoked the first church councils, beginning with Arles in 314. He decided when such councils were over, and whether their decisions were valid and had the force of law. He also drew ecclesiastical districts,

Roman emperor Constantine the Great (ca. 274-337) issued the Edict of Milan, which accorded Christianity equal status with the other religions of the empire. He intervened zealously in theological disputes of his day in the interests of unity in his realm.

appointed bishops, and heard appeals on ecclesiastical matters. Given what we know of the early papacy, a clash between emperor and pope was inevitable.

In 381 the Council of Constantinople decreed that no bishop could interfere in the affairs of another diocese. While this was directed at Arian bishops, who were notorious meddlers, it also excluded the bishop of Rome from interfering in the affairs of Constantinople. Pope Damasus attempted to counteract this by introducing the Petrine theme at a Roman synod which met the following year. The Petrine theme was the notion that Rome was the See of Peter, which implied superiority to other dioceses. This had been previously mentioned by Cyprian in the mid-200s, and even earlier by Tertullian.

Other factors led to the embellishment of Roman independence as opposed to control by the emperor in Constantinople. Among them was the translation of the Bible into Latin (c. 350 AD). This provided a Bible that put such terms as to bind and to loose into legal language: *ligare* and *solvere*. Another contributing factor was the invasion of barbarian tribes from regions to the east, that caused the Roman government (in Constantinople) to abandon the west, leaving the only effective government in the hands of the church.

With Leo I (the Great), Bishop of Rome from 440–61, the papal position was consolidated by a combination of biblical, theological, and juridical arguments. Leo claimed that the pope inherited the office, the legal status, and the *objective* powers of St. Peter, but not Peter's personality or *subjective* merits. Thus the person of the pope is separated from the office of the pope—an argument found not surprisingly a generation following St. Augustine's parallel argument for the objective content of sacrament vs. the subjective worthiness of the minister. By principles of Roman law, the pope as office-holder was indistinguishable from St. Peter. He followed St. Peter directly, and not his (the pope's) predecessor. There was no intermediary between the pope and St. Peter. Thus Pope John Paul II did not obtain his power from Pope John Paul I (as a hereditary monarch would), but from Peter himself. Furthermore, the office of the papacy could be measured by objective criteria. This meant that the validity of a papal decree did not depend on the holiness of an individual pope, but on legal grounds.

Next, Leo daringly drew Ambrose's distinction of power to its logical conclusion: since the pope's office was directly connected to Peter's, which had been given directly to Peter by Christ, the pope's authority is clearly superior to the emperor's, which is either inherited or the result of a coup. If this is the case, the pope has jurisdiction in ecclesiastical matters over the emperor, who is merely a member of that church. The emperor, for his part, had civic jurisdiction over the pope insofar as the pope is a citizen of the empire. Leo may rightly be called the first theologian of the papacy.

Thus pope and emperor began to go their separate ways. In the west, the pope was supreme. Kings and tribal chiefs sought to draw the connection between their rule and God's rule—i.e., their rule was given to them by God—and needed the blessing of the pope. They would seek the pope's approval as God's approval. In the east the emperor rejected Leo's argument and remained supreme. This is called *caesaro-papism*, where the emperor also claimed the authority to run the church, which he did in the east until 1453, when Constantinople fell to the Turks.

What the pope needed next was physical security. It was one thing to make broad claims, no matter how historically and theologically they were rooted, but it was quite another to put them into effect. In 496 the Frankish king Clovis converted to Christianity, and with him his entire tribe. This was the secure base from which the popes would begin to operate in the west. Gregory I (the Great), pope from 590–604, had served as ambassador to the imperial court in Constantinople and knew the futility of waiting for the emperor to submit to the claims of Rome. So on his election to the papacy Gregory decided to concentrate his authority on those areas of Europe beyond the reach of Constantinople: Britain, Spain, and France. He would use the new monasticism as his organizational and driving force.

Unfortunately for the popes, Italy was still within reach of the emperor, who arrested Pope Martin I in 649 and exiled him until he died in 655. The pope had defied an imperial order for-

The Baptism of Clovis. Clovis (466–511) was the first king to unite the Frankish tribes under one ruler. Through the influence of his wife, the Princess Clothilde, he became a Christian. Clovis and his Franks were the first barbarian tribe to convert to Catholic rather than Arian Christianity.

bidding further discussion of the wills or energies of Christ. It would be another one hundred years before the popes would gain the security they desired. This security would come from the dominant tribe, the Franks. Charles Martel, the king of the Franks, defeated the Muslims at the Battle of Tours in 732. His son, Pippin, was recognized by the pope as the legitimate ruler of the Franks. Charles then gave the pope land in central Italy.[7] In 800 the pope crowned Charlemagne head of the Holy Roman Empire, effectively dividing the empire in two. While this was inevitable, it still came as a shock to the easterners.

The First Christological Councils

Once the persecution had ended in 311, the church found itself with the freedom to reflect on its own beliefs and debate them in public. Previously its time had been taken up almost completely by the fight for survival. Now that the fight had been won, the church had to examine what it really believed. The first serious questions concerned what it really believed about Jesus Christ.

The Council of Nicaea (325)

Arius was an eastern monk who thought that he detected a contradiction in the nature of Christ. While there was ample evidence that Christ was human—he ate, for example, and drank, and wept, became weary, suffered, and died—there did not seem to be a corresponding amount of evidence that he was God. Besides, there was the logical problem of the oneness of God. Since there cannot be two Gods, Christ the Son simply could not be God in the same sense that the Father was God. Christ, according to Arius, was therefore a mere created human being—a great man, and one who was greater than all others, but a man nonetheless.

We forget how seriously all of this was taken. Disputes such as this one were not restricted to scholars, but were discussed by everyone. One writer of the period (Gregory of Nazianzen) said that if you went to the baker, he would not tell you the price of bread, but would "argue that the Father is greater than the Son."

Sometimes this even led to rioting. Rival bands of monks would roam through the cities harassing the populace, threatening councils with violence until they got their way. So violent could this all become that the settling of the dispute was not only a matter for theology, it involved public order. Public officials often became embroiled in these debates and convoked councils in order to settle them, even to the point of dictating terms to the councils.

Arius was called in by his local bishop (of Alexandria), and when his answers proved unsatisfactory, he was excommunicated. Arius, however, was not to be put off so easily and appealed to another bishop, who backed him. This escalated the affair into something regional rather than local, and the bishop of Alexandria summoned a synod of all Egypt in 319, about 100 bishops, which condemned Arius and issued an encyclical which was sent to *all* the bishops of the church. This now made the disagreement universal and caught the eye of Emperor Constantine, who wished to resolve the difficulty quickly by summoning a council of the church. It was to be held at Nicaea in Asia Minor, close to Constantinople, so that the emperor could keep a close watch over the proceedings.

Despite the universality of the problem, Arius's difficulty was primarily an eastern issue, and was addressed in the east by eastern bishops. Of the nearly three hundred participants at the council, only five bishops came from the west, among them a representative of the pope. They decided, after reviewing all the scriptural evidence and logical deductions from that evidence, that Christ had two natures—a human nature and a divine nature—and that he was, in fact, God. Did this mean, as Arius thought, that the church believed in two Gods? The council fathers were not as simple as that. They maintained a delicate balance between the oneness of God and the divinity of Christ by positing some philosophical distinctions: The Father and the Son (Christ) are one in substance or being *(ousia)*, but distinct in person *(prosopon)*.[8] Thus Nicaea affirmed that there was only one God, but that this God could be distinguished in person.

The council drew up a list of statements which held that Christ was "God from God, Light from Light, True God from True God, Begotten not made, One in being with the Father." Anyone who did not accept these statements was excommunicated. The followers of Arius (or Arians, as they became known) initially gave in and signed the creed, but later some recanted and the problem lingered. The Arians found their strength in the fringe areas of the Roman Empire—especially barbarian lands in northern Europe and the area of Arabia. From this latter area would arise Islam, one of whose major tenets is, not surprisingly, that Christ is not God.

It is instructive that the Second Age of the Church both began and ended in controversies about Christ, from the denial of his divinity by Arius to the similar denial by Muhammad three hundred years later. The church would never suffer more than in defending this basic doctrine—that Jesus Christ is God—which it defined formally at Nicaea in 325.

The Council of Constantinople (381)

Toward the end of the fourth century, it was evident that another council was needed to reaffirm Nicaea. Political and ecclesiastical chaos had resulted from the earlier council as emperors took various sides and rival bishops forced out their competitors. In fact, the fourth century might be called the most chaotic century the church has had to endure. Athanasius, the bishop of Alexandria, was exiled five different times and was threatened with kidnapping at least once.

The new council at Constantinople, presided over by a new generation of fathers, basically underlined what had been done at Nicaea. Certain statements were added to the creed of Nicaea which bolstered the earlier statements and made them more explicit. The council declared that Christ was "born of the Virgin Mary and became man...was crucified under Pontius Pilate...and is seated at the right hand of the Father." Moreover, statements were added about the Holy Spirit, stressing that he, too, is God, "the Lord the Giver of Life, who proceeds from the Father, with the Father and the Son he is worshipped and glorified; he has spoken through the prophets." Thus the creed that we recite today is a combination of statements from these two councils.

The basic argument at both Nicaea and Constantinople was over the creatureliness of Jesus Christ. The Arians claimed he was

St. Athanasius (ca. 295–373), bishop of Alexandria, attended the Council of Nicaea and fought vehemently against the heretics of his day. St. Gregory Nazianzen (330–390), bishop of Caesarea and then of Constantinople, staunchly opposed Arianism. Both these doctors of the church suffered considerable abuse for their championing of the truth.

created, although they nuanced this to say that Christ became *flesh*, and not fully man—that he had the body of a man, but the soul of God. But the problem here was that it made Christ into something changeable and inferior. If he had to be created, something (which created him) was superior, and thus the council fathers insisted that Christ was uncreated—"begotten, not made." To emphasize the point, the liturgy was used to convey the idea that all three persons were on a par. Doxologies (mention of the Father, Son, and Holy Spirit) were added at the end of the opening prayer of the Mass, at the end of the canon of the Mass, and at the end of psalms recited each day as the prayer of the church.

The Council of Ephesus (431)

Some people thought that the two councils had cleared the air but had not solved the problem. Nestorius, the bishop of Constantinople, was one such, and he attempted another formulation hoping to avoid the errors of the Arians, but also hoping to avoid the idea that Mary was the Mother of God. After all, the Greeks were Platonists for the most part, and Plato thought that worldly things were imperfect because they were created by something higher and because they were limited.[9] It would not do to have a human being give birth to God Almighty, or, for that matter, to have God Almighty doing things like being born, walking the earth, eating, drinking, dying. So Nestorius said that Christ had two "personalities," or was two distinct persons—that he was God and had always been God, but that for a time he put this divinity aside and became man. After the resurrection, he reverted to being God and ceased being man. In other words, Christ could be one or the other, God *or* man, but he could not be both at the same time. The conclusions to be drawn from this are that the child born in Bethlehem was not *God*, the person who died on the cross was not *God*, and Mary was not the Mother of *God*. She was the Mother of *Christ*. According to Nestorius, *Christ*, not God, was born in Bethlehem; *Christ*, not God, had died on the cross.

Cyril, the Bishop of Alexandria, went after Nestorius with a vengeance. Both men had their problems: Cyril was a schemer and a dirty politician, while Nestorius was arrogant and intolerant. Add to this personality conflict the rivalry between the cities of Constantinople and Alexandria, and you have the makings of a huge quarrel, and a huge quarrel is exactly what occurred. Pope Celestine, once again showing the long arm of the bishop of Rome, ordered Nestorius to recant within ten days, and he made Cyril his agent in this matter. Cyril then added twelve of his own propositions to the recantation which, of course, Nestorius refused to sign. Emperor Theodosius felt the need to summon a council, which was held at Ephesus in Asia Minor, in 431.

The council began and ended in chaos, thanks largely to Cyril, who began the council before the Nestorian party from Syria and the Roman delegation had arrived. In all, 150 bishops assembled, although Nestorius and a few friends stayed away, saying they would attend when everyone was present. At this meeting Nestorius was deposed and was declared "the new Judas." Four days later the Nestorian party arrived and held its own meeting (composed of fifty bishops) and deposed Cyril. A second session was held—presumably with both parties present, including the pope's delegates, and the majority condemned *all* of the Nestorian bishops, who, in turn, excommunicated the whole of Cyril's group. The emperor's representative then arrived and, seeing the confusion, invalidated the entire proceedings and deposed both Nestorius and Cyril.

The amazing thing is that, given all the intrigue and disagreement, quite a lot was accomplished at the council. The Nicene/Constantinople Creed was declared normative, and all later developments would be measured against it. In addition, Cyril's *Second Letter to Nestorius* was declared to be in harmony with Nicaea, and thus orthodox. In this letter, Cyril had said two key things: a) that what happens to Christ as a man happens to him as God;[10] and b) that Mary was the Mother of God. This first claim is crucial because it holds for a radical unity in Christ. Cyril argued that if Christ did not come to earth as God, and die and rise as God, then there was no saving action; then we are not redeemed. In his argument, he attacked the illogic of saying that God could put aside his divinity for a time. One cannot be God one minute and then not God the next. And this reasoning led to the second claim—that Mary was the Mother of God. Nestorius had said she was the Christ-Bearer, the *Christotokos*, but Cyril and the council affirmed that she was the God-Bearer, the *Theotokos*. They did this on the basis of logic more than anything else. If Christ was indeed God, then Mary was God's mother. These decisions made at Ephesus had immediate liturgical consequences. The first known depiction of Christ on the cross is on the wooden door at the church of Santa Sabina in Rome, built about the year 450. The first church dedicated to Mary was also in Rome, Saint Mary Major, built about the year 435.

Though it was Cyril's opinion that prevailed, he would never be remembered well by the Nestorians. When he died, one Nestorian bishop wrote:

> The living are delighted. The dead, perhaps, are sorry, afraid they may be burdened with his company....May the guild of undertakers lay a huge, heavy stone on his grave, lest he should come back again and show his faithless mind again. Let him take his new doctrines to Hell, and preach to the damned all day and night.

The Council of Chalcedon (451)

Not long after Nestorius had been dealt with, there arose a further interpretation about the nature of Christ that came from another monk, named Eutyches. And so another council was duly assembled in Chalcedon—again in Asia Minor—in the year 451. Of the five hundred bishops present, only four came from the west. Eutyches held that there was only one *nature* in Christ—which was a divine one. Christ, therefore, only *seemed* to be human: he did not need to eat, nor was he really eating; he was only play-acting. The Greek verb for "to seem" is *dokeo*, and thus this interpretation was called "Docetism."[11] It was an explanation that had the merit of maintaining the divinity of Christ throughout his earthly ministry, but made problematic his human existence and his honesty. If God is truth, after all, then why this elaborate hoax?

The council simply reaffirmed Nicaea. Thus, with Eutyches, the full circle of theories about the natures of Christ had run its course. Arius had begun the discussion with a doubt about Christ's divinity, Nestorius had compromised and said that Christ was human and divine—but in two different persons—and Eutyches claimed that Christ was not human at all, but that he was *only* God.

The Development of Doctrine

The church was beginning to gain a sense of how doctrine or dogma develops, of how doctrine gradually comes to be defined and refined. Doctrine, or a statement about what we believe, did not come ready-made out of the New Testament. Scripture provided a body of material which, when placed in a different cultural setting, required some adaptation. The church was fortunate in having its original revelation in a form that could be described as culturally or philosophically neutral. At least Jewish concepts were simpler than Greek concepts, and so the initial message was not weighed down by very much cultural or philosophical baggage. It was left to each individual culture to accept the raw material and give it a particular shape. The Greeks were the first to do this in any significant way, being the philosophers they were.

The pattern of development that became evident was that of an oscillation between challenge and definition. Very few doctrines held by the church have been defined unless they were first challenged. Even then the definition has been a cautious narrowing of the boundaries: The church might not say what was precisely or exclusively right; but it knew what was wrong. Arius's case is a good example: It was not until Arius challenged the divinity of Christ that the church *defined* Christ's divinity. Only when Eutyches challenged Christ's humanity did the church provide some definition of that. These doctrines were there all along, but in an implicit and unwritten form. When the doctrine was threatened, the church made the doctrine explicit.

Some people have looked on the lack of a formal doctrinal definition as proof of a doctrine's nonexistence. They claim, for example, that Mary was not regarded as the Mother of God until 431. The fact is that no one bothered to question her as the Mother of God until 431. One modern evangelist, Jimmy

Swaggart, has given voice to a similar misunderstanding: "Actually, throughout the entire New Testament period, *and for three hundred years afterward*, there was no Catholic Pope. Further, during these same three hundred years, there was no Catholic Church!"[12] St. Irenaeus, who was the bishop of Lyons in the second century, would have been surprised to hear this. If Swaggart's reasoning were strictly adhered to, then it would be equally true to say that the church did not believe Christ was God until the year 325. All that such *lacunae* mean is that a specific doctrine had not been attacked until a certain date, and required no reasoned defense until then.

Because the council fathers came to the evidence honestly and did not attempt to impose their beliefs on Scripture, their definitions were cautious and left much ground for debate. Scripture can be ambiguous, confusing, and contradictory, and the early church fathers gave it a wide berth. Even the twentieth-century church debated about the limits of the divinity and humanity of Christ—specifically how much Christ actually knew.

As the church proceeded through the centuries, the limits of certain doctrines slowly narrowed, though never came to a point, since human language will never be able to describe fully or finally a divine mystery. The development of doctrine does not mean a rigid adherence to one idea, but rather a delicate balance between two extremes. The church could hold for the humanity of Christ on the one hand and his divinity on the other. If it was to respect Scripture, it had to balance both sides. And it did so in any number of areas: marriage and celibacy, pleasure and abstinence, freedom and obedience. G. K. Chesterton, in his book *Orthodoxy*, observed that the history of the church was like a wild ride down a mountain road, with the carriage careening from one guardrail to another: "The heavenly chariot flies thundering through the ages, the dull heresies sprawling and prostrate, the wild truth reeling but erect."[13]

St. Augustine (354–430)

Next to St. Paul, the most influential person in the Christian Church—at least in the Western Church—was St. Augustine. He was born in North Africa in 354 and was thoroughly western. He came to Christianity slowly, and only after going through successive stages first of worldliness and then of asceticism. In his early life he became enamored of the classics and the Roman way of life.

Augustine taught rhetoric in Carthage and later in Rome, at the same time taking a mistress, by whom he had a son. He became dissatisfied with what he thought was a dissolute life and turned to Manicheism, a sect that denied the goodness of physical and material things. After hearing St. Ambrose preach in Milan, Augustine experienced a conversion not altogether different from Paul's: A child's voice came to him in a garden which repeated, "Take it and read it." Augustine went to an open copy of the New Testament and read from Paul's Letter to the Romans: "Not in reveling and drunkenness, not in lust and wantonness, not in quarrels and rivalries, rather, arm yourselves with the Lord Jesus Christ. Spend no more thought on nature and nature's appetites."

The Church in North Africa

It is important to realize that north Africa was not "African" in the sense that we know it today. Africa north of the Sahara Desert was an extension of Europe. Christianity, south of the Sahara, hardly existed except in Ethiopia, which became cut off in the 600s by the advance of Islam. An independent form of Christianity survived in Ethiopia, when it was rediscovered in the nineteenth century by European explorers and missionaries. In Lalibela, there are eleven churches carved into solid rock, the most spectacular of them being St. George, which was constructed in the thirteenth century. It goes forty feet down and is carved from a single rock.

Augustine wrote later, "I had no wish to read more and no need to do so, for in an instant as I came to the end of the sentence, it was as though the light of confidence flooded into my heart and all the darkness and doubt was dispelled."[14]

Augustine did not do things by halves; not only did he convert to Christianity, but he became a bishop in 395—of Hippo, in North Africa. He remained in this post until his death in 430. His two most famous works are the *Confessions* and *The City of God*. Rome had fallen in 410, sacked by Alaric and his Visigoth soldiers, and the western world was shocked. Aristocratic Romans wept at the loss of their once-great nation, and even Christians reacted with feeling. St. Jerome wrote, "If Rome can perish, what can be safe?" Explanations were looked for, and Augustine sought to answer the accusations that Rome had fallen because of the presence of Christianity. For Augustine, the fall of Rome was a tragic thing, but symbolic of the inevitable fall of the earthly city. So Augustine wrote *The City of God* to explain the fall of Rome in Christian terms. There was, he said, a fundamental difference between the City of Man which, no matter how great it became, was still a passing thing, and the City of God, which was eternal and indestructible. His point was platonic: The real earthly kingdom is by its very nature imperfect and prone to destruction, whereas the heavenly kingdom is perfect and everlasting. While we must live in the world, we must set our sights on heaven and not be too discouraged by the passing of an earthly civilization.

Augustine's *City of God* was written for the Roman aristocracy which had been arriving in North Africa as refugees, and it was a masterpiece of classical literature. It was filled with allusions to Latin authors and, as Peter Brown has written, it used arguments "to show that he [Augustine], also, could move among the cumulus clouds of erudition."[15] But Augustine added Christian authors as well—*our* authors as he calls them—because they had gone beyond the inadequate ideas of the pagan authors. These pagan authors, great as they were, could not answer the great question of life; only Christian authors could.

Augustine's treatment of the fall of Rome borders on the sympathetic. He says that the Romans had created an earthly city

St. Augustine of Hippo (354–430) converted to Christianity after a wayward life and lengthy search for the truth, and became bishop of this north African town. Possessor of one of the greatest minds of all time, he wrote prolifically. Among his greatest works are his *Confessions* and *The City of God*.

and, because they knew nothing else, were forced to worship their handiwork. Peter Brown comments:

> Committed to the fragile world they had created, they were forced to idealize it; they had to deny any evil in its past, and the certainty of death in its future. Even the most honest of their historians, Sallust, had lied in praising the ancient days of Rome. This was inevitable, "for," as Augustine said poignantly, "he had no other city to praise."[16]

This attempt by Augustine to explain historical events in religious terms is known as the theology of history. In an earlier age the Jews possessed a similar, though more basic, approach to history. Their notion was that God was on their side in victory, fair weather, abundant harvests, and large families, and furthermore that God punished their sinfulness in military defeats, bad weather, famines, childlessness, etc. The Jews saw every historical or natural event in terms of their faithfulness or unfaithfulness to God. Augustine was more sophisticated than this, having had the benefit of a classical education. Nations, he said, must of necessity pass away because they are of this world and must deal with this world. As a result, Augustine did not share in the growing optimism about a Christian state, as promoted by St. Ambrose. So great was the gulf between heaven and earth that no human institution such as the state, however Christian in its policy, could hope to bridge the gap.

The *Confessions*

The *Confessions* was an earlier work, one that Augustine wrote just before he became the bishop of Hippo. It was shorter and more personal than the dense *City of God*, and it is therefore more accessible to modern readers. It is regarded as the world's first autobiography. Just as Augustine had traced world events in terms of a plan of God in his *City of God*, so he traced his personal life in terms of a plan of God in the *Confessions*. God led him somehow, inexplicably, through a life of sin to Christianity. Much like St. Paul had been led by God—despite his doubt and sinfulness—so had Augustine been led.

Augustine was a man of contrasts who not only thought in contrasts, but who saw contrasts in his own life: good vs. evil, God vs. human weakness. The *Confessions* was a cogent witness to that contrast—an admission by Augustine that he had come to realize the error of his past, the weakness of his present, and the possibility of the future under the guidance of Christ. As bishop of Hippo, Augustine had to deal with errors other than his own youthful ones; he faced three major and widely divergent heresies, and his response to them set the course of the church's moral and sacramental doctrine to the present day. Before we enumerate these three heresies, it is important to note that western Christianity and eastern Christianity were concerned with matters of almost no interest to the other. This was owing to the very different approaches to life which had grown up in west and east. Easterners, as we have seen, were speculative and philosophical, and concerned themselves with things as they are, such as the nature of Christ. The westerners, on the other hand, had always been more practical and legal, concerned themselves with how things work, and found themselves arguing more about the duties of the Christian. The

west has social doctrine, east doesn't

east wanted to know who Christ was, and the west wanted to know what Christ wanted them to do. Their respective enthusiasm about Christian doctrine followed those directions.

Manichaeism

The first serious heresy to confront Augustine was Manicheanism, which sought to answer the problem of evil—i.e., why do the innocent suffer? The Manicheans, who had been founded in the east by a preacher named Mani (d. 277), posited the existence of a good God and a bad God. It was Platonism in the extreme, because spirit was again equated with good and matter was equated with evil. All material things were corrupt and subject to decay or destruction, while all spiritual things were perfect. But something had to create these evil things, and that would have to be some sort of evil God or Force of Darkness. At one time in his life, Augustine had been attracted to this doctrine because it answered so many questions about life so easily, and he actually went so far as to become a Manichee before he became a Christian. He knew, therefore, the weaknesses of the Manichean argument. The first weakness was logic—Augustine argued that there must be *one* God, because any division would render God "divided against himself," and would mean that God was neither perfect, nor all-powerful.

Augustine's argument from logic did not end there. If this one God is perfect (he reasoned), then he is also good (because goodness is a positive element whereas evil is only the lack, or privation, of good), and therefore everything he has created is good. The creation itself must be, of its very nature, imperfect because it is finite and has been created by a superior being. But only humanity can make this imperfect creation into something immoral and refuse to accept the order God intended for creation. What causes evil, therefore, is not an evil God, but humanity, who misuses creation. Humans themselves are creatures, but have the dignity of freedom, so that while humans are necessarily weak and prone to misuse creation, they are not *determined* to do so.

Augustine's teaching here was astonishing, given his own innate distrust of human activity, because his logic forced him to concede the goodness of creation. Physical pleasure is good, he argued, because God created it, but we can misuse it—and, in fact, the greater the pleasure, the more likely we are to abuse it. Thus sexual pleasure and marriage were two things which Augustine staunchly defended, even though he knew they would be frequently abused—"Nothing is so powerful," he wrote, "in drawing the spirit of a man downwards as the caresses of a woman."

But Augustine found even more problems with Manichean teaching on evil. Not only was it illogical, but it made evil to be the only dynamic—interesting—force in the universe. Goodness for the Manichees was a bland absence of evil. In the Manichean universe, evil kept breaking in to a passive, good world, and this was unacceptable to Augustine. Goodness, if God was good, was dynamic and had tremendous powers. Finally, this Manichean emphasis on the force of evil did not allow one to grow in holiness. One simply avoided evil, or pleasure, but there was nothing one could do to increase one's love of God or closeness to God.[17]

Donatism

The Donatist controversy grew out of the persecutions. A bishop, Felix of Aptunga, who apostatized during Diocletian's persecution, ordained Caecilian as the bishop of Carthage. Other African bishops questioned the validity of this ordination, and so they elected a rival bishop whom they regarded as the real bishop of Carthage. This man was succeeded by Donatus, and hence the name of the controversy. The basic issue was whether an apostate or a notorious sinner could validly administer the sacraments. The Donatists took a rigorist position on this and insisted that the minister must be holy or pure in order to perform the sacraments.

Augustine saw the danger of elitism in this, and, as the controversy wore on, the Donatists did, in fact, become more and more elitist. Augustine taught that the church is holy, not because its members are holy but because its founder and its purposes are holy. Sacraments are valid because of their inner purity and sanctity, not because of the sanctity of the minister. Thus baptism, if administered according to the proper form and intention (however minimal that intention might be), is valid whether the minister is "worthy" or not. It is not Peter who baptizes; it is Christ. Sacraments, as a result, are available to all, and not merely to an elect group.

The Donatist controversy remained restricted to North Africa, but was greatly divisive nonetheless. Basilicas were taken over by Donatists, acts of violence were committed against bishops and priests loyal to Rome, and some Donatist bishops even led extreme groups of Donatists called Circumcellions into combat with government forces. The government, after going back and forth on the issue, finally outlawed the Donatists in 405. The controversy ended surprisingly easily. The orthodox bishop in each diocese was declared the ordinary (or principal) bishop. If there was a Donatist bishop in the same diocese, he (because he was validly ordained as well) was declared the coadjutor, or the bishop with right of succession. Any bishop who disagreed with this arrangement (and there were a few Donatist bishops who did) were imprisoned and thus rendered incapable of ordaining anyone else and perpetuating the problem.

Pelagianism

Like many heresies, Pelagianism was named for a man, Pelagius, who had little interest in a fight and whose main ideas were championed by his followers. There is even some question today about whether Pelagius was really a Pelagian himself. He was trying to correct the tendency to be superstitious about sacraments—people, for example, who thought that baptism *guaranteed* their salvation. He also tried to counter the notion that the human condition is *so* hopeless that we cannot help but sin, a notion that leads to passivity toward sin. These were notions that needed correcting, but Augustine thought the corrective measures proposed by the Pelagians went too far to the other extreme.

Pelagianism was a rigorist movement, but in opposite ways to Manichaeism and Donatism. Rather than being pessimistic about human nature and created things, it had great optimism about them. So confident was Pelagianism in the possibility of human achievement that it taught the individual had all the means necessary to ensure his own salvation. Adam, in other words, had not committed an "original" sin—affecting all generations; his sin was no more than a personal fall and served only as a bad example. Infants, therefore, did not need to be baptized; and baptism itself did not appear to be especially necessary to the process of salvation. If mankind was truly free, then the whole concept of original sin was illogical.

This was not all. If original sin does not exist, the Pelagians taught, then death and ignorance are not the consequences of sin, but rather the results of nature. Furthermore, Christ's coming was not necessary, but served only as an antidote to the bad example set by Adam. The operative word in all of this was "necessary." Was Christ's coming necessary for our salvation, or are we merely aided by his words and deeds? Is our own initiative and conversion all that is necessary for salvation? The Pelagians were not laxists and were not promoting a "bare minimum" approach to Christianity. If anything, they promoted the opposite: they claimed that whatever good an individual was capable of doing, he was *obligated* to do. Anything short of that was sin.

Against this, Augustine said that Scripture makes it clear that Adam's sin affected mankind generally, making it necessary for Christ to come and reconcile the human race to God. One implication of this is that all people—even infants who were personally sinless—needed baptism, since this was the sign on their part that they were responding to Christ's saving action. We cannot *merit* eternal life. We can only respond to God's call, and even that response is the result of grace, or a gift from God. Augustine tended to exaggerate the inevitability of the action of grace, a position which bordered on predestination and was rescued from that extreme only by later commentators.

One interesting aspect of this controversy is that the Pelagians appear to be the optimistic party, while Augustine seems to be the harsh and unbending advocate of man's innate sinfulness. And yet, the actual situation is the reverse of this. Because the Pelagians were confident about the possibility of human activity, they were also impatient and condemnatory of those who did not measure up. Augustine, on the other hand, knew first hand that sin was more complicated than a simple cold decision to oppose God. He recognized factors that might influence a sinner: upbringing, environment, human passions, the spirit of a particular age—all of which detracted from absolute human freedom. Augustine had an intimate knowledge not only of the actions and results of sin, but of the motivations that were behind a sin. Consequently, his approach was always more patient and forgiving than that of the Pelagians.

This is very nearly an anomaly, given Augustine's own harshness and distrust of human possibility, and makes Augustine all that much more remarkable. No one, perhaps, understood the psychology of sin better than Augustine. He knew intimately the forces that played on people and the need to have compassion on the sinner. Hence, he instinctively hesitated to condemn those who did not measure up. He wrote: "Many sins are committed through pride, but not all happen proudly....They happen so often by ignorance, by human weakness; many are committed by men weeping and groaning in their distress."[18]

This sympathy for the sinner presented the church with a legacy of Christian forgiveness and a greater awareness of its mission in distinguishing hatred for sin from love for the sinner. Had Augustine done nothing else, this alone would have earned him the gratitude of future generations.

The Veneration of the Saints

There was very little that the mind of St. Augustine did not touch upon during his career as bishop of Hippo. One final subject that concerned him was the veneration of saints, and he, along with other bishops of the time—especially Ambrose and Martin of Tours, ensured that such veneration would not go astray.

All of the first saints were martyrs, i.e., those who had died witnessing to the faith.[19] The veneration of their remains grew out of the Christian reverence for their deeds and the Roman practices in honoring their dead. Every year on the anniversary of a person's death, the Roman practice was for the family of the deceased to gather at the tomb to celebrate a memorial meal. This was called a *refrigerium*. Christians quickly adapted this and began celebrating a eucharistic meal instead—the origin of saints' days in the church's calendar.

When barbarians began threatening the city of Rome in the fourth century, many of the martyrs' remains were transferred into the city itself for greater protection—since the catacombs lay outside the city walls. Most often, the bodies of these martyrs were placed in the main altar of a church, and thus added significance to the Mass: Not only was Christ's sacrifice being commemorated, but the sacrifice was taking place directly over the body of a person who had given his or her life precisely in defense of the name of Christ. To this day, altars still contain the relics of martyrs for the same reason.[20] Competition for these bodies was acute and appeasement came sometimes only after some of the bodies were dismembered and their parts distributed to various churches. Thus, the church of St. John Lateran in Rome contains the heads of Sts. Peter and Paul, while their bodies lie in St. Peter's Basilica and St. Paul's Outside the Walls respectively, above their original resting places.

The problem of how properly to venerate these saints became more problematic as the church became free. Rich families joined in the competition for saints' remains (or relics) and sought to enhance their family burial plots with the addition of a prestigious saint. Such an addition, it was thought, would bring about a physical proximity to the saint resulting (it was hoped) in a spiritual proximity. If St. Cyprian is in heaven, and I am buried next to him—the argument ran—then my chances of being in heaven are greater. Family pride also played a part in this; if our saint was more famous and influential than your saint, then our family is more famous and influential than yours. It was simple, primitive reasoning, and soon gave way to boasting, ostentation, and rivalry between warring families. It also posed the danger of making the veneration of saints an entirely private affair—one limited to the owning family—and one which would be exclusively in the domain of the rich.

This came to a crisis in the late 300s, and the bishops—especially Augustine and Ambrose—were quick to react. The question was one of control: Who had control over the expression of beliefs about the saints—rich patrons or the bishops? Augustine and Ambrose insisted that the saints belonged to the whole church and could not become the exclusive property of a rich minority. The first test case came in Milan, when the bodies of the soldier-martyrs Gervase and Protase were discovered outside the city. Before the usual competition over the bodies could even begin, Ambrose confiscated them and had them brought to his cathedral in Milan, where they are buried today. He is buried next to them.

From this point on (c. 400), the veneration of saints became more public: Miracles could be documented and recorded, liturgies enhanced, shrines constructed, and existing shrines made more elaborate. It is important to note, as Peter Brown has noted in his superb book on this subject, *The Cult of the Saints*, that these practices did not entail something substantially new, but involved practices of veneration which went back to earliest Christianity, which were now given a new direction as a corrective for abuses. The bishops had simply regained control of the veneration of the saints.

Pilgrimages, long a Jewish practice on the high holy days, became a phenomenon associated with saints. With the growth of shrines and other public places of worship, the faithful began making trips with the intention of venerating the remains of a saint and asking for special favors. These pilgrimages were revolutionary insofar as they combined social groups which would otherwise never have mingled on an equal basis. Rich and poor, male and female, slave and freemen, city folk and peasants all mingled together during these extended marches—a sort of public socializing which was not otherwise acceptable.

The reverse of the pilgrimage was the cult of relics, where the remains of the saints were carried to the people. Despite the abuses which crept into this particular practice over the years, from the duplication of relics and the veneration of bizarre relics to the theft of relics by custodians of rival shrines, the origins of relics are quite respectable. Because of the growth of the church, certain provinces (especially those in northern France and Britain) were in danger of losing touch with their Roman traditions. Saints' bodies, or fragments of these bodies, were looked on as one way of retaining continuity with the Rome of the martyrs— reminding people that they belonged to the same church as the martyrs. This was accomplished by "translation"—the transferring of a martyr's bones from one place to another. The arrival of such remains in a city often occasioned great civic celebrations.

Relics are mementos and resemble the mementos of loved ones that we honor today: locks of hair, photos, articles of clothing or furniture, etc. These articles are worthless in themselves, but in the eyes of those who remember the deceased, they are priceless reminders of a person and of times gone by. They are sacred, and the church has long recognized that these mementos are especially sacred when they remind us of a truly great or heroic saint.

Canonization of Saints

A lot of religions venerate human beings. Only Rome has a process by which they are formally recognized, and for making "new" ones. As Kenneth Woodward pointed out in his insightful book *Making Saints*, the Catholic Church does not make them as such, but "does claim...the divinely guided ability to discern from time to time that this or that person is among the elect. The purpose in identifying these holy men and women is to set them before the faithful for their emulation."[21]

To *canonize* means to declare that a person is worthy of public and universal veneration. The church found that it needed a process to test the authenticity of a proposed "saint." Up until the tenth century, it was the voice of the people which decided, with the bishop in the role of providing a veto. The first recorded account of a saint being proclaimed by a pope was in 973 (St. Uldaricus). It became more common for bishops to request that the pope announce the saint in Rome, and eventually (in 1234) the pope reserved the right to canonize to himself. In 1588 the Congregation of Rites was established, to oversee the canonization process. This became further refined in 1734, when Pope Benedict XIV wrote a four-volume work on the "Beatification of the Servants of God and their Canonization." Now the process is under the Sacred Congregation for the Causes of the Saints, which also oversees the preservation and validation of relics.

Pope John Paul II revolutionized the saint-making process in two ways: he made it more historical and less legal, and he introduced a new category of saint—the martyr for charity. The making of saints had become too legalistic and unwieldy, with lawyers dragging out the process (literally a *processus*) much longer than necessary. Only certain kinds of saints—founders of religious orders—seemed able to survive such a long procedure. So Pope John Paul II asked that historians take a more active role in determining the merits of a proposed saint.

But he also created a new category of saint: the martyr for charity. Previously, the only person who could be declared a saint without going through the normal process was a martyr for the faith, one who had given his or her life against a challenge to belief. But Pope John Paul II expanded this concept to include those who were challenged in terms of their charity. Thus, the Franciscan priest Maximilian Kolbe, who offered his own life in exchange for a Jewish man about to be executed at Auschwitz, has been declared a "martyr for charity."

The Rise of Monasticism

Christian monasticism is an attempt to live a life of perfection, specifically in imitation of Christ. Until the early 300s martyrdom had been the most available means of imitating Christ, but with Constantine's toleration of Christianity, this preferred way was no longer possible. Something else heroic had to be found to take its place, and this turned out to be monasticism—an "unbloody martyrdom" of sorts. The idea of going to the desert for a period of time to prepare for one's life was not new. Christ had done it for forty days before beginning his public ministry, and Paul spent two years in the desert preparing for his. Also, people become accustomed to escaping to the desert during times of persecution. What was new about Christian monasticism was its permanence. People were beginning to do it for a lifetime.

Antony and Pachomius

The founding of Christian monasticism is traditionally attributed to a man named Antony, although we know that he was not the first monk. Antony, in fact, spoke of going to the desert to seek a hermit who lived nearby as a spiritual guide. But Antony was the first great charismatic monastic figure, a great leader and advisor. He lived from 251 to 356 and decided to become a monk

Eastern Monasticism

when he heard the lines, "Give up everything you have and follow me." The first monks were hermits, or anchorites, and lived by themselves.[22] Their goal was to meditate on the Lord without distraction, and this they did most conveniently in the deserts of Egypt and Asia Minor. But the idea quickly spread, and soon there were loose groupings of monks—usually centered around a spiritual father, but without the structure of a rule. There arose a need to organize them in some way lest they become a mob, quarreling over scarce supplies. This task was taken up by a man named Pachomius (c. 287–346), who organized the monks into walled monasteries where they ate and prayed together and lived under a rule and a superior. The typical Pachomian monastery was not a continuous building, but rather a series of houses which held thirty to forty monks each, presided over by a dean or superior.

Uniformity in a Pachomian monastery was the order of the day—everyone was to practice the same discipline in regard to

Western Monasticism

fasting (twice a week, and no meat or wine except for the aged), clothing, furnishing of cells, common prayer (five times a day), and manual labor. Duties consisted of service to the community: there were weavers, gardeners, bakers, fishers, shepherds, etc. The goods they produced were sold for the good of the community. Much of this was enacted in order to reduce the bizarre ascetic practices and fierce ascetic competition toward which the early monks were prone. A complete renunciation of personal property and a pledge of unconditional obedience to a superior allowed this arrangement to work. The Pachomian rule was known for its practicality and moderation, but its very success caused problems. Houses grew so large that the superior of the entire monastery (abbot) could not possibly fulfill his role as spiritual director to everyone. Also, the accumulation of property and wealth needed to run the monastery destroyed the ideal of poverty. Finally, the number of leadership positions became the object of competition and politics. Still, by the time of his death in 346, Pachomius had founded nine communities of men in Egypt, and two communities of women.

Western Monasticism

Monasticism spread to the west largely through the efforts of St. Athanasius, the bishop of Alexandria, who was exiled to Germany during the Arian controversies. He knew Antony and wrote the *Life of Antony*, which quickly attracted westerners to monastic life. Several men, from Cassian to Augustine, wrote their own rules and gave monasticism their own peculiar emphasis. One unique feature of western monasticism is that it combined the monastic ideal with the priesthood. Pachomius had not been a priest and deliberately kept the number of priests in each community to a minimum, so as to avoid disputes over rank. But Augustine saw the monastic life as the best way to live out the priesthood, so he was responsible for about thirty monasteries being founded in northern Africa—monasteries which served not as convenient gathering places for hermits, but as centers of apostolic and intellectual life.

Benedict of Nursia (c. 480–560)

Even though he did not write the first rule, Benedict is known as the "Father of Western Monasticism" principally because his rule dominated in the west for the next several centuries. And with good reason. Previous rules had been written for specific houses and emphasized certain characteristics of monasticism, whereas Benedict's rule, which was a synthesis of several rules, could be applied to any number of monasteries and locations. Its major contributions could be reduced to three: a) moderation, b) the integration of prayer and work, and c) the socialization of monastic life.

    A. Moderation. Despite Pachomian attempts to eliminate ascetic competition, eastern monasticism remained severe. Irish monasticism, probably founded directly from the east, was famous for excruciating penances: standing chest-deep in ice-cold water, making pilgrimage either on bare feet or knees, etc. Benedict sought to modify this, retaining self-discipline (fasting, for example) as an important part of the Benedictine regime, but reducing the severity of the practices. Benedict's whole *tone* is moderate. Chapter 40 of Benedict's rule contains a section on how much a monk should drink:

> Every man has his proper gift of God, the one in this way, the other in that. We hesitate therefore when we have to decide how much others should eat or drink. Nevertheless, keeping in mind the weakness of the less robust, we think that half a pint of wine is sufficient for each. But those on whom God bestows the gift of abstinence must know that they will have a reward. But if local conditions, or work, or summer heat demand more, let the abbot decide, taking care that neither surfeit nor drunkenness result. We read, indeed, that wine is no drink for monks; but since nowadays monks cannot be persuaded of this, let us at least agree on this, that we drink sparingly and do not take our fill, for "wine maketh even the wise to fall away."[23]

B. **The Integration of Prayer and Work.** In the Benedictine monastery, everything and every part of the day was ordered to prayer. Formal prayer was carried on several times a day, though practices differed in different monasteries. Normally the day began at 2 a.m. with Matins, followed by Lauds at daybreak, the minor hours of Prime, Terce, Sext, and None at 6 a.m., 9 a.m., noon, and 3 p.m. respectively. Vespers was held at sunset and Compline concluded the day after the evening meal.[24] These hours consisted of a recitation or a chanting of the psalms, followed by readings from Scripture and the fathers of the church, and various prayers. As the centuries wore on the office, as it was called, became more and more elaborate, despite repeated efforts to keep it simple. Benedict mentioned that some of his elders were known to recite all 150 psalms every day, and this he sought to make more manageable and realistic. His success can be measured by the fact that the Divine Office today follows the same moderate pattern outlined by Benedict in the sixth century.

Work was distinct from prayer but was meant to complement it. Work could be manual (farming, building, and shop work), educational (copying manuscripts, teaching, studying), or artistic (singing, illuminating manuscripts)—but it was always meant to provide for the maintenance and self-sufficiency of the monastery. Thus each monk felt that he was contributing to the welfare of the entire community. Because of the number of monks in each house, not everyone was needed for the business of survival, and thus some monks were free to perform tasks that were not materially productive—tasks that we would describe as leading to the development of civilization. Thus culture was a hallmark of Benedictine monasteries, something almost totally unknown to previous generations of hermits.

The typical monastery would have reflected this association of prayer and work (*ora et labora*, which is the Benedictine motto). David Knowles describes what such a monastery would have looked like:

> The monastery is a relatively small building of stone with a tiled or shingled roof and around it are offices, outhouses and, at a distance, farm sheds. All rooms are on the ground floor and none is large, for dormitory and refectory and oratory need to give space for no more than fifteen monks. The oratory has a simple altar, and there are benches or stools of wood. Kitchen, novices lodging and guesthouses are either separate or small appendages to the main block. There are no cloisters, but there are a work-room and a reading room.[25]

C. Socialization. Benedict envisioned a family working and praying together, all sacrificing themselves for the common good—a self-contained social unit. It was a socialism or communism of sorts, but one that sought for a higher goal—namely the complete attention to one's God. The religious habit, perhaps better than anything else, symbolized this communal aspect of Benedictine life. The habit reduced everyone in a community to a visual sameness, so that no one could distinguish rich from poor. It also clothed the monks in a practical garb that eliminated the bother of a wardrobe. Finally, it gave the monks an identity not only to the outside world (which immediately recognized them as Benedictines), but to themselves—as family. Despite their differences, they all belonged to the same religious family and, hopefully, to the same mission of Christ.

In addition to wearing the same habit, the monks were all required to renounce ownership of property, to deny themselves sexual activity, and to obey the abbot and rule, and these are the vows of stability, conversion of life, and obedience. The abbot was especially important to the successful operation of the monastery. His job was to act as spiritual guide for the entire house and to interpret the rule. Yet he was also under the rule. His term of office was for life, and he frequently became the most important person in a diocese or province.

The Spread of Monasticism

Once the idea of monasticism was introduced to the west by Athanasius, it spread quickly. We see it in Africa and France in the late 300s, and even as far away as Ireland at about the same time. How it came to Ireland is a matter of some debate. The liturgical and literary evidence is strong that it came directly from Egypt without the moderating influence of the Roman Church. Both Celtic monks (Ireland and Scotland) and Coptic monks (Egypt) held Antony in great esteem. In a seventh-century antiphonary from the Irish monastery of Bangor, we read:

This house full of delight
Is built on the rock
and indeed the true vine
Transplanted out of Egypt.[26]

Liturgical similarities between Copts and Celts are striking. Among other instances, the Irish litany of saints remembers the "seven monks of Egypt [who lived] in Disert Uilaig" on the west coast of Ireland. Celtic monks always held for the eastern dating of Easter (14th Nissan). In addition, the austerities of Celtic monks were extreme—a feature of eastern monasticism rather than western. Finally, Celtic artwork, as seen in the Book of Kells or the Lindisfarne Gospels, is decidedly eastern.

As the Romans withdrew from Britain in 400, the church—mostly through the work of St. Patrick (d. 460) and the monasteries—carried Christianity through the transition from a Roman Britain to a Germanic Britain. In fact, Christianity in Ireland was almost synonymous with monasticism. Indeed, the structure of the church in Ireland depended very much on the monastic system. Oftentimes, bishops in Ireland were abbots of large monastic houses. In cases where an ordinary monk was chosen to be the bishop, his abbot often remained in charge of the administration of the diocese. Irish monasteries were like small cities which provided not only shelter for the populace, but also education, charity, and sacraments.

From Ireland monasticism (and Christianity) spread to Scotland by Columba (Columkille), who established a monastery on the Scottish island of Iona in 563.[27] From here monasticism spread east and south, and eventually back to the continent in the 700s, thanks to the work of St. Boniface, who was probably the greatest missionary since St. Paul. Ireland's peculiar brand of monasticism, known as Celtic monasticism, reached a turning point in the mid-600s, when it met the Roman variety, promoted by Pope St. Gregory, who was himself a monk, at the Synod of Whitby. This Roman monasticism, so strongly influenced by the

Iona, where Columba built his monastery. St. Columba (521–597) was one of several itinerant Irish missionaries who worked to convert Northern Europe. The Irish monks deliberately chose bleak and isolated spots for their monasteries to remain close to God and to nature.

Benedictine ideal, overcame its Celtic counterpart and eventually became the norm in the British Isles.

The Contributions of Monasticism

It would be difficult to exaggerate the effect of monasticism on western culture. Part of its contribution was passive—a mere copying of classical manuscripts—but even this had the enormous effect of providing a link between Europe and its classical past. However, much of the monastic achievement was dynamic: The monks enriched the world by developing art, architecture, and music. For a period of time, it might be said that monasticism *was* western culture. Benedict could not have imagined the astonishing achievements of his monks—wishing only as he did, that they direct their thoughts to God. Yet the genius of his rule made these accomplishments possible, and the western world will be forever in his debt. John Henry Newman wrote about this great saint:

> St. Benedict found the world, physical and social, in ruins, and his mission was to restore it in the way not of science, but of nature, not as if setting about to do it, not professing to do it by any set time, or by any rare specific, or by any series of strokes, but so quietly, patiently, gradually, that often till the work was done, it was not known to be doing....Silent men were observed about the country, or discovered in the forest, digging, clearing and building; and other silent men, not seen, were sitting in the cold cloister, tiring their eyes and keeping their attention on the stretch, while they painfully copied and recopied the manuscripts which they had saved. There was no one who contended or cried out, or drew attention to what was going on, but by degrees the woody swamp became a hermitage, a religious house, a farm, an abbey, a village, a seminary, a school of learning and a city.[28]

The End of the Second Age

The Second Age of the Church saw Christianity survive three major crises: theological controversy in the east, moral controversy in the west, and the destruction of Rome. Through all this there rose up individuals who charted a course that would benefit the church not only in their own time, but well into the future—and an institution, monasticism, that would carry the church and western civilization through the dark days ahead. By the year 600 the western world was in a steep decline. Rome had become exhausted, and barbarians flooded in from the north— Vandals, Franks, Goths, and Slavs. But even more ominous was the news from the east: that Jerusalem had fallen and that Islam was on the march.

Recommended Readings

(C) Peter Brown, *Augustine of Hippo* (Los Angeles, 1967). This is still considered to be the best biography of St. Augustine.

(B) Peter Brown, *The Cult of the Saints*, esp. Chapters 1 and 2 (Chicago, 1982). This book shows how the veneration of saints began and developed. It is not a systematic work, but rather answers traditional Protestant objections to the veneration of saints, especially those objections which arose during the Age of Reason.

(B) William Dalrymple, *From the Holy Mountain* (New York, 1996). This fascinating book about Christianity in the Mideast is part travelogue, part history, part current events.

(C) J. N. D. Kelly, *Early Christian Doctrines* (New York, 1960). This dense book is essential to any serious student of the christological controversies.

(B) David Knowles, *Christian Monasticism* (New York, 1972). A short helpful book with many maps and illustrations.

(B) Boniface Ramsey, *Beginning to Read the Fathers* (Mahwah, NJ, 1985). This book features good introductions to subjects treated by the fathers, from the nature of Christ to poverty, prayer, ministry. There is also a helpful reading list in the back of the book.

(B) Helen Waddell, *The Desert Fathers*, Introduction (London, 1936). This introduction is considered a classic.

(B) Kenneth Woodward, *Making Saints* (New York, 1990). A balanced and interesting account of how saints are canonized, and how John Paul II has changed the process.

Notes

1. As far as we know, none of the fathers was Jewish, which shows how quickly the Jewish influence disappeared from the early church.

2. See Henry Chadwick, *Early Christian Thought and the Classical Tradition* (London, 1966), p. 1.

3. Jerome's edition was known as the Vulgate, named because the common people (the *vulga*) could read it.

4. William Jurgens, *The Faith of the Early Fathers* (Collegeville, 1970), p. 189.

5. For a concise discussion of this issue, see Raymond Brown's article "Hermeneutics" in the *Jerome Biblical Commentary* (Englewood Cliffs, 1968), No. 71.

6. Christopher Dawson, *The Making of Europe* (New York, 1945), pp. 44–45.

7. This would later be known as the Donation of Constantine. It would be expanded and remain under the pope's control until the mid-1800s, though not be officially ceded to Italy until 1929 in the Lateran Treaty.

8. The word "person" did not mean for the fathers at Nicaea what it means for us today. Rather they meant "a rational being with an individual nature."

9. First of all, a chair is made by a chair maker, which means that the chair maker has a superior intelligence and ability. It also means that as soon as the chair is given a certain shape, it is limited. It is made out of wood, for example, and nothing else; it looks like a rocking chair, and nothing else. Thus it is limited and therefore imperfect.

10. This is called *communicatio idiomatum*, or "communication of idioms." If Christ eats as a man, he is also eating as God. If he dies on the cross as a man, he dies as God. Thus it is true to say that "God died on the cross."

11. It is also known as Monophysitism, named after *mono physis* or "one nature."

12. Jimmy Swaggart, *A Letter to My Catholic Friends*, 1982, p. 29 (the italics are mine).

13. Chesterton, *Orthodoxy*, p. 187.

14. Augustine, *The Confessions of St. Augustine*, Book 8, Ch. 12.

15. Peter Brown, *Augustine of Hippo* (Los Angeles, 1967), p. 304.

16. Ibid., p. 309.

17. There is a dangerous tendency in modern fundamentalism toward this passivity in holiness. Once one has been saved, there is very little talk about where one is to go afterward. After all, how can a person improve on being saved?

18. Augustine, *De Natura et Gratia* XXIX, 33.

19. *Martyr* is the Greek word for "witness."

20. This is why the priest kisses the altar before and after the Mass—as a sign of respect not only for the place where the sacrifice is to be reenacted, but as a sign of respect for the martyr who is buried there, even if only symbolically.

21. Kenneth Woodward, *Making Saints* (New York, 1990), p. 17.

22. The word "anchorite" comes from the Greek word *enkrateia*, which is the exercise of poverty, chastity, and obedience. The word *monus*, from which the word "monk" is derived, means alone.

23. *The Rule of Saint Benedict*, Chapter 40, in David Knowles, *Christian Monasticism* (New York, 1972), pp. 34–35.

24. Lauds and Vespers were the major hours, while the other hours took their name from the Roman hours of the day: Prime was the first hour of the day, Terce the third, Sext the sixth, and None the ninth. These hours generally reflected the hours of the first Good Friday (See the Gospel of Mark 15:1–39). See Josef Jungmann, *Christian Prayer through the Centuries* (New York, 1978).

25. Knowles, *Christian Monasticism*, p. 35.

26. William Dalrymple, *From the Holy Mountain* (New York, 1996), p. 418. In a letter to Charlemagne, the educator Alcuin of York describes the Celtic *culdees* as *"pueri egyptiaci"* (Ibid., p. 418).

27. Recently, Gilbert Markus, OP, has claimed that Christianity was already present in Scotland when Columba landed. See Dauvit Brown and Thomas Owen Clancy, eds., *Spes Scotorum: Hope of Scots* (Edinburgh, 1999), pp. 115–38.

28. John Henry Newman, *Historical Studies* II.

THE THIRD AGE OF THE CHURCH (650–1000)

The Dark Ages

> It would be truer to compare the Dark Ages to a dark room, with certain chinks in the shutter through which particular rays of light could pierce. But the light was daylight, what there was of it; and not even a dull or troubled daylight. It was broad daylight that came through a narrow hole. (G. K. Chesterton, *Chaucer*)

The Third Age of the Church began amid a genuine crisis. The entire Roman world was crumbling, and not slowly. Only Constantinople remained to carry on the vestiges of ancient Rome while the western world sank into darkness, and Constantinople was becoming more and more isolated. It was not for nothing that the Dark Ages are so named, because everywhere there was war, invasion, violence, and chaos. The permanence and peace so necessary for the propagation of culture and civilization were gone, and the world strove simply to survive. Yet it would be a mistake to write off the age so easily, for there is another side to its dark face. Christopher Dawson wrote almost defiantly that, despite its upheaval, "It was the most creative age of all."[1] While the west did not produce much in the way of cultural achievement during this age, it produced the means by which later advances would be gained. In some ways, it created the very culture itself. Thus it is important to examine the forces that were at play in the beginning of the age.

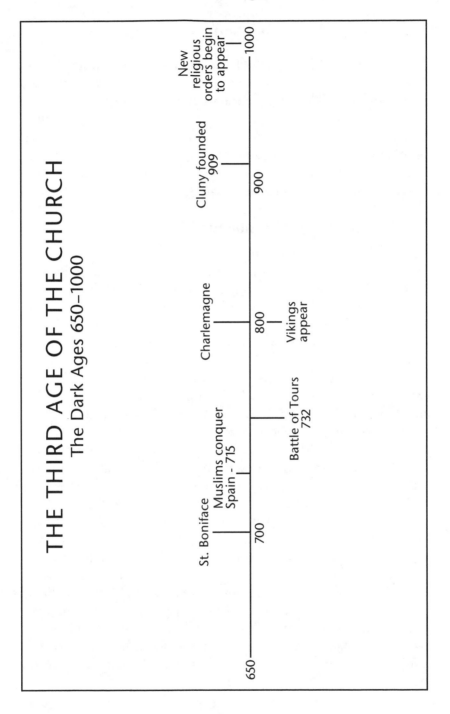

THE THIRD AGE OF THE CHURCH
The Dark Ages 650–1000

650

700

St. Boniface

Muslims conquer
Spain - 715

Battle of Tours
732

Charlemagne

800

Vikings
appear

Cluny founded
909

900

New
religious
orders begin
to appear

1000

Islam

The word "Islam" comes from the word *aslama*, which means "surrender" and has the connotation of "Peace that comes with surrender to God." The origin of the word is in Abraham's consent to sacrifice his own son Isaac (Gen 22:1–14). The word "Muslim" means a "believer," an adherent of Islam. "Muhammadism" is another word applied to this religion, but this is considered a misnomer by Muslims, since it identifies the religion as a heresy (like Pelagianism) rather than a legitimate faith.

Muhammad

Muhammad was born in 570 to a wealthy family from Mecca in Arabia. The Arabia into which he was born was barbaric. The principal social unit was the nomadic tribe, and tribal life could be raucous. The religion of these tribes was naturalistic and superstitious and had little bearing on the moral lives of the nomads.

Muhammad's early life was marred by the deaths of successive guardians. His father died a few days after he was born, his mother when he was six, his grandfather when he was nine; thereafter he was raised by an uncle. The entire experience produced in Muhammad a deep reliance on God. When Muhammad was twenty-five years old he entered the service of a rich widow named Khadija, who was in the caravan trade. He so impressed her that she married him despite being fifteen years his senior. Around this same time, whether coincidentally or not, he started to frequent a cave, where he had a vision. The exact nature of the vision is not known, but Muhammad claimed that he was told to preach. Muhammad never claimed to work miracles. He claimed only that he spoke with the voice of God. What God (or Allah— *the* God) told Muhammad he recorded in the Koran, the Muslim bible. The Koran consists of a retelling of several Old Testament stories, some homiletic material borrowed from early Christian and Jewish sources, and some principles of Islamic law and morality. Muhammad claimed that the material was not his own, but came to him directly from God. He merely transcribed what he had received.

Muhammad's tomb. Muhammad (570–633) was the founder of Islam, which, almost from its beginning, was a force to be reckoned with by the church. Through their rediscovery and translations of the works of Aristotle, Islamic scholars paved the way for Scholasticism and thereby for the work of St. Thomas Aquinas and other great medieval theologians.

The Beliefs of Islam

The tenets of Islam can be reduced to three: a) monotheism, b) strict morality, and c) radical equality.

A. Monotheism. The outstanding doctrinal belief of Islam is that there is only one God. This was held in direct opposition to the prevailing Arabian orthodoxy of the time, which maintained a panoply of ineffective gods—much like Rome's collection of deities. Muhammad's belief came in conflict with Meccan shrines (said to number 360) and their accompanying businesses. But this belief also conflicted with Christian orthodoxy, which held for one God, but with the nuance that this was to include Jesus Christ as God. Muhammad did not accept this. For him, Jesus Christ could *not* be God, simply because God was one and the recognition of Jesus as God implied a dual Godhead. Thus Muhammad allied himself with the Arians, who contended that Christ's humanity, even though it was a superior type of humanity, was irreconcilable with any claim to divinity. This similarity between Islam and Arianism is not surprising when one realizes that Arianism flourished on the fringes of the Roman Empire—from northern Europe to Arabia, far from the center of power in Rome. Nor is it surprising that the early church regarded Islam as it

91

regarded Arianism—as a Christian heresy—and gave it the name of its founder, "Muhammadism."

In the Islamic system Jesus is a prophet—a great prophet who ranks above all the Old Testament prophets and who will judge the earth on the last day. Muhammad, on the other hand, is the last of the prophets and therefore the bearer of the most complete revelation. Muhammad never claimed to be God, and he has never been regarded as God by his followers.

One of the weaknesses of Islam is also its strength: simplicity. In reducing the number of beliefs to a minimum—and those few beliefs were simple ones—it has had to explain away evidence that would lead to complications. Thus, while most of the Old and New Testament stories are accepted as true, all of the events taking place after Christ's Last Supper are believed to be fictitious. Christ, therefore, was not crucified, did not rise from the dead, and did not appear to any disciples after he rose. As far as Islam is concerned, the inclusion of this material in Scripture was a result of a case of mistaken identity or an attempt by disappointed disciples to salvage a vanished hope. What *did* happen to Christ? Islam says that he ascended to heaven before all of these events, and not afterward, as the Christians claimed.

B. Strict Morality. Muhammad called on his followers to live a strictly regulated life. Even today, Islam tends to be puritanical—forbidding alcoholic drink, imposing strict fast laws on its adherents and strict clothing regulations on its women. Each Muslim is called on to practice the Five Pillars:

1) a profession of faith

2) ritual prayer

3) almsgiving

4) a strict fast during the holy month of Ramadan

5) a pilgrimage during one's life to Mecca

Such a regime did not meet with instant approval in Arabia, which had to be taken by force by Muhammad's followers. But even after Muhammad died, the Muslim world was quickly divided into the fundamentalist Shiites and the loose-constructionist Sunnites.

C. Equality. Immorality and unbelief were not the only two problems Muhammad tried to remedy. Inequality was a significant problem in seventh-century Arabia—where slavery was common and women were treated like animals. Muhammad sought to erase this with one bold stroke by declaring, "We are all equal in the sight of God." All races were to be treated as equals, and women were given rights of inheritance and consent in marriage. This idea of equality met with instant opposition and, of all his projects, this was the one that has never been realized.

In fact, all of Muhammad's ideas met with violent opposition. Even his own tribe disowned him and he fled for his life to Medina—the famous *hejirah* of 622. There he made a name for himself by easing Arab-Jewish tensions and by organizing a small army. Using Medina as a base, he sent this army against Mecca twenty-seven times before conquering it in 630. Two years later he died. His success was staggering: he had unified all of Arabia both religiously and militarily. In doing so he would let loose one of the most powerful movements in the history of the world.

The Expansion of Islam

Muhammad had no vision of a campaign to take over the world. He had conceived of the idea of the *jihad*, or holy war, but only on a limited scale. It was not until after he died that the idea took on a global meaning. Just why Islam expanded so explosively is not easy to explain; several factors probably contributed. Poverty and drought may have motivated the Arabs to move so quickly. Another factor was the heady victory over Mecca. The army, once assembled and victorious, was not easily dispersed. Instead, a military confidence resulted which became uncontrollable. Added to this was the centuries-old division within the Arab world, which Muhammad had only recently united. It was a fragile unity and required a "cause" to keep it united. That cause would be the takeover of the Christian world.

Islam, associated in the beginning with Arabia, was immediately and stunningly successful. A brief look at its victories tells the tale: Syria fell in 636, Jerusalem in 638, Caesarea in 640, Alexandria in 642, Iraq and Persia (Iran) in 642, Carthage in 697, and all of Spain by 715. Europe and Constantinople were in a state of shock at this onslaught but managed to stem the tide. In 717 the Arabs threw themselves at the gates of Constantinople in an enormous and desperate attempt to take the city, only to be convincingly defeated. There is evidence that nearly two thousand vessels took part in the battle, which was decided partly by a mysterious weapon known as "Greek fire"—probably some mechanism resembling the modern-day flame thrower. In Europe the issue was settled in 732 at the Battle of Tours where the Frankish king, Charles Martel, defeated the Saracens and sent them eventually back into Spain. What the Muslims had accomplished was, from a Christian point of view, catastrophic. All of the Mideast, all of northern Africa, and all of Spain were securely in the hands of Islam—seemingly overnight. It would take Europe another four centuries to mount a counterattack. Constantinople would survive for another 700 years, but it would never recover its prior greatness.

Why were the Muslims so overwhelmingly successful? Part of the explanation is religious. The Mideast and North Africa had been plagued by doctrinal division for so long that they were not only susceptible to attack by a unified enemy, but they were also susceptible to a straightforward and simple solution to their doctrinal quarreling. God was God, and Christ was not God, and that was the end of it. Any territory long oppressed by the various debates found such simplicity to be a welcome relief. Many terri-

---

Saracens

"Saracens" was a word used by writers in the Middle Ages to denote Arabs. It is important to note that not all Muslims are Arabs (and not all Arabs are Muslims), and in fact most Muslims today are *not* Arabs. In the first great expansion of Islam, however, the two terms "Muslim" and "Arab" were synonymous.

tories were still divided along tribal lines, and no tribe was strong enough to oppose the Arab invasion, even had it so desired. Islam offered peace, order, and a superior culture and this had a great appeal to a world exhausted from years of warfare. The church could not deal with the Muslims as it had the barbarians because the former were neither culturally bankrupt nor desirous of anything Roman. In fact, the Muslims looked down on the west and had a belief system already the rival of Christianity. Thus there were no gaps for the church to fill, no opportunity to take advantage of, no one to educate. Muhammad had supplied a spiritual foundation which gave this Islamic revolution a sense of direction and an enduring quality which made it irresistible.

The Achievements of Islam

The Arabs excelled in the areas of art, philosophy, and mathematics, and in these areas made contributions to the west which significantly influenced the Middle Ages. Because Muhammad had looked on the reproduction of the human form as idolatrous, no significant portraiture or statuary has ever been produced by an Islamic country.[2] Instead Islamic art tended to limit itself to geometric patterns designed to calm the believer and create an atmosphere of serenity. Arab philosophy had also outdistanced the west and made great discoveries in the areas of science and mathematics. The Arabs had received much of Greek thought from the early Christians, who not only spread the message of the Gospel but also preserved the writings of ancient Greek philosophers and scientists. These writings found a home in Arabia, where Islamic theologians were attempting to give a reasoned defense of their religion. It was an attempt which failed, largely because fundamentalists gained the upper hand and forced Arab intellectuals to pursue philosophy for its own sake. As a result the Muslim world has never produced a great theological thinker. It is unfortunate, though perhaps inevitable, that Muslim theology could not build on Muslim philosophy as Christian theologians had built on Greek (and even Muslim) philosophy.

Greek thought, in some ways, had come full circle. Having first been passed to the Arabs by the early Christians, it was now about to be passed back to the Christians of the Middle Ages by Arab philosophers. Greek texts often did not come to the west directly, but had been lost for several centuries and then rediscovered in Arabic translations. These translations, in turn, were translated into Latin by Jewish scholars in Spain. This contact with Greek philosophy, especially the work of Aristotle, touched off a revolution of thought in the west which gave the Middle Ages its driving theological spirit.

The highest achievement of Islamic culture could probably be found in Spain, which in the 900s was the richest and most populous area of Western Europe. Christopher Dawson describes it:

> Its cities, with their palaces and colleges and public baths, resembled the towns of the Roman Empire rather than the miserable hovels that were growing up in France and Germany under the shelter of an abbey or a feudal stronghold. Cordova itself was the largest city in Europe after Constantinople, and is said to have contained 200,000 houses, 700 public baths, and workshops that employed 13,000 weavers, as well as armourers and leather workers whose skill was famous throughout the civilised world. And the intellectual culture of Moslem Spain was no less advanced. Moslem princes and governors rivalled one another in their patronage of scholars, poets, and musicians, and the Khalif's library at Cordova is said to have contained 400,000 manuscripts.[3]

The Byzantine Church and the Eastern Schism

There are several reasons why Constantine may have decided to move the capital of the Roman Empire to the east in the early 300s. For one thing he was a barbarian himself and probably felt inferior living amid the Roman nobility. This nobility could also have made life difficult for any outsider seeking to govern it. Constantine was not a member of the club. It is also possible that Roman corruption had gone too far and the best solution was simply to start over again. Finally, there is always the desire on the part of great men to build their own great cities and monuments. Hence Constantinople. The endeavor was much more than an attempt on the part of Constantine to put some distance between himself and Rome; he meant to resurrect the Greek nation on a Roman model. The Greek system of city-states would be replaced by an *imperium*, a united empire based on a common language, common culture, and common religion. The language, in this case, was to be Latin, the culture Roman, and the religion Christianity.

It did not work. Byzantium, as the new empire was known, was a Greek enterprise from start to finish. Its boundaries were those of ancient Greece—encompassing the Balkans, Asia Minor, Palestine, southern Italy, Sicily, and portions of northern Africa. Its language remained Greek. And its religion, while Christian, was something very different from its western counterpart.

Byzantium became more and more isolated as the barbarians migrated from the north—especially the Bulgars and Slavs moving into the Balkan Peninsula and thus creating a land barrier between east and west—and Muslims encroached from the east. With this isolation came a growing need for self-preservation. But in its glory, Byzantium was glorious indeed, especially when compared to the dismal atmosphere of the west. Constantinople was magnificent, like the Rome of old—prosperous and populous—and it was the envy of the west. When Charlemagne visited Ravenna, a Byzantine colony in northern Italy, he was so impressed with its exquisite buildings that he ordered a chapel to be built along similar lines in his capital of Aachen. The best examples of Byzantine art, noted especially for its development of mosaics, iconography, and the dome, can still be seen in Ravenna, Venice, and Constantinople (modern-day Istanbul). But Constantinople's growing isolation caused this culture to become static. Constantinople regarded the barbarians and Muslims as inferior and successfully held them at bay, but at the gigantic cost of stagnating. This isolation eventually brought on the religious split between east and west, known as the Eastern Schism.

There were three major factors which led to this religious split: cultural differences between east and west, political differences, and religious differences.

San Vitale Church, Ravenna, built between 526 and 547, is an outstanding example of Byzantine architecture. During the reign of Emperor Justinian (ruled 527–565) Ravenna was an important seat of government in the Byzantine Empire.

Cultural Factors

The cultural differences that separated ancient Greece from ancient Rome still applied in the new Christian context. Language was one such difference, and it was so important a difficulty that the Christian world split almost precisely along the Greek-Latin language boundary. Words, and consequently thoughts, could not be translated exactly, and words often meant much more in one language than in another. But the language problem was also symbolic of the difference in cultural temperament between Greece and Rome. As we have already seen, the Greeks had always been more philosophical, theoretic, and theological, while the Romans were practical, technological, and concerned with law. Even the Greek and Latin fathers of the church did not concern themselves with what the others were doing. The Latin fathers accused the Greeks of being the founders of most of the early Christian heresies, while the Greeks did not think their Latin counterparts capable of lofty thought or of theological disagreement.

The Greeks definitely felt superior to the westerners, which was natural enough given their edge in philosophical and literary tradition, but they were also extremely touchy and were quick to take offense. The barbarians of the west felt inferior to the easterners, but they had already conquered the Roman world and now sought some independence from this shrinking and endangered empire to the east.

Political Factors

Once a dominant tribe emerged from the barbarian invasions, this independence from Constantinople became a very real possibility. The Franks of the 700s, under Pippin and Charlemagne, possessed the military might to accomplish this independence, and they succeeded. Remember that the so-called *eastern* emperor regarded himself as emperor of the entire Roman Empire—both east *and* west. So it came as a great shock when Charlemagne had himself crowned Holy Roman Emperor by the pope in 800. This event served notice to the emperor in Constantinople that he no longer had jurisdiction over the lands west of the Balkan Peninsula. And, as we shall soon see, Charlemagne never missed an opportunity to widen this separation.

The western bishops and especially the pope supported the Franks in this endeavor. It would serve the purposes of the church very well to have more independence, and this is precisely what the eastern emperor had not been willing to grant the church. Ever since the days of Constantine, the Roman emperor regarded himself as a quasi-pope, having the care of the church as well as the state among his responsibilities. He had traditionally summoned councils of the church, supervised the proceedings of these councils, and decided when they were over and what about them would be valid and binding. He frequently appointed bishops (including the Patriarch of Constantinople) and decided on the extent of dioceses. In short, the emperor regarded himself as having authority over church and state and, in a sense, became the Christian equivalent of the old Roman emperor-God, a notion which became known as *caesaro-papism*.

Ever since the emperor moved to Constantinople in the mid-300s, the popes opposed this meddling firmly, but with little success. But in Charlemagne they had at last found a champion who had the military might to throw off the yoke of this eastern emperor. It is no coincidence that, at this very time (c. 800), a document appeared that would help the popes in their quest for ecclesiastical freedom from the east. It was known as the Donation of Constantine, and it was a forgery. It was supposedly given by Constantine to Pope Sylvester I, conferring on him all sorts of authority, both episcopal and secular, and was widely regarded as authentic until the fifteenth century. It was probably drawn up by Roman clerics anxious to justify the claim to the land in Italy recently donated to the pope by Pippin, a donation which would, of course, make the pope more independent of Constantinople. But it was particularly important because everyone believed it to be true, including opponents of the papacy.

Religious Factors

The papacy was, and still is, *the* issue that divided east and west. The primacy of Peter, and consequently of the pope, had never been satisfactorily settled. The issue centered on the interpretation of "primacy." The easterners claimed that the bishop of Rome deserved respect only because he inherited an episcopal see made historically important because Peter was its first bishop. But the capital had moved, and so should the head of the church, as Peter had done. The primacy of the Roman pope, in other words, was honorific.

Rome, however, saw the primacy as legal because it was apostolic. Peter was the bishop of Rome and possessed a certain primacy; his successors were bishops of Rome and possessed the identical primacy because of apostolic succession. Actually, Rome was supported in this by the other patriarchates of Jerusalem, Alexandria, and Antioch, while they still existed, all of whom looked on the Patriarch of Constantinople as an artificial creation—a man who lacked apostolic roots and was, at worst, a usurper. Islam simplified the problem by destroying all the eastern patriarchates except for Constantinople, which had the effect of locating all the rival claimants to Rome in the eastern capital. The question quickly became: Who was primary—Rome or Constantinople? Or was there to be dual leadership? It is a question that has still not been settled.

A second religious matter ran alongside this problem over authority. Known to us as the *filioque* question, it is a good example of how seriously the east took its theology. In the Nicene Creed there was a phrase that concerned the Holy Spirit, which stated that he proceeds from the Father: *[Credo] in Spiritum Sanctum…qui ex Patre procedit.* In Spain, because the Arians there so downplayed the divinity of Christ, the bishops decided to add a phrase to the creed that would underline Christ's divinity and underline his equality with the Father. That phrase was *filioque*, and meant that the Holy Spirit proceeds from the Father *and* the Son.

The east was immediately offended, partly because the phrase first appeared in the west, which was incapable of comprehending the theological subtleties involved, but mostly because it altered the creed, which (it claimed) only a council could do. And thus the east never included the *filioque* clause in its creed—on the grounds that it was an illegal addition and because of what it said. Charlemagne saw the disagreement as another way to drive a wedge between himself and the east, so he took up the cause with some enthusiasm and proclaimed that *filioque* should be included in the creed throughout his empire.

The final religious factor really should never have concerned the west at all. It was called *iconoclasm*, and became an east-west problem only when the pope tried interfering. Iconoclasm was the tendency to look on images of any kind as idolatrous. It was mostly an eastern phenomenon. Muhammad taught that images were sacrilegious and he forbade their production, which is why Islamic art is almost entirely symbolic. But even further back, the Jews were prohibited from creating and worshipping images in the book of Exodus (20:4–5): "You shall not make for yourself a graven image, or any likeness of anything that is in heaven above, or that is in the earth below, or that is in the water under the earth; you shall not bow down to them or serve them."

While that is straightforward enough, there is an account *in the very same book* of Moses building a tabernacle filled with images of angels (Exodus 36:8, 35). But, even so, the sense of the Old Testament is that the making of images is forbidden because it usually leads to idolatry. Somehow this infected the world of Constantinople, again possibly because of its platonic distrust of the physical. Two parties emerged: the iconoclasts, who were against the making and displaying of images (icons), and the iconodules (or iconophiles), who regarded images as helpful in the aid of worship. At issue was the respect shown these images. The iconoclasts saw the veneration of images as tending almost necessarily to idol-worship and superstition. "What," they asked, "is being worshipped—the image or the person it is supposed to represent?" Too often it seemed that the image itself was the object of worship. Certainly the large number of abuses called for the elimination of images altogether.

Against this, John of Damascus (John Damascene) wrote a tract defending the veneration of images. There was a distinction, he suggested, between worshipping God and venerating his image. One prayed to God himself, not to a piece of wood or mosaic. The picture was there, however, to focus one's prayer, much like the Gospel accounts focused one's prayer. John Damascene's comparison of images to the Gospel was crucial to his argument, and was the most ingenious part of it. The Gospels, he wrote, were verbal accounts of the Lord's words and actions, while icons were pictorial accounts; reject the latter and you are in danger of rejecting the former, because their content is identical. Finally, much as the Gospels were shown public respect (standing,

---

Mosaics in Rome

One good effect of iconoclasm in Constantinople was that unemployed mosaic-workers fled to Rome in the 700s, where they were put to good use by the pope. Several mosaic-laden churches still survive in Rome as a testament to the magnificence of Byzantine art, the most spectacular of them being Santa Prassede, near the basilica of Saint Mary Major.

---

bowing, processing, holding candles to either side, incensing, etc.), so too icons deserved similar public honor.

For a time (early 700s), however, the iconoclasts gained control of Constantinople and began a widespread purge of iconodules and their images. They also withdrew southern Italy from the pope's jurisdiction, which was the immediate reason for which the pope turned to Charlemagne and made him Holy Roman Emperor—the direct and official opponent of the eastern emperor. Charlemagne's (or some western king's) crowning was inevitable, but it stunned the east nonetheless.

But this was not enough. The iconodules regained power for good in 843 and were faced with the pressing question of what to do with the conquered iconoclasts. The extreme wing of iconodules wanted to punish the defeated iconoclasts severely, while the moderates, led by the Patriarch Photius, were for less stringent measures. Even though Photius had been elected patriarch in the presence of two papal delegates, the pope refused to recognize him, under pressure from the extreme party, and declared his election invalid and Photius himself excommunicate. Photius responded by excommunicating the pope.

But even this was not enough. Photius's protector, the Emperor Michael III, was assassinated, and Photius was soon deposed by the former patriarch, Ignatius. A few years later Ignatius died and Photius was once again back on the patriarchal throne. Rome approved him this time, but the damage had been done.

The Final Break

After Photius, the feud between Rome and Constantinople simmered for another two hundred years before breaking out in a new and final dispute. Southern Italy, long a Greek stronghold, was being heavily colonized by the Normans, a tribe of Viking origin now settled in France, and they were demanding the Roman liturgy in their churches. The pope ordered those Greek churches that still remained in the south to change to Latin and the Roman rite of liturgy. This included the use of unleavened bread and the *filioque* clause in the Creed. The Greek patriarch,

---

Uniate Churches

Some eastern churches chose to recognize the pope as the legitimate head of the church, remained within the jurisdiction of Rome, and continued their own particular rites and practices. These are known as Uniate churches. They include the Ukrainian Catholic Church, the Ruthenians, etc.

Michael Cerularius, retaliated by ordering all the Latin churches in Constantinople to accept the Greek rite, or be suppressed.

Rude letters were exchanged between pope and patriarch, and the pope sent a rude envoy to carry a papal bull to the east. The legate was insulted as soon as he arrived. The legate immediately excommunicated the Greeks, despite having no authority to do so, and then was himself excommunicated by the patriarch, who also burned the papal bull for good measure. This happened in 1054 and made the Eastern Schism a permanent fact. From then on, Christianity would be divided into a Roman Church and an Orthodox Church.

The Barbarians

The barbarians were those people who lived outside the borders of the Roman Empire. The name "barbarian" connotes a savagery which was not necessarily a characteristic of any given barbarian tribe. They were simply outsiders, foreigners. Their society was tribal, based on kinship rather than on citizenship, and was largely nomadic and unsettled. The Romans tried to harness this unwieldy and unpredictable mass of people in three ways: a) destruction, b) transplantation, or c) incorporation.

A. Destruction. Barbarian tribes, especially the smaller ones, could be isolated from other tribes and then destroyed or forced to flee by superior Roman military force. Julius Caesar's *Gallic Wars* is a chronicle of just such an activity. It was a policy which could only succeed on a limited scale—owing to the sheer numbers of barbarian tribes and the great distances from Rome at which they had to be fought.

B. Transplantation. Many tribes, having been subdued by force or by negotiation, were moved to frontier lands as a conciliatory gesture and as a means of further population (thus creating more markets), but also as a buffer on the borders against even more threatening tribes. Most tribes were troublesome only when in search of food, and the Romans sought to diffuse their hostility (and their hunger) by giving them the land they so greatly needed. The Romans became famous for this policy of colonization, which served not only to reward barbarian tribes for their cooperation, but also to make productive land which hitherto had been wilderness.

C. Incorporation. The Romans, being a pragmatic people, soon realized the futility of holding the barbarian migrations at bay either militarily or diplomatically. So they armed the barbarians and made them Roman soldiers (or auxiliaries) and thus Roman citizens. Some compromise was inevitable if Rome was to survive, but the arming of the barbarians was a tactic which proved to be only a delaying action, and one which eventually ended in disaster. It was a disaster which was not far off in any event, since Rome was doomed by exhaustion. It no longer had the will to fight and it no longer had anything to fight for except, perhaps, its own survival.

Too much has been made of the fact that these barbarian tribal armies were now "Roman" armies. Historians have claimed that there was no invasion of barbarian hordes, that Rome was never "sacked" by Alaric and his Visigoths, but that what happened was no more than the ancient Roman ritual of coup d'etat or civil war—much the same thing a Julius Caesar or a Constantine would have engaged in.[4] The fact is that the barbarians were significantly different from Romans, citizenship or no. Even though Alaric had a commission in the Roman army, he and his men were identifiable as barbarians, which was to say as heathens and aliens. When the Rhine froze in the winter of 406, the barbarians quite simply poured into Roman territory, spurred on by an extreme lack of food and by pressure from marauding Huns to the east. Henri Daniel-Rops describes this movement:

They came. They came not simply as men had been accustomed to see them come of old—as regiments of soldiers, more or less—but as whole tribes, with their womenfolk, their children, their wagons, their bundles of belongings, their reserve cavalry, their herds, and their flocks. The word "invasion," which brings to mind primarily the entry of an army into a specified area, is something of a misnomer here. The term which exactly describes the phenomenon is the German *Völkwanderung [sic]*, i.e., a migration of peoples.[5]

The Christian Response to the Barbarians

The church would have been swept away by this flood of barbarians had it, like Rome, been solely a tangible thing. Rome's spiritual component was long gone, so that Rome was little more than buildings and armies, and the buildings and armies could be destroyed. But the church was more than buildings, and had no armies. Granted several monasteries were destroyed and some bishops put to death, the church managed to survive because structures and personalities were not essential to its continuance. The most famous monastery to be overrun was Monte Cassino, south of Rome, which was overwhelmed and sacked by the Lombards in 585, only fifty years after it was founded. Physical assault could not threaten it as it had the Romans. Church government, what there was of it, was fluid and possessed an intangibility which made it particularly immune to attack.

What especially aided the church was that the barbarians were desirous of anything Roman—and that included Christianity. They might overrun Roman cities, but this was in the hope of possessing the Roman "thing." They were anxious to be a part of Rome's stability, wealth, and style of life. Because Christianity was increasingly a part of Roman life, the barbarians wanted to embrace it as well. Roman institutions and armies had to be gotten rid of because their continuation threatened the existence of the tribes, while Christianity posed no such threat and still maintained an aura of *Romanitas*. Hence the barbarians readily converted to Christianity. The normal pattern was for the tribal leader to be baptized and then for all his troops to follow suit. It is said that when Clovis, the Frankish chief, converted to

Christianity in 496, three thousand of his troops converted as well. These conversions were unquestionably marriages of convenience. Cooperation between bishops and tribal leaders assured both the political control of a region and its spiritual life as well.

Much of the church's role in this cooperation was educational. Herbert Butterfield commented, "Far from being the cause of cultural backwardness of the Dark Ages, the Church through the medieval centuries performed the great task of educating the barbarians."[6] The church was in a position to do this because it still held onto classical culture. Paul Johnson notes:

> The western church found itself the residual legatee of Roman culture and civilization, and the only channel by which it could be transmitted to the new societies and institutions of Europe....It had the chance to recreate the secular framework of society *ab initio*, and in its own Christian image. It was the only organized international body left with ideas, theories, a sophisticated hierarchy and advanced cultural technologies, in an empty world which possessed little but tribalism.[7]

Nothing could have been more opportune for the church than this fusion of a young and malleable society with the church's tradition-bound civilization. In the meeting between the barbaric Atlantic world and the civilized Christian Mediterranean world, the barbarians were being tamed and educated and Christianized, but the church also benefited, for it was saved from stagnation and was infused with new life. The church also received one of the world's great emperors as its defender, the Emperor Charlemagne.

Charlemagne

Charlemagne was heir to the Frankish military gains of the eighth century. His grandfather, Charles Martel, had defeated the Muslims in the Battle of Tours in 732, and his father, Pippin, had subdued the Lombards—thus ridding the Frankish Empire of one of its principal enemies and bringing to Europe a semblance of peace. Charlemagne further consolidated these gains and sought

The Vikings

Nearly at the same time Charlemagne was being crowned, a new threat to Europe's unity was being launched from Scandinavia in the form of Vikings. In 793 they sacked the northern English island of Lindisfarne. Two years later they harried the coast of Ireland and founded the city of Dublin. Their conquests were concentrated in the north Atlantic: by 900 they controlled the Shetland and Orkney Islands, the Hebrides, Iceland, Greenland, and by the year 1000 had landed on the coast of North America in Newfoundland.

In France they were defeated at Chartres in 911 and their leader (Rollo or Rolf) was baptized and given land along the Seine River in return for protecting the interior from any further Viking invasion. This land became known as Normandy, or the "Land of the Northmen."

But their restlessness was not so easily tamed. Between 1050 and 1100 these Normans conquered England, Sicily and southern Italy, and helped greatly in the First Crusade. Their presence in southern Italy would help to cause the Eastern Schism.

to make them permanent. What he achieved is known as the Carolingian Renaissance, a bright and brief candle in the midst of darkness. Charlemagne's goal was to create a truly Christian kingdom, with himself as the ideal Christian king. His subjects compared him to the biblical King David, a comparison he no doubt encouraged. He was the first Christian emperor in the west, and attempted to duplicate what Christian emperors had done in the east: make his kingdom physically and spiritually one. Dawson points out:

> The Carolingian Empire represented an ambitious but premature attempt to realize the unity of Western Christendom. It consequently had to reconcile two fundamentally conflicting ideals. On the one hand was the ideal of the Frankish

> Imperialism, founded on the wars and conquests of Charles
> Martel, Pepin and Charlemagne....On the other hand, it
> represented the ideal unity of the whole Christian people,
> united in a common Faith and in obedience to a common
> religious law.[8]

The word "Christendom" denotes an international unity, the bond of which was Christianity, and could be said to be the result of Charlemagne's efforts. He did it mostly through education. He had an amazing ability to attract great educators and authors, most of whom were Churchmen. Alcuin of York was the greatest of them. He undertook the reform of a nearly non-existent and chaotic educational system by attending to the structure and content of the subjects taught. He even saw to such details as how manuscripts were to be copied accurately.

Politically, Charlemagne knew well that the church could serve his own ambitions—it could legitimize his family's usurpation of the Frankish crown, and provide the unifying factor for a great empire, which he hoped to set against the eastern empire. Without the church, Charlemagne could do none of this. But the church did not have things its own way; it relied on Charlemagne for protection against the Lombards and for a defense against the claims of Constantinople. The church and Charlemagne needed each other, and so they forged an alliance which was mutually beneficial. In an action which symbolized their mutual need, the pope crowned Charlemagne in the year 800. This alliance was potentially dangerous for the independence of the church. While the pope regarded Charlemagne as being inferior in authority, Charlemagne saw himself as another Constantine who ruled over both church and state. But the church in the west had a high theology of the papacy already in place for centuries, so that Charlemagne's attempt to assert ecclesiastical power was ultimately thwarted.

What Charlemagne actually accomplished was not nearly as great as what he had envisioned. Physically the Carolingian period did not last long; the empire was split up by Charlemagne's sons and ended with the death of Charles the Fat in 888. The unified system of laws never had much effect owing to the long

Christ with Pepin, Charlemagne, etc. The Frankish dynasty known as the Carolingians ruled from the mid-8th to the end of the 10th century. They included Pepin of Herstal, Charles Martel, Pepin the Short, and Charlemagne, who was crowned ruler of the Holy Roman Empire in 800. Depicting them with Christ was a way of legitimating them as anointed rulers by divine right.

distances between cities and town. Even an ingenious system of runners proved ineffectual.[9] Renewed invasions from the north by Vikings contributed to the vanishing of Charlemagne's dream. A darkness ensued, which Dawson has described as "the darkest age of all."[10]

The Papacy (955–1057)

The Frankish Empire revived under the Ottos in the mid-900s, who engaged in a tug-of-war with Italian noble families over control of the papacy. The popes, after distancing themselves from the easterners and crowning Charlemagne in 800, now found that their authority problem simply moved from east to west. Between 955 and 1057 there were twenty-five popes—no fewer than twelve were outright appointments by the emperor, the others were creations of the Roman aristocracy. Five popes during this period were deposed or dismissed by the emperors. Two (and probably three) were assassinated.

The pattern was for the emperor to impose his candidate as pope, order the Romans never to interfere without his (the emperor's) permission, then, as soon as he returned to Germany, the Romans would depose the pope and impose *their* candidate. Benedict IX was pope three different times! During this time

---

Pope Joan

It has long been a cherished legend that a female pope reigned from 855–57. This legend first appeared in the 1240s and was widely believed to be true, even as late as the nineteenth century. The legend was effectively demolished in the 1600s, by a Protestant historian, David Blondel. J. N. D. Kelly writes, "Not only is there is no contemporary evidence for a female pope at any of the dates suggested for her reign, but the known facts of the respective periods make it impossible to fit one in" (*Oxford Dictionary of the Popes*, p. 329).

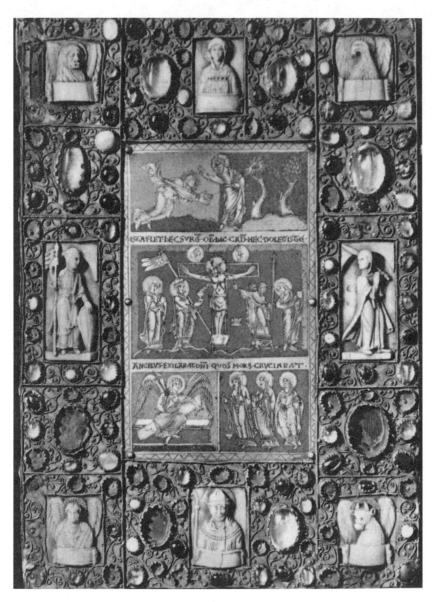

Cover of the Hildesheim Gospels. The Hildesheim Gospels are just one example of the beautiful creations of medieval artists. They were supposedly written and illuminated by St. Bernward or Berward (ca. 960–1022), bishop of Hildesheim and chaplain and tutor to the young emperor Otto III.

there were also three antipopes. It was a century which might be justly regarded as the low point of the papacy. What brought this to an end? Four things combined to get the papacy out of this mess: 1) the revival of monasticism, 2) the organization of canon law, 3) the Crusades, and 4) the revolution of religious life known as the friars. Only the first of these will be treated in this chapter.

The Gregorian Reform

In the mid-600s the popes began to grant privileges to certain monasteries, and these privileges were known as "monastic exemption" (Bobbio was the first in 628). The idea was to take control of the monastery away from the bishop and local lay leaders and, at the same time, give the papacy an income and thus some independence. This would begin to bear serious fruit with the founding of Cluny in 909. By 1150, Cluny had 460 monks. Exemption was the key. In the eleventh century 270 religious houses were granted exemption. In the twelfth century 2000 were made exempt! The monks could now control their own monastery and initiate reforms so badly needed: reemphasis on prayer life, celibacy, stricter morality, study, the avoidance of simony, etc. Needless to say, almost all of the reformers and saints of the eleventh century were monks.

This reform did not stop with the monasteries. Popes who had contact with such monasteries tried to effect such reforms on the larger church. Pope Leo IX (1049–54) made the first significant break with the German emperors, even though he was related to the Emperor Henry III, who appointed him. He sought the advice of the abbot of Cluny (Hugh), and Peter Damien, then called to Rome several outstanding men including Hildebrand, who came from a Cluniac monastery.

The job of these reformers was to do away with the proprietary system (including simony), to restore celibacy, and to establish an electoral *college* of cardinals, or electors, who would be responsible for electing the popes. In 1073, Hildebrand himself was elected Pope Gregory VII. He was bright, efficient, experienced, and reform minded. Thus monasticism and the papacy came together.

The College of Cardinals

At the time of the founding of the College of Cardinals (1059) there were seven cardinal-bishops (who were bishops of the seven dioceses surrounding Rome), 28 cardinal-priests (today they are also titular pastors of parishes in Rome), and 18 cardinal-deacons, one from each region of Rome (today they are usually heads of curial positions, and thus more powerful than some cardinal-priests, a vestige of their former power. Also, the senior cardinal-deacon enjoys the privilege of investing the newly-elected pope with the *pallium*).

The actual number was normally between 20 and 30 and sometimes fell as low as 10. In 1586 Sixtus V raised the number to 70 in imitation of the 70 chosen by Moses (Ex 24:1) and by Jesus (Lk 10:1). Until 1958 there were usually between 60 and 70 cardinals, although when Pius XII died, there were only 55. John XXIII ignored the limit and the college grew to more than 80 members. In 1970 Paul VI raised the limit to 120, not counting those over 80 (who cannot vote). By October 2003, there were 195 cardinals (135 electors and 59 over the age of 80), of whom John Paul II has created 176.

However, an independent papacy did not come about immediately or easily. Gregory VII wrote the *Dictatus Papae* as a list of demands which attempted to establish the pope's rights: to depose, reinstate, or transfer bishops; to depose emperors and to release their subjects from their fealty, etc. It was a declaration of war. And it was resisted by the emperor (Henry IV), who did not like these ideas at all. So the question remained, "Who is boss in Christendom?" Gregory's reign ended chaotically. After excommunicating Henry IV, and getting him to seek absolution, Henry eventually called a synod and elected an antipope. He then attacked Rome, and Gregory fled first to Castel Sant'Angelo, a fortress near the Vatican, then to the Benedictine monastery Monte Cassino, where he died on 25 May 1085.

The End of the Third Age

Noting the events of the Third Age of the Church, it is amazing that the Catholic Church had survived at all, given the external assault of the barbarians, the internal feuding between east and west, and the weakened state of the papacy. But underneath the surface a great movement of the two cultures, Atlantic and Mediterranean, was combining like geological plates which would emerge as what some claim was the church's greatest age. After Gregory VII died, it took another ten months to elect a legitimate pope. Ten months later he accepted. A year later he died. He was replaced by Pope Urban II, who called the First Crusade.

The *Dictatus Papae* of Pope Gregory VII (selections)

3. That the Roman Pontiff can alone depose or re-instate bishops.
5. That the pope may depose the absent.
7. That for the pope alone it is lawful to enact new laws according to the needs of the time, to assemble together new congregations, to make an abbey a bishopric, and to unite the poor ones.
12. That he may depose emperors.
13. That he may transfer bishops, if necessary, from one See (diocese) to another.
16. That no synod may be called a general one without his order.
18. That no chapter or book may be regarded as canonical (i.e., officially approved) without his authority.
25. That, without convening a synod, he can depose and reinstate bishops.
27. That the pope may absolve subjects of unjust men (e.g. kings) from their fealty.

The Seeress. Hildegard of Bingen (1098–1179), German visionary and preacher of church reform, founded Benedictine communities at Bingen and Eibingen. Her writings include descriptions of her extraordinary visions, letters of admonition to emperors and bishops, songs, and treatises on the natural world. Her theological writings are enriched by metaphors drawn from the beautiful Rhineland countryside in which she lived.

Recommended Readings

(B) Geoffrey Barraclough, *The Medieval Papacy* (New York, 1968). This book stretches into the next age as well, but is a good overview.

(B) Yves Congar, *After Nine Hundred Years* (New York, 1959). An excellent summary of the split between the Western and Eastern Churches.

(B) Christopher Dawson, *The Making of Europe* (New York, 1945). This landmark book, written in 1952, was one of the first in English to speak about the *contribution* of the Dark Ages to western civilization.

(B) Christopher Dawson, *Medieval Essays*, Chapter 12, "The Vision of Piers Plowman" (Garden City, 1959). A good example of how a church historian can use literature to demonstrate a point.

(B) Patrick Granfield, *The Limits of the Papacy* (New York, 1987). An excellent summary of the development of the papacy from the beginning of the church, as well as a clear discussion about the limits on papal authority.

(C) Jaroslav Pelikan, *The Spirit of Eastern Christendom*, Chapter 3, "Images of the Invisible" (Chicago, 1974). A good explanation of the Iconoclast controversy.

AUDIO-VISUALS:
   Civilisation, by Kenneth Clark, Episodes 1–3. BBC Production, 1969. Still available through Home Vision Arts, though with diminished sound quality.

Notes

1. Dawson, *The Making of Europe*, p. xv.
2. See H. W. Janson, *History of Art*, 5th ed. (New York, 1995), pp. 266–83.
3. Dawson, *The Making of Europe*, pp. 167–68.
4. Paul Johnson, *A History of Christianity* (New York, 1976), p. 130.
5. Henri Daniel-Rops, *The Church in the Dark Ages* (New York, 1959), p. 61.
6. Butterfield, *Christianity in European History*, p. 19.
7. Johnson, *A History of Christianity*, p. 127.

8. Christopher Dawson, *The Formation of Christendom* (New York, 1967), p. 186.

9. The normal procedure was for two runners, one a cleric and the other a lay person, to be sent to a town to promulgate laws and maintain communications. If the laws or news were unwanted, the messengers could be ignored or even put to death.

10. Dawson, *The Formation of Christendom*, p. 188.

THE FOURTH AGE OF THE CHURCH (1000–1450)

The Middle Ages

The Fourth Age of the Church began roughly in the middle of the eleventh century, and it saw a burst of activity in every conceivable area—from theology and religious life to art and architecture, science and engineering to music and literature. It was a movement which is difficult, if not impossible, to explain unless one does so in terms of spiritual energy. Europe had come of age. The forces of the Atlantic peoples had mixed with both the ancient Mediterranean culture and Christianity and produced something very new and very dynamic. We may call it Christendom or Europe. Whatever its name, the west was more unified than at any time since the reign of Constantine. And this unity would produce stunning results.

The Crusades

This unity would encompass Constantinople as well. Even the grave differences which existed between east and west were not sufficient to prevent them from cooperating in one of the most astonishing military ventures the world has ever seen: the Crusades. Both east and west felt the need to do something about the inroads made by Islam. Constantinople especially was hard-pressed, and watched as its traditional stronghold of Asia Minor fell to the militant Turks. Nicaea, the closest fortified city to Constantinople itself, was taken by the Turks in 1084, creating so urgent a crisis that eastern pride had to be put aside and western help sought.

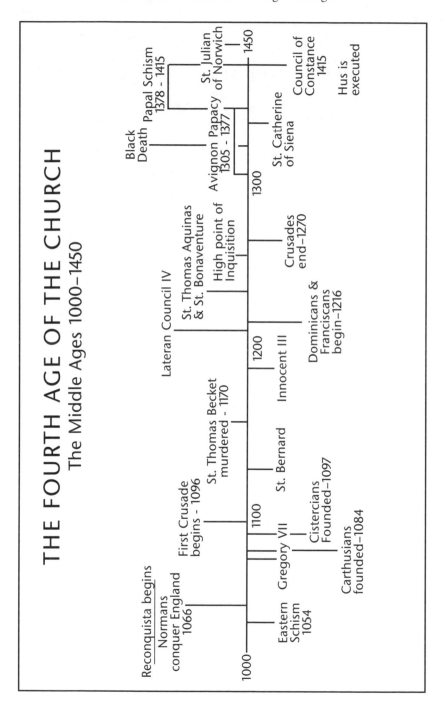

THE FOURTH AGE OF THE CHURCH
The Middle Ages 1000–1450

1000

Eastern Schism 1054

Reconquista begins

Normans conquer England 1066

Gregory VII

Carthusians founded–1084

First Crusade begins - 1096

Cistercians Founded–1097

1100

St. Bernard

St. Thomas Becket murdered - 1170

Lateran Council IV

Innocent III

1200

Dominicans & Franciscans begin–1216

St. Thomas Aquinas & St. Bonaventure

High point of Inquisition

Crusades end–1270

1300

Avignon Papacy 1305 - 1377

St. Catherine of Siena

Black Death

Papal Schism 1378 - 1415

St. Julian of Norwich

1450

Council of Constance 1415

Hus is executed

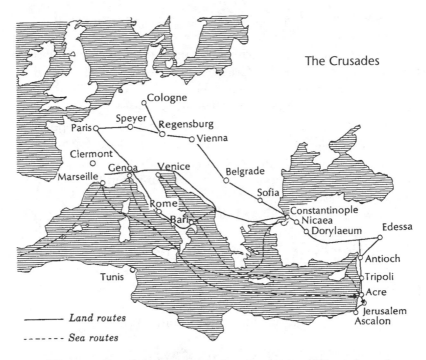

The Crusades

Cologne
Speyer
Paris
Regensburg
Vienna
Clermont
Genoa
Venice
Belgrade
Marseille
Sofia
Rome
Bari
Constantinople
Nicaea
Dorylaeum
Edessa
Antioch
Tunis
Tripoli
Acre
Jerusalem
Ascalon

——— *Land routes*

- - - - - - *Sea routes*

The westerners were more than happy to oblige, though not out of any affection for Constantinople. The west had reasons of its own. Earlier in the eleventh century, the Turks, under the Caliph Hakim, had begun a ten-year pogrom against Christians, restricting their movement, mandating the wearing of distinctive clothing, etc. Church property was confiscated, crosses were burnt, and little mosques built on church roofs. In 1009 Hakim ordered the destruction of the Church of the Holy Sepulcher in Jerusalem and, by 1014, some 30,000 churches had been burnt or pillaged. Christian pilgrims, who had peacefully coexisted with Arab rulers of Jerusalem, now found themselves harassed by the Turks, and reports and rumors of beatings, robberies, and molestations began to filter back to Europe, creating an atmosphere of collective outrage suitable to the beginning of a war, similar to that experienced after the news of Pearl Harbor or the destruction of the World Trade Towers in September 2001.

There were lesser reasons as well. Europe was overpopulated and a crusade was looked on as a productive way both of expanding and also of channeling the violence that comes with overpopulation to a good end. The pope, also, saw a crusade as an opportunity to reconcile the great kings of Europe to the church. For in the year 1095, when the Crusades finally began, the German emperor, the French king, and the English king had all been excommunicated. In addition to bringing these men back to the church, a successful crusade would demonstrate the pope's primacy over the kings of Europe, since he would be the only one capable of bringing them together to fight a common enemy. Popes had called for crusades before, beginning in the year 1000, but Europe was never quite ready to answer the call.

It was ready now. The most immediate and proximate problem was Spain, which was still almost completely in the hands of Islam and had been so for nearly 350 years. In the mid-1000s the reconquest *(reconquista)* of Spain began. It was to be a long, drawn-out war, lasting more than four centuries but would ultimately succeed. Toledo was taken by the Christians in 1085. Cordova and Seville would have to wait until 1236 and 1248

Christ leading a crusade. The Crusades were a series of wars undertaken between the eleventh and thirteenth centuries, to free the Holy Land from Muslim control. Artwork such as this would have served to convince Christians that their cause was just, for Christ was on their side.

respectively, and Granada, the final city to fall, surrendered in 1492. Eight hundred years of Muslim rule in Spain were at an end. There has been considerable discussion about the role of the Muslims in Spain, most of it tending to see Muslims as tolerant and progressive. The most recent scholarship questions this, however, and claims that their rule may not have been as pacific as has been portrayed, and that a certain ruthlessness went with Muslim control. As Edward Rothstein noted, citing several recent studies of the time:

> Issues of succession were often settled by force. One ruler murdered two sons and two brothers. Uprisings in 805 and 818 in Cordoba were answered with mass executions and the destruction of one of the city's suburbs. Wars were accompanied by plunder, kidnappings and ransom. Cordoba itself was finally sacked by Muslim Berbers in 1013, its epochal library destroyed....[Christians and Jews] were subject to special taxes and, often, dress codes. Violence also erupted, including a massacre of thousands of Jews in Grenada in 1066 and the forced exile of many Christians in 1126....Even in the Umayyad tenth century, Islamic philosophers were persecuted and books burned....[The Muslim philosopher] Maimonides and his family fled Muslim fundamentalism in Cordoba in 1148 when he was barely in his teens. Averroes [another great Muslim philosopher] was banished from Cordoba about fifty years later.[1]

But more spectacular was the call to crusade given in 1095 at the Council of Clermont by Pope Urban II. Armies were to be raised to conquer the holy city of Jerusalem for Christianity. So high was the enthusiasm in Clermont that the red material used for the making of the five red crosses—symbolic of the five wounds of Christ and of crusade and to be known as the Jerusalem Cross—soon ran out, and people demanded to be tattooed or branded with this red cross. The church tried keeping this enthusiasm in check in order to ensure the success of the crusade and to guarantee its sacred character by issuing a special blessing and, more practically, by keeping a strict control over volunteers to the armies. Those wishing to enroll had to be approved by their

Mosque in Cordova. In the early Middle Ages Muslims from North Africa gradually made their way into Spain, establishing their hegemony in Andalusia with Cordova as their capital. This Islamic civilization became an extraordinary center for the arts and sciences; the great mosque at Cordova is a marvel of Islamic engineering.

parish priest, and a crusading vow had to be taken. Desertion meant excommunication. Unfortunately, these precautions were not enough to prevent the inclusion of undesirable types, both men and women, who followed every crusade.

Enthusiasm certainly got the better part of a large group of people who were whipped into a near-frenzy by a man known as Peter the Hermit. This mob, said to number as many as 40,000 to 50,000 when it left Germany, was undisciplined, untrained for war, and knew nothing about supply and strategy. This fact did not prevent it from terrifying people in their way, especially Jews. They brawled with whoever was unfortunate enough to be in their path, leaving 4,000 dead in Hungary, and sacked the city of Belgrade. The emperor in Constantinople was so nervous about their arrival that, after they refused his advice to wait for the main armies, he had them shipped over to Asia Minor as soon as possible. There they met the Turks, who promptly slaughtered all but 2,000 to 3,000 of the nearly 40,000 assembled, only a quarter of whom were actual fighting men. Thus the People's Crusade came tragically to an end. Peter the Hermit survived and would join the next crusade.

In hindsight, the People's Crusade proved beneficial to the western leaders. It is probable that the Turks were lulled by their easy victory into thinking that the main body of the western army had been eliminated, and that any further interference from the west would be just as easily routed. So they returned to their internal feuding, which had increased recently due to the splitting of the Turkish Empire in four parts. What they did not and could not know was that one of the greatest and most extraordinary military operations in the history of the world was already headed in their direction.

The First Crusade

The idea of crusade did not only catch on with religious fanatics or the more desperate elements of society; it caught on with professional soldiers. They both agreed to fight, and knew the business of fighting. Being realists, they set out to retake Jerusalem in a methodical and sober way. Four main armies amounting to nearly 70,000 soldiers were led by leaders who proceeded by different routes to their rendezvous point of Constantinople.[2] They were scheduled to arrive in August of 1096. In fact, the first troops arrived in late December of 1096, and the rest arrived in April and May of 1097. This gathering of western armies was not especially comforting to the Byzantine Emperor Alexius Comnenus, because a few of the western leaders (especially the Norman leader Bohemond) were openly hostile to him and would happily fight against him at the least provocation. They had not come to save Constantinople; they had come to conquer Jerusalem. But it was a gathering nonetheless, and one still unified in purpose.

The first engagements were successful, but boded ill for the future. Nicaea, the first Turkish fortification to be attacked, was practically empty of all fighting men, who were off fighting other Turks. A short siege of six weeks was enough to reduce the town, but just as the crusaders were about to storm the walls and claim their spoils, the Byzantine flag was seen flying from the turrets. The Turks had surrendered secretly to the Greeks. This infuriated the western generals and armies and ever afterward there would be talk of "Greek treachery." The Greek emperor then promptly made matters worse by fêting the sultana, who governed the town in the absence of her husband, and by sending her away laden with gifts.

This was chivalry of a type unknown to the westerners and it only added to their resentment and distrust. The ancient warning "Beware of Greeks bearing gifts" seemed to be true after all.

The Greek army did little to allay these hostile feelings and, soon after the victory at Nicaea, headed due east along the Black Sea to retake its former possessions amid little resistance. The westerners, on the other hand, headed inland and directly into the path of the Turkish Sultan of Nicaea, who was belatedly returning to relieve his besieged city. The two armies collided head-on at Dorylaeum, where Bohemond's Normans were both taken by surprise and outnumbered. Bohemond proved his fighting mettle, however, and with the aid of reinforcements surrounded the Turks and earned a complete victory. Neither army had ever fought this way before. The Turks were lightly clad and were used to fighting on small, fast horses, while the westerners favored the larger draft horses and armored knights, who were seemingly impervious to arrows and sword cuts. Surrounding these "moving fortresses" would be five to ten soldiers who would serve as a platoon to cooperate with their knight on horseback.

But most engagements were not on an open field. The next major encounter came at Antioch and was as close to tragicomedy as warfare ever comes. First the crusaders laid siege to the city, a tactic which had worked quickly on unsuspecting Nicaea, but would take seven and a half months against a well-fortified and prepared city. No sooner had the crusaders entered the city when, two days later, a large Turkish army arrived—not in time to save the city, but in plenty of time to begin a siege of their own. Thus the besiegers became the besieged. Tempers became frayed, desertions occurred, and it seemed that defeat was certain. One western general, in fact, deserted and warned an advancing Greek army just two days away not to bother to continue, since the city was certainly in the hands of the Turks by the time it would arrive. But this was not the case. So confident were the Turks of their strength, and perhaps eager for a quick end to the siege, that they allowed Bohemond and his Normans to come out and fight them, which Bohemond did and duly won.

Here the crusade faltered, however. Bickering took place as Bohemond claimed Antioch for himself and refused to go a step further. Several months passed, in fact, before anyone could be persuaded to leave Antioch and press on with the crusade, and then only a comparative handful set out—only 6,000 in number. Reinforcements pushed this number up to 10,000, and it was with this army that Jerusalem was approached and invested in the summer of 1099. The Greeks, needless to say, were not among the number.[3]

Interestingly enough, the crusaders who went to Jerusalem were not facing Turks any longer, either. Egyptian (Arab) Muslims, who distrusted the Turks, had taken over Jerusalem while the latter were busy at Antioch. The Egyptian leader was given to compromise and offered the crusaders a peace plan: safe passage for all unarmed groups to the Holy Places. But the crusaders had come too far to settle for a peace treaty; their goal all along had been the takeover of Jerusalem. As Zoé Oldenbourg says in her history of the Crusades, "The Crusaders did not come to Jerusalem merely to pray and to worship. They were there to fight and to snatch the city from the infidel."[4] What ensued was one of the most puzzling episodes in the history of Christianity. The siege lasted a mere forty days before the crusaders breached the walls. An estimated 40,000 people lived in the city—soldiers, men, women, and children—and the crusaders, for reasons that are still debated, put many of them to death.

Historians have tried to explain this as the result of several things: the rage and hysteria of a conquering and long-suffering army, the soldiers' frenzy so often whipped up by powerful preachers, and the Jerusalem garrison itself, which for weeks had baited the crusaders by performing various indignities against Christian symbols. What is most likely is that word had spread among the new conquerors that an Egyptian army had landed at nearby Ascalon. The crusaders, not wanting to repeat the near-catastrophe of Antioch or to leave a potential enemy in their rear, needed to eliminate all noncombatants and bring the project to a resolution. They marched off to Ascalon, surprised the Egyptians, and won the final victory of what would prove to be the only "successful" crusade.

The Second Crusade

Once the threat of Turkish and Egyptian resistance was eliminated, the Christian armies began to wither away. Only two princes remained in Jerusalem with their forces, while all the rest either returned home or set out to establish Christian principalities in the Mideast. This had the effect of weakening the Christian strongholds to the point where they could be recaptured by the forces of Islam. In 1144 Edessa was once more in the hands of the Turks. Edessa was key because it was the last stronghold before Antioch. Thus the Second Crusade came to be preached, the relief of Antioch as its goal. It was a fiasco from the start. By this time, the emperor in Constantinople feared the crusaders more than he feared the Turks, and had reached a treaty with the Turks, who were consequently free to concentrate on the westerners. These consisted mostly of Germans and French, who did not fight together, but allowed the Turks to attack them one army at a time. The Germans were routed at Dorylaeum in 1147, and the French managed to survive with enough of an army only to cause more internal feuding when they arrived in Antioch.

The Third Crusade

This was to be the crusade of great names. On the Turkish side there was the great Turkish general Saladin, who had united the Turks and recaptured Jerusalem in 1187. This provoked the call for a third crusade, which would be led by Frederick Barbarossa of Germany, Richard the Lionhearted of England, and Philip II of France. But, great as their names were, greatness was not a hallmark of the crusade. The first tragedy was accidental as Barbarossa, who was seventy years old and the best of the generals, died en route, probably the victim of a heart attack. The allied armies captured Jerusalem's port town of Acre, but the ordeal of laying siege cost them at least half of their men (mostly through disease), and those who remained seemed little disposed to fight on. The king of France went home with his men, and Richard the Lionhearted was left in charge. He promptly slaughtered the 3,000 prisoners who had been captured when Acre fell, less from cruelty than from an impatience to get on with the fighting.

While considerable land along the Mediterranean coast was reconquered for the west, Jerusalem itself remained in the control of Saladin.

The Final Crusades

The crusading spirit was difficult to sustain and the final five crusades were ineffective. Resentment against the Greeks finally got the better of the westerners and the Fourth Crusade, which set out in 1202, managed to get only as far as Constantinople, which it first sacked and then established a Latin government, which lasted only a few years. It was at this time that the Venetians, who orchestrated the attack on Constantinople, stole the body of St. Mark and the famous four bronze horses that now stand atop the entrance to St. Mark's Cathedral in Venice. This only increased the bitterness between east and west, and weakened Constantinople for its ultimate contest with the Turks.

The Seventh and Eighth Crusades are worth mentioning because they feature the great Louis IX of France, who is known to us as St. Louis. One intriguing theory is that he was anxious to go on crusade partly to escape his overbearing mother, so that he and his wife could be alone together. In any event, Louis's idea was to attack Jerusalem from the coast of Africa, and he failed both times—first, because his army was slaughtered on the banks of the Nile, and next because of disease, which killed Louis himself in 1270.

Acre fell to the Muslims in 1291 and this marks the official end of the Crusades. Never again would Jerusalem be the focus of a crusade. But crusades as such did not end. It should be pointed out that when the eight "official" crusades were taking place, there were smaller armies leaving all the time.[5] But even after 1291, the Turkish threat persisted and made inroads into central Europe, Greece, and Italy itself. One typical battle between Christians and Muslims took place in Nicopolis (in Hungary) in 1397.[6] Constantinople fell to the Turks in 1453. In the next century the Renaissance popes were continually calling for the Italian cities to band together to fight the Turks. This resulted in the enormous sea battle of Lepanto in 1571, when the Christians ended Muslim incursions along the northern Mediterranean. But it was not until 1683 in a battle outside of Vienna, that the Turks were defeated by a Polish army and never threatened Europe again.[7]

Summary of the Crusades

On balance, what did the Crusades accomplish? Militarily they accomplished very little. Jerusalem was still in the hands of the Muslims, as were Asia Minor and North Africa. Furthermore, eastern and western Christianity were still divided—the reconciliation of the two, even if by force, being one of the goals of several popes. But the Crusades were not a total failure. The historian Thomas Madden makes a convincing case that the combination of crusader occupation of considerable land in the east for almost two centuries, and persistent attempts to take Jerusalem and to expand those gains, kept the Muslims on the defensive and probably bought time not only for Byzantium, which lasted until 1453, but for Europe itself.[8] The fact that the countries of Europe could come together to fight at all was a sign that Europe had finally come together, that it possessed a fundamental inner unity enabling it to cohere in a way it had never done before. The fact that it was the pope who called the Crusades was no coincidence. It meant that the Crusades were above all a spiritual phenomenon, and it highlighted the pope's ability as an international leader.

Henri Daniel-Rops has described the Crusades as a mystical fact, "the manifestation of a spiritual impulse springing from the depth of man's soul, the heroic expression of a faith which found no satisfaction unless in sacrifice, an answer to the call of God."[9] Even a less romantic writer such as Zoé Oldenbourg would have to agree with this. The Crusades simply make no sense unless they are understood spiritually. They were, if ever there was one, a holy war. Madden observes:

> If, from the safety of our desks, we are quick to condemn the medieval crusader, we should be mindful that he would be just as quick to condemn us. Our infinitely more destructive wars waged for the sake of political and social ideologies would, in his opinion, be lamentable wastes of human life. In

both societies, the medieval and the modern, people fight for what is most dear to them....For medieval men and women, the crusade was an act of piety, charity, and love, but it was also a means of defending their world, their culture, and their way of life.[10]

Despite the fact that, as Kenneth Clark once said, the Crusades had "all the factors that make for a goldrush," it never degenerated into one.[11] While there were plenty of opportunists on crusade who wanted land and riches, most of the leadership stood to lose the most—often selling off land and valuables in order to finance their army. For the vast majority of participants, the Crusades were a religious affair, and were undertaken in a spirit of pilgrimage. When the western generals became entrenched in Antioch after their miraculous victory, and seemed hesitant to move on, the common soldiers mutinied and said they had not come all this way merely to capture Antioch.[12] They wanted Jerusalem and they would force their leaders, if necessary, to take them there.

Why then, did the Crusades fail? The spirituality that motivated the Crusades and that was largely responsible for their initial success was also largely responsible for their ultimate failure. Religious fervor may be able to lead men to capture a hill in a mass attack, but it cannot convince them to keep the hill for any length of time, especially if the hill is far from home. Capturing Jerusalem was a simple matter compared to keeping it. Jerusalem was too far away. Supplies and reinforcements had to come from long distances—again, a possibility in a short campaign, but nearly impossible to sustain in a protracted stay. Besides, by being so far away, Jerusalem had lost its romantic hold on Europe. News of its fall was able to arouse the crusading spirit, but news of its fall again and again deadened the sensibilities of Europeans who had never seen it.

Another cause of failure was the inability of the westerners to incorporate themselves into the Middle East. They were regarded as foreigners and they treated the conquered peoples as subjects and vassals. When the crusaders first arrived, they were hailed by native Christians as liberators, but their policies too often proved to be brutal and inconsiderate of the natives. Granted, theirs was a martial government and attention had to be given to the constant threat of war rather more than to the niceties of cultural blending, but Christian populations soon realized they had merely substituted one slave owner for another.

Internal conflict also led to failure. The suspicion of Byzantium led western leaders, in their reordering of the Middle East, to bypass the one power whose proximity and historical ties to the region could lend permanence to a Christian rule. Almost all of the western leaders despised Byzantium and did nothing to restore it to its former provinces in Asia Minor, seeking to carve out Frankish or Norman kingdoms instead. This proved to be ultimately suicidal. To the west, it did not matter much if the enemy was Constantinople or Islam, so that when Constantinople fell in 1453, a loss akin to the fall of Rome in 410, the west hardly noticed.

All things considered, however, the Crusades had an impact on the west. One example is that returning crusaders brought back with them attitudes toward women that were new to the west. Until this time, women were treated as little more than property, while women in the east, while they were by no means the equal of men socially or legally, were treated with far more respect. This seems to have caught on with the crusaders, and the plight of women in the west improved dramatically. Thus were born chivalry and courtly love. This affected religious practices as well. Nearly all the churches being built in France at this time were named for the Blessed Virgin, and the popular recitation of the rosary began at this time.

The New Religious Orders

The Fourth Age of the Church saw development in religious life as well. Three basic directions were taken: the revival of Benedictine life, sometimes under slightly new forms; the introduction of a completely new form—the friars; and the appearance of women's religious orders.

The Revival of Benedictinism

Thanks to the monastic revival at Cluny, founded in southern France in 909, several reform movements sprang up throughout France and Italy, spawning new religious orders. Cluny had insisted on a return to a strict observance of the rule, with emphasis on celibacy, prayer in choir, splendid liturgies, and independence from lay control. Its influence was felt keenly in the middle of the eleventh century, by which time the famous Benedictine monasteries of Monte Cassino and Subiaco had been reformed. But new religious orders emphasized the hermetic life as well. The *Carthusian Order* was founded in 1084 by St. Bruno and vows its monks to a virtual hermit's life, permitting them to meet in common for Mass, office, and meals only on feast days.

Not long after the Carthusians appeared, the *Cistercians* were founded in 1098. Again, the emphasis was on seclusion, strict poverty, and manual labor. St. Bernard of Clairvaux became its most famous son and was partly responsible for the order's meteoric rise in popularity. When he died in 1153, there were already 343 Cistercian abbeys; by the year 1300 that number would be more than doubled.[13]

Another order, taking their name *Premonstratensians* from the French town of Prémontré where they were founded by St. Norbert in 1119, also attempted to live a live of apostolic poverty.[14] Norbert was an itinerant preacher who was getting on the nerves of the bishop of Laon, who eventually helped Norbert to found his own house.

The Friars

As the universities and towns grew in the Middle Ages, a new form of religious life was called for that could adapt to the different demands being made on Christianity. The monks, often secluded in remote parts of the countryside, could not adapt to the demands of university and city life. The most popular and thriving religious orders, in fact, were those that had deliberately chosen a quasi-hermetic style of life. But almost all monks had taken a vow of stability, which confined them physically to one abbey. Even the *Augustinian Canons* (or Austin Canons), who had been founded one hundred years before Dominic to bring some monastic life to the secular clergy, were relatively immobile as a preaching force. Dominic (1170–1221), an Augustinian Canon himself at the time, was en route from Spain to Rome when he passed through an area of France particularly bothered by the Albigensian heresy, and realized that very little was being done to combat the spread of this heresy. He envisioned an order that would combine the communal ideals of monastic life with an intellectual focus and a mobility that would allow his "monks" to travel freely from town to town and university to university. Thus we find Thomas Aquinas, at various times in his career, teaching at universities in Naples, Bologna, Paris, etc. Dominic's order, officially approved in 1216, was called the Order of Friars Preachers, but quickly became known as the *Dominicans*.[15]

It was known for two other innovations: 1) an international system of governance and 2) democracy. Just as Rome was centralizing power under the pope, so Dominic envisioned an order that was interconnected by priories and provinces, headed ultimately by a Master General. Houses with sufficient numbers would elect a prior, who had a term of office (usually of three years). These priors, along with other delegates, would elect a provincial. The provincials, in turn, would elect a Master General. *Franciscans* would adopt this same method of governing in time.

St. Francis of Assisi (1181–1226) may have met St. Dominic in Rome—they were contemporaries. Francis has always been portrayed as a poet given to extreme poverty, an impractical man given to unrealistic whims (he went off to preach to the Muslims for a time, thinking this would convert them) and not disposed at all to found an order. But he was a little more determined and politically astute than history has judged him. He wanted to combat heresy by example, rather than by argument—especially those heresies (Catharism and Waldensianism) which were practicing extreme poverty and implying that the official church had renounced its original mission. Francis showed that poverty could be lived within the context of the orthodox church.

In getting his order established, he knew what political contacts to make in Rome and had a very capable cardinal as a sponsor.

St. Dominic (1170–1221) founded the Order of Friars Preachers (Dominicans), largely to combat the Albigensian heresy then sweeping Europe. A gentle man who embraced a life of simplicity, he once declared, "heretics are more easily won over by examples of humility and virtue than by external display or a hail of words. Should we not rather arm ourselves with devout prayers and, carrying before us the standard of true humility, proceed in our bare feet against Goliath?"

St. Francis of Assisi (ca. 1182–1226) renounced a frivolous life to follow Christ's call to "build the church." Living at a time when the church sorely needed reform, Francis, along with St. Clare of Assisi (ca. 1193–1254), founded religious communities to call Christians to lives of radical simplicity and poverty. Francis also embarked on several missionary journeys.

When he was asked to accept into his care several communities of religious women, he refused to be affiliated to any except Clare's in Assisi. Francis could be justly accused of being unconcerned administratively about his new order, which may have caused it to splinter immediately upon his death—the argument was over what degree of poverty to practice. Yet Francis provided a vision of religious life that was magnetic and that has inspired millions of men and women, lay and cleric, Catholic and non-Catholic down through the ages. When he died, there were 5,000 Franciscan men. He remains among Christianity's most popular saints.

Women's Religious Orders

Religious enthusiasm was not restricted to men. Communities of women called *beguinages*, with a religious superior and temporary vows, began to emerge in the Low Countries around 1200 in order to live a life based on Gospel poverty and apostolic work. These women (or *beguines*) remained single. They were expected to make a living, support themselves, and help with the care of the beguinage. They did not take a vow of poverty. They taught reading, weaving, and needlework, and wrote spiritual works, usually in the vernacular. They were free to leave at any time. There were two kinds of beguinages: 1) a small house (five to fifteen beguines) governed by a mistress (or "Martha" in German). They did not have a church or chapel of their own, but attended the nearby parish. They were often founded and main-

---

Beguine

The word "beguine" has disputed origins. Some claim it was a term of derision, originating from "La Begue" (the Stammerer), a reference to a priest named Lambert, who supposedly founded the movement. Others suspect it is a derivation of "Albigensian." Still others say that it derives from the German stem "Begg," which denoted one who muttered prayers.

---

tained by a wealthy patron. At their high point in the 1200s, some cities had dozens of these houses.

2) The second kind was a large complex of buildings resembling a monastery, but offering beguines different kinds of living arrangements. Wealthier beguines could own their own house; but communal arrangements were also possible, as well as assisted living for the elderly. The beguines were not free of controversy. The loose structure of a beguinage made the Roman authorities nervous. The religious enthusiasm of the beguines placed them on the "edge" of theological debate, along with the Cathars and Waldenses. So Rome sought to affiliate these women with existing religious orders, either placing them under the care of Dominicans and Franciscans, or forcing them to become Dominican or Franciscan nuns. Beguinages fell into decline until they revived in the 1600s as a result of the Catholic Church's reformation. The French Revolution suppressed them again, but today several beguinages still exist in the Low Countries.

Dominican and Franciscan Nuns

Women's groups would be officially approved in 1216, when James of Vitry was consecrated bishop by the new pope and obtained approval for women to live together in community in the diocese of Liège and all of France and Germany. Women's groups other than the beguines sought to align themselves with men's groups—both in order to obtain *cura animarum* (care of souls, or the benefit of the sacraments and spiritual direction) and official approval. The men (Norbertines and Cistercians) successfully resisted this, so it was left to the emerging mendicants to serve their spiritual needs. Francis wanted nothing to do with women's groups except for Clare's, and was quite angry when he returned from his trip to the Middle East to find that the curia had foisted several women's houses on his order in his absence. These were immediately removed. But the curia won out in the end and eventually found a sympathetic master general, who accepted the houses after Francis's death. Dominic saw the possibility of including reformed Albigensian women, who were often single, in religious houses, thus allowing their religious fervor to continue. In fact, he seems to have founded a house of Dominican women, led by a woman named Diana, before he founded his own order of men.

Scholasticism

Scholasticism is a system of reasoning which has as its object the whole of scientific learning, but which is most closely identified with knowledge about God. It began in the early 400s, as Augustine applied classical logic and the classical method of learning to Christian doctrine. It stems from the assumption that faith is something not only to be believed, but understood as well. If God is Truth, in other words, then he can be known not only through revelation, but through reason as well. Under revelation God speaks to the world about his nature and mission; but under reason, the world uses its own devices to learn about God.

Several great names developed this idea in the west: John Scotus Erigena (c. 810–877) said that Christians had a duty to reflect on Scripture; Anselm (1033–1109) said that the mind had a right to inquire into the truths of Scripture; Abelard (1079–1142) perfected the technique of theological investigation at the time, whereby *quaestio* (the question itself) led to *interrogatio* (the investigation itself) and was followed by the *disputatio* (the argument and final resolution). He also thought that theology could be synthesized under the headings of faith, morality, and sacrament, a division which proved helpful throughout the Middle Ages. Peter Lombard (c. 1100–1160) summarized the wisdom of the previous centuries in a book called the *Sentences*, which remained the primary text for all theologians for the next four centuries.

St. Thomas Aquinas

By far, the greatest name in scholasticism was that of Thomas Aquinas, a Dominican friar from Italy, whose *Summa Theologiae* is the high point of scholastic theology. In using the newly rediscovered texts of Aristotle, Thomas so revolutionized the study of theology that his teaching on free will was condemned for a time by the Archbishop of Paris. His method followed roughly that of the medieval disputation, the method by which a professor would present a certain problem, answer objections, and then arrive at some solution.

Thomas divided his *Summa* into three parts: a) God as God; b) God as he relates to man; c) Christ as mediator between God and man. Let us take a look at a typical question taken up in the *Summa* and see how Thomas approaches it:

1. Thomas states the question: *"Can it be proved that God exists?"*

2. Then he lists the objections to this question:

   a) *It is an article of faith that God exists.*

      Faith is about the unseen. As the Letter to the Hebrew states: "Only faith can guarantee the blessings that we hope for, or prove the existence of the realities that at present remain unseen." What cannot be seen, therefore, cannot be proved.

   b) *We do not know the essence of God.*

      We only know of what his essence does *not* consist.

      (Here there is a quote from John Damascene supporting this.)

      Therefore, we cannot prove that God exists.

   c) *If we could prove the existence of God, we would have to do so through God's "effects"—i.e., creation.*

      But creation is finite and God is infinite.

      Therefore, we cannot prove that God exists.

Having set out the objections, Aquinas then responds "On the Contrary" and quotes someone himself, as if to say, "If you want to argue from Scripture, then I will take you on your own ground." In this case, he quotes St. Paul's Epistle to the Romans: "The invisible things of him are clearly seen, being understood by the things that are made" (Romans 1:20).

What follows—the response—is vintage Aquinas. He begins by making a distinction, namely that there are two ways to prove something: a) to start with the cause and prove the effects, or b) to start with the effects and work backward to the cause. Put simply, this means that you can start at the beginning and prove that what follows was caused by what came before, or start at the end and prove that something caused it to happen. In the case of God, because we cannot know him directly, we must do the latter. We must look at his creation and work our way backward to discover that "someone" has created it. Thomas then concludes by answering each objection one by one.

What is important here is that Aquinas is building a case *systematically*. Look at the questions he asks, and see how he progresses from basic ones to more difficult ones. Aquinas's answers are in parentheses:

1. Is the existence of God obvious to everyone? (No)

2. Can we prove that God exists? (Yes)

3. *Does* God exist? (Yes)

4. What is God like? Does he have a body? (No)

And on and on it goes. Thomas's theology is considered the only *complete* theology, in that he begins at the beginning and ends at the end, and asks all the questions in order. The casual observer might think that this is only logical, but, in fact, it was an immense undertaking, and St. Thomas Aquinas is the only one ever to accomplish it. This is why this method is called *systematic* theology. His answers tend to be measured and moderate. One favorite quotation ascribed to Aquinas is, "Never deny, seldom affirm, always distinguish," and indeed he was always making important and necessary distinctions.

He is known for other things as well. He questioned the prevailing notion, taken from Augustine, that humanity is fundamentally debased. For Aquinas, the opposite was true—humanity is fundamentally good. He drew this from his view of creation, which states that all created things are good precisely because God made them. He explained evil by saying that we can (and do) misuse these created things. Things that give us pleasure, for example, can be used to give us the kind of pleasure that wrongs another person. In doing this, Aquinas was revolutionizing morality because he was placing tremendous importance on individuals to judge for themselves what was inappropriate and what was not. Aquinas would never go so far as to say that morality was relative, but he did recognize that people were made differently and required different disciplines in their pursuit of virtue. This had the effect of making the individual person much more important in western culture, and sowed the seeds of what would become the glorification of the individual in the Renaissance.

St. Bonaventure

As a balance to the intellectualism of St. Thomas Aquinas, a Franciscan friar named Bonaventure attempted to do two things: a) to rescue the good name of Plato (and Augustine) and b) to reassert the importance of love and devotion as opposed to knowledge and science. This is not to say that Bonaventure was anti-intellectual. Far from it. Bonaventure thought that knowledge and science were useful, but that they followed from the experience of love and devotion, much like love follows from infatuation. St. Thomas would have argued that love and devotion followed from knowledge. In any case, Bonaventure's language, which was an attempt to describe the philosophy of Plato in Aristotelian terms, was much more affective than Thomas's. Bonaventure wrote, "The best way to know God is through the experience of sweetness; this is more perfect, excellent, and delightful than through rational inquiry."

Medieval Mysticism

By the fourteenth century there was some dissatisfaction with Scholasticism, which was looked on as too arid, too dogmatic, and too absorbed with minutiae. This reaction took the form of mysticism. There are four kinds of prayer: the prayer of praise, petition, thanksgiving, and union. This last prayer—the prayer of union—is what is aimed at in mysticism. Its ultimate goal, a "mystical union," is not accessible to all but a very rarified few. However, some form of contemplative prayer is accessible to everyone, and it was to such as these that the mystics addressed themselves. Mysticism is an experience of God gained through prayer and, even though the vast majority of worshippers would never reach its emotional heights—what might be described in today's language as a "runner's high"—some experience of God was available to all.

At first, the medieval mystics sought to complement the work of the theologians by placing more emphasis on emotion. A group of Dominicans known as the Rhineland Mystics (Meister Eckhardt, Johann Tauler, and Henry Suso) sought to synthesize the work of Thomas Aquinas with their own emphasis on charismatic assent to God. But this quickly gave way to an anti-intellectualism that stated that we cannot know God through human reason. *The Cloud of Unknowing*, whose very name suggests anti-intellectualism, appeared in the 1300s, and claimed that we cannot know God through our human reason, but must come to him through contemplation and experience. Walter Hilton (d. 1396) reinforced this, as did Julian of Norwich (c. 1342–1413). This mystical movement culminated in the classic *Imitation of Christ* by Thomas à Kempis (1380–1471), which is filled with practical advice on how to pray and live a Christian life, but repeatedly warns against the dangers of scholarship and learning.[16]

The Medieval Inquisition

Unfortunately the friars, because they were so well-educated, became quickly entangled in a process which sought to eliminate heresy, known as the *Inquisition*. There are several things that must be understood about the Inquisition, however, before we can proceed. To begin, the Medieval Inquisition is usually confused with the *Spanish* Inquisition, which is a later and different phenomenon. The Inquisition in the Middle Ages was the normal method of trial law in the church, much like a military tribunal is the normal method of trial law in the military. Its object was not merely the elimination of heresy. Several items fell under the jurisdiction of the Inquisition, such as marriage and divorce. Henry VIII's attempt to dissolve his marriage with Catherine of

Aragon, for example, came under the purview of an Inquisition trial. Its concern, in other words, was not merely with heresy, but with any number of things that could possibly have endangered the faith of the people. The extent and danger of heresy, however, made the Inquisition procedure develop quickly.

The Inquisition as a heresy-hunting operation should be examined, because this is how it is most often remembered. Punishment for heresy in the Christian world began about the year 325 with the Emperor Constantine. Fines, imprisonment, and flogging could be inflicted on heretics. The first execution for heresy came in 350, although the pope, Ambrose, and Martin of Tours all protested vehemently. Most theologians saw punishment for heresy as therapeutic rather than punitive. Punishment for heresy should be purposeful: to turn sinners away from their sin, and thus it should fall short of execution. Killing a heretic was an admission of defeat and lost a sinner for all eternity. Still, Augustine saw capital punishment as occasionally necessary. John Chrysostom (d. 407), on the other hand, wrote, "To kill a heretic is to introduce upon earth an inexpiable crime."

The state was generally more severe than the church in seeking to punish heretics. While imperial law identified heretics as the equal of barbarians in their contempt of the law and worthy of capital punishment, the church urged caution and encouraged preachers rather than the police to attack the problem. The takeover of western society by barbarians ended the drive for the execution of heretics (since so many of them were heretics), and forced the church to focus on conversion rather than enforcement.

Consequently, punishment for heresy was almost unknown until the early 1000s, when religious fervor was on the rise. As in all religious movements, enthusiasm was multidirectional—some of it falling along traditional lines, but some of it heading into uncharted territory. Several heretical groups emerged in the 1000s, which posed a threat not only to the church, but to society as well. In 1022, the first known case of a trial for heresy took place in Orleans, where a group of eight priests had denied that creation came from God. This meant that sacraments were useless, at best. It also implied that marriage and sexual pleasure were sinful. One of these priests was the confessor to the queen, so one can only imagine the king's interest in prosecuting them. All eight were burned at the stake.

There were two main groups of heretics, whose common thread might be evangelical poverty—a life of poverty based on the Gospel. Not that this was a bad thing in itself, but it led to excesses that were problematic. The south of France was particularly fertile ground for these heretics. Its closeness to Spain, where Muslims and Jews had lived together for centuries, plus the addition of migrating Bogumils from the Balkan peninsula, made for a religious diversity and toleration which was dangerous. One group which emerged was called the *Waldenses* after their founder, Peter Valdes, or "Waldo." Their program involved poverty and lay preaching. Such groups were legion in the 1100s and took such names as the "Poor Preachers." They got into trouble as they increasingly ignored their bishops, and became elitist in whom they recognized as legitimate (i.e., worthy) ministers of sacraments. St. Francis tried to combat them with his own version of evangelical poverty and preaching.

The predominant heretical group was called *Albigensians*, as their center was in the city of Albi. Albigensians (or Cathars or Manicheans, as they were otherwise known) were dualists. They believed that a good God could not possibly create an evil world. This implied not only that the world was evil, but that all created things were evil, which meant that a human Christ was not really a man and he did not suffer and die on the cross or rise from the dead. They also introduced an alternative to baptism called the *consolamentum*, which was a baptism in the Spirit. Suicide was commendable and usually occurred by inducing pneumonia or starvation. As extreme as it sounds to us today, it had a following and was threatening the fabric of the society as well as the church. By the end of the twelfth century there were four Albigensian bishops in southern France, in Carcassone, Albi, Toulouse, and Agen.

Resistance to Albigensians came from two sources: the church, which sought legislation against them and encouraged preachers to combat heresy by persuasion; and the northern French, who initiated a crusade against the southerners. In 1208 a papal delegate was murdered and the northern French, led by

Simon de Montfort, invaded the south. It was a particularly brutal crusade; the northerners were not patient when it came to heresy. In one episode, 140 Albigensians were burned to death at one time in the town of Minèrve. The Albigensian Crusade, as it became known, lasted until 1219. The pope, Innocent III, was a lawyer and saw both how easily the crusade had gotten out of hand and how it could be mitigated. He encouraged local rulers to adopt anti-heretic legislation and bring people to trial. By 1231 a papal inquisition began, and the friars were given charge of investigating tribunals. The friars were perfect for the job: They were well-educated, they were devoted to the pope, and they were not swayed by local interests.

The method of the Inquisition was for a tribunal (or threesome) of friars to arrive in a town and "preach" the Inquisition, that is, to explain why heresy was so harmful and why people should come forward and give information about the activities and whereabouts of heretics. Sometimes everyone was summoned to speak to the inquisitors—all males over fourteen years old and all females over the age of twelve. They had one week to appear. If a person did not appear, he or she would be provisionally excommunicated. After one year, a penal sentence would be added. Many people who were summoned and knew that they were guilty or strongly suspected of heresy would flee during this time.

Inquisitors were both the investigators and judges. They began with an *inquisitio generalis*, which determined whether some form of heresy had actually occurred, whether it was worth pursuing, whether the accused was "triable." This might best be described as a "pretrial hearing" today. If a person was deemed "triable," then the *inquisitio particularis* began. The accused was given a list of the charges against him or her, witnesses were summoned, and a trial held in secret.

The degree of heresy was first determined. There were several degrees, some more serious than others. People who aided or concealed heretics were considered to be heretics themselves, though the nature and extent of their involvement had to be determined by the court. Then there were those who showed an interest in heresy by attending meetings, speaking with known heretics, taking part in ceremonies. Finally there were heretics themselves—those who preached heresy, believed in the heresy, encouraged others to join their group, etc.

The investigation then went forward. Ideally, as today, the inquisitors hoped for an admission of guilt. Such admissions saved time and the accused was usually given a lighter sentence. If the accused did not admit guilt, judges gained information through witnesses, spies planted in prisons, or tests. For example, if a suspected Cathar ate a piece of meat, which Cathars were not allowed to do, he or she could be cleared. One man pleaded: "Lords, hear me, I am no heretic, for I have a wife and lie with her, and have children. And I eat flesh and lie and swear, and am a faithful Christian."[17]

Only two types of proof were recognized: partial proof and full proof. Only full proof could convict. Proof was regarded as "full" when the accused confessed, or if the accused was caught in the act, or if there were two eyewitnesses of a heretical act. All other evidence was considered to be partial proof, and no amount of partial proof could add up to full proof. However, a great body of partial proof, or circumstantial evidence, could lead the inquisitors to suspect a person of heresy, and so torture might be used to extract a confession.

When the investigations were complete, the inquisitors, in solemn ceremony in front of the townspeople, civic officials, and nobility, pronounced judgment. The ranking inquisitor preached a short sermon, then proclaimed "decrees of mercy," or commutations of punishment, or what we might call "suspended sentences." These could be frequent. In 1246 the Dominican inquisitor Bernardo Gui sentenced 207 heretics. None of them were burnt at the stake, 23 received prison sentences, and 184 were commuted and had only to wear crosses for a period of time.

The extent of the Inquisition trials for heresy has been highly exaggerated. In fact, the word *inquisition* itself has come to mean "an unfair trial" or a "kangaroo court." Karen Armstrong, in her popular history, *Holy War*, expresses well the common misconceptions of the Inquisition: She calls it "One of the most evil of all Christian institutions...an instrument of terror in the Catholic Church until the end of the seventeenth century" (p. 456), "this noxious offspring of the Crusades" (p. 457), "iniquitous

byword of orthodoxy" (p. 459), and a "fanatical extreme" (p. 461).
She continues:

> Its methods were that "heretics" should be hunted out by a
> panel of inquisitors, who in the Catholic Church were usu-
> ally the Dominicans....These bloodhounds of orthodoxy
> sniffed out the heretics in the community and people who
> held unacceptable views or were accused of "unchristian"
> practices were arrested and flung into prison. There they
> would be tortured with unbelievable cruelty and made to
> "confess their crimes."...They were forced to confess that
> they worshiped the Devil or took part in monstrous sexual
> orgies; once they had been tortured beyond endurance, they
> had no further strength to deny the charges....Once the
> heretic had confessed his error he might be released, but that
> was not always the case. After confession, the heretics were
> handed over to the secular authorities and were then either
> hanged or burned at the stake. (p. 457)[18]

Fortunately, modern scholarship on both the Medieval and
Spanish Inquisitions has made clear that almost everything
claimed by this author is not true. But favorite bigotries die hard.
One historian at the State University of New York was inter-
viewed for the History Channel's documentary on the Inquisition,
and said that, *despite all the evidence to the contrary*, the Inquisition
"is every bit as vicious as it has been painted."[19] Better, apparently,
to have inaccurate history.[20]

The facts are quite different. One author has recently pointed
out that between 1249 and 1257 the Medieval Inquisition sentenced 230 people to prison and only 21 to the "secular arm," i.e.,
death. This means that, throughout the whole of Europe in an
eight-year period—when the Inquisition was at its peak!—less than
three heretics a year were burned at the stake. Of the 900 cases
heard by a long-time Dominican Inquisitor Bernardo Gui, only
forty were given over to the secular arm for execution. This same
author concludes, "Once the Inquisition was established...the
pyromania which had characterized lay attempts to suppress heresy
came to an end."[21] Ninety percent of the sentences were "canonical" or church-related penances: fasting, pilgrimage, increased

attendance at Mass, the wearing of distinctive clothing or badges, etc. The number of those who were put to death was very small indeed.[22] The best estimate is that, of every hundred people sentenced, one person was executed, and ten were given prison terms. Even these latter could have their sentences reduced once the inquisitors left town.

This does not mean that the Inquisition was without problems. For one thing, religious orders were nervous about their men participating in the Inquisition tribunals. These men became a separate caste. They might regard themselves as above the rule of a local superior, and their visits disrupted community life. Secondly, bishops did not always welcome the appearance of the Inquisition. He, after all, had to stay behind and live with the people who might not be too happy with the proceedings. But, even more, he often resented the interference of a religious order in the workings of his diocese. In 1279, for example, the Bishop of Padua was reprimanded by the pope for not cooperating with the visiting friars.

Then there were the rivalries between the Dominicans and Franciscans. Members of one order might use the Inquisition to get rid of members of the other order or to gain turf. In 1266 the Dominicans of Marseilles brought false witnesses against the Franciscans. Sometimes the people could be hostile. Several Inquisitors were killed, the most notable being the Dominican Peter of Verona (Peter Martyr) on his way from Como to Milan. In 1242, all the inquisitors of Toulouse were murdered.

Abuses of the Inquisition system also took place. Overzealous inquisitors occasionally overstepped their authority. Conrad of Marburg was notoriously cruel and was eventually murdered by the populace. In one outrageous case in 1239, Robert the Bugre sentenced 180 heretics to death in Montwiner, including the bishop. His own Dominican order suspended him from his office as inquisitor, then sentenced him to life in prison.

Safeguards existed, but were not always effective. The Dominican Bernardo Gui, much maligned by Umberto Eco's book, *The Name of the Rose*, and the even cruder movie by the same name, was actually quite meticulous in ensuring the fair treatment of heretics. His guidelines for inquisitors are still used in the train-

ing of FBI agents to this day! He urged the inquisitor to be dili-
gent for the truth, neither given to anger or laziness, always open
to appeals for delay or lesser sentences, and to be merciful, hon-
est, consistent, and not cruel. Papal directives also warned inquisitors against abuse.

But abuses were not limited to inquisitors. Politicians could
use the Inquisition as a tool to get rid of their enemies. Property
was also confiscated as part of a capital sentence, and even though
it was usually dispensed from, it could prove a tempting target for
politicians. In a few cases, an accused person's land was sold before
he was found guilty of heresy. Occasionally a dead person could
be tried for heresy—this was done usually with property in mind.

An Assessment of the Medieval Inquisition

Inquisition trials for heresy in the Middle Ages were mostly
confined to southern France and northern Italy. Scandinavian
countries escaped them entirely. England saw almost no trials for
heresy, the trial of Joan of Arc in 1431 being a notable exception—
she was actually tried in northern France. Most of France and
Spain also saw little Inquisition activity, in the case of Spain until
the late 1400s. Trials for heresy began to recede significantly by
the year 1300, mostly because of a lack of suspects. Several factors
combined with the Inquisition to eradicate heresy in the thirteenth century. Simon de Montfort's Albigensian Crusade,
assisted by the preaching of the friars and papal legislation channeling new religious orders into existing and orthodox institutions, all helped to end the threat to medieval society and the
church.

The Medieval Inquisition was actually a considerable
advance in the treatment of criminals. Manuals were produced
which guided judges in investigating cases and provided suspects
with some legal recourse. Mob vengeance, so prevalent at the
beginning of the thirteenth century, came to an end and the number of those put to death for heresy was reduced dramatically.

The Spanish Inquisition

Two hundred years after the Medieval Inquisition had almost ceased, the rulers of Spain were anxious to unify their country along ethnic and religious lines. They looked to the apparatus of the Inquisition—i.e., its trial procedure—as the best means of accomplishing this. The Spanish Inquisition was essentially about conformity to Catholicism. It targeted those recent converts (or new Catholics—mostly Jews, called *conversos*, and Muslims, called *moriscos*) whose conversion was suspected of being insincere, and those old Catholics who could be charged with any number of minor offenses, ranging from blasphemy, to various sexual offenses (bigamy, homosexuality, bestiality), and solicitation from the confessional.

The first sixty years of the Spanish Inquisition, beginning in 1480, concerned mostly the former (converts from Judaism and Islam) and witnessed most of the executions—about 3,000 in number—while Inquisition activity over the next 300 years involved mostly the latter. In fact, sixty percent of Inquisition trials in Spain did not involve Jewish or Muslim converts at all. But it is their persecution which has attracted most of the notice of historians and most of the criticism of the whole system of inquisition, and is worthy of some attention here.

By turning on converts to Catholicism, the Spanish courts essentially changed the terms of enforcement from religion to race. Ferdinand and Isabella, the rulers of Spain, were not anti-Semitic, nor was the nobility, but the lower classes were, so it is possible that the new rulers seized on this attitude as a means of uniting the country.

The history of attacks on the Jews of Europe is a long and storied one and cannot be adequately summarized here. But serious problems began for the Jews in the late 1200s, when they were expelled from England in 1290 and then from France in 1306. In the mid-1300s Jews were suspected of spreading the Black Death. In the late 1300s the archdeacon of Seville led an assault on the ghetto and tore down synagogues, an act which was repeated in Valencia. Jews could escape only by being baptized. In 1412 to

1414 the preaching of the Dominican Vincent Ferrer touched off rioting directed at Jews.

Nor was this activity restricted to Spain. Throughout the 1400s we see the Jews being expelled from Vienna and Linz (1421), Cologne (1424), Bavaria (1442), Perugia (1485), and all of Tuscany (1494). While they were persecuted locally in Spain, the crown tried to protect them. One pope (Nicholas II) wrote a bull denouncing the exclusion of Jewish-Christians from political office on the basis of race. The Archbishop of Toledo forbade the existence of guilds organized on racial lines. But the Dominican prior of Seville (Alonso de Hojeda) pressured Queen Isabella into beginning the Inquisition, which she did in 1481. It quickly spread to other cities. The first *auto da fe* (the ceremony at which the condemned were sentenced) occurred in the same year, when six people were burnt. Hojeda preached. A year later more inquisitors were appointed, the Dominican Tomas de Torquemada among them.

The pope (Sixtus IV) did not take kindly to these goings-on and objected both to the use of church courts and government controls in the persecution of Jews. He even went so far as to have the Spanish Ambassador to the papal court arrested. This same pope demanded that the accused be allowed to appeal to Rome, be told the names of hostile witnesses, and be allowed to have legal counsel. Furthermore, personal enemies and former servants of the accused should be disqualified. Ferdinand flatly refused and the pope lost all control over the process. In 1492 a decree was passed requiring all Jews and Muslims to convert or leave the country. There were not many Muslims left in Spain, as they were defeated in Granada in the same year. Of the estimated 80,000 Jews, about a third fled the country (seeking shelter in Poland and Eastern Germany), about a third converted willingly, and a third unwillingly. Attention focused on this last group, who were suspected of continuing Jewish practices secretly and conspiring with Muslims in North Africa for another Muslim invasion.

The Inquisition in Spain was a national phenomenon, in which the king appointed the Grand Inquisitor, his council, and declared what was heresy and what was not. Jews were not the only ones affected by this Inquisition. Ignatius Loyola was imprisoned twice for being an *alumbrado*—an "enlightened one"—a code word for a "charismatic." Teresa of Avila was accused of misconduct and one of her works placed on a list of forbidden books. Even the Archbishop of Toledo, who had written a catechism approved by the Council of Trent, found his book forbidden and spent eight years in prison for writing it.

Two recent historians of the Spanish Inquisition—made perhaps more authoritative because they are Jews themselves—have modified the views generally held about this Inquisition.[23] First, the Spanish Inquisition was not a monolithic efficiently organized pogrom of twentieth-century dimensions. Rather, it seems to have been quite inefficient and porous. Secondly, its cruelty seems to have been highly exaggerated by propagandists, especially after Protestants were defeated by the Spanish king in the 1560s. Torture was hardly used in Spain and there is evidence that criminals in state prisons would deliberately blaspheme in order to be tried by the Inquisition and moved to a more humane Inquisition prison. There were also attempts to settle matters out of court. Thirdly, the numbers executed are far less than the hundreds of thousands (or millions, by some estimates) previously thought affected by the Spanish Inquisition. Historians previously have been misled by the number of "executions." While 100 people might be "sentenced" to death, only one or two would actually be executed, while the others would be hung in effigy as a warning to themselves and others. In its whole existence, between three and four thousand people were burned at the stake in Spain, three-fourths of these before 1540. This is not to defend the Inquisition in Spain, but it is important to give it some perspective. The last execution was carried out in Seville in 1781.[24]

Innocent III

The high point of papal power was reached under Pope Innocent III (1198–1216). It was he who managed to put the *Dictatus Papae*, the list of the prerogatives of the papacy composed by Gregory VII one century earlier, into effect. The pope now had the right and authority to examine emperors who were

---

Transubstantiation

The phrase *transubstantiation*, used to describe scientifically the action which happens at the consecration of the Mass, has its roots in Aristotelian language. Aristotle saw the world as composed of "substance" and "accident." Substance was that which identified a thing as what it was. A chair had a "chairness" about it. This was its substance. The materials it was made from, the color, the smell—all of these things were accidents. If you changed the accidents: had the chair reupholstered from cloth into leather, painted it a different color—you would be enacting an "accidental change." You still had a chair. But if you destroyed the chair, so that it was no longer a chair, you had brought about a "substantial change."

When it came to the Eucharist, the church thought it had finally found a language which described what happened: the accidents remained the same, but the substances changed. Thus, while the accidents of bread and wine remained—e.g., it still looked like wine and tasted like wine—it was no longer wine at all. It was the blood of Christ.

---

elected. The pope was once again the one who crowned the emperor. Innocent saw his office in a semidivine light "set in the midst between God and man; below God, but above man." He was the first to use the phrase "the Vicar of Christ." He began the Fourth Lateran Council, which proved to be one of the most important councils in the history of the church.

The Fourth Lateran Council emphasized the individual's response to the Gospel, drawing a relation between the vertical (*pietas*) and horizontal (*caritas*) which affected everyone. Thus, monasticism was de-emphasized and more attention given to lay spirituality. Along these lines, the council legislated annual confession for the faithful and the "Easter Duty," defined "transubstantiation" as the official explanation for the action of the Eucharist (see inset), and reaffirmed the number of sacraments at seven. The council also did a lot to improve the state of the clergy. It demanded better *ministers* and ended the proliferation of new religious orders. At the same time it approved the formation of Dominicans and Franciscans.

The Decline of the Papacy

The political power attained by Innocent III was bound not to continue. A succession of lawyer popes in the thirteenth century saw papal power erode at the hands of the Germans and then the French. By the end of the century, the papacy was headed for a crisis. In 1292 Nicholas IV died. For more than two years (twenty-seven months) the cardinals could not come to a two-thirds majority on any candidate. Finally they agreed on an eighty-five-year-old hermit named Peter Marrone. He took the name Celestine V, and disliked his new job so much that it is said he cried every night. Six months later he consulted a canon lawyer about the legality of abdicating. The lawyer told him that there were precedents, which was not true. Celestine thereby resigned, and the lawyer was elected to take his place. He took the name Boniface VIII.

He was both brilliant and arrogant, and thought he could turn the clock back to the time of Innocent III, where he thought he would be an international force. But those days were over. He proclaimed the first Holy Year in 1300 and wrote a bull, *Unam Sanctam*, which was famous for its claim that every person needed to be subject to the Roman Pontiff in order to be saved.

Avignon Papacy (1309–77)

The next pope, Benedict XI, died after being pope for only nine months. The cardinals met in Perugia in 1305 and elected a Frenchman, the archbishop of Bordeaux, who was not present. He took the name Clement V and was a rather weak pope, being dominated by the French king. He created ten cardinals in 1305, one of whom was English and nine French. He was crowned in Lyons and settled in Avignon in 1309. The curia became nervous about returning to Rome because of the disturbed condition of Italy, antipapal risings in Rome, and the growing need for French support and security. As the papal court remained in the bishop's palace in Avignon, a vast fortified palace housing an elaborate administrative machinery was gradually established, and this added to the curia's reluctance to move back to Rome.

This arrangement caused several problems. Most importantly, it was a perpetual scandal that the Bishop of Rome should reside permanently (not to mention affluently) outside his diocese. Secondly, the papacy in Avignon was deprived of a financial and military independence it enjoyed in Rome. Thirdly, the Avignon papacy was the occasion of the Great Schism, and an aid to its continuance.

This arrangement was immediately condemned by Petrarch, who was more scandalized by the sumptuousness of the papal court than by its location, calling Avignon "the Babylon of the west." Later on, Catherine of Siena upbraided one pope until he finally made the move back to Rome. Most of the seven Avignon popes were men of personally devout life, and some of them seriously attempted curial and ecclesial reform, making the curia the

Catherine of Siena (ca. 1347–1380), a lay Dominican, was one of the great medieval mystics and a prototype of today's social activist—she unstintingly served the poor and the sick, especially those ill from the Black Death then sweeping Europe. A committed reformer of the church as well, she persuaded Pope Gregory XI to return from Avignon to Rome.

most administratively and financially efficient government in Europe. Some of them (Urban V [1362–70]) even tried moving the curia back to Rome. In fact, Urban succeeded for a time, but military necessity forced him out. His heart was probably always back in Avignon. He created eight cardinals in 1368—six of them were French and only one was a Roman.[25] But Gregory XI (1370–78) was fairly determined to return to Rome. It wasn't until 1377 that he was able to overcome the financial, diplomatic, and military obstacles and accomplish the deed.

The Black Death

During the Avignon papacy, the world's greatest peacetime catastrophe struck. It was called the Black Death and its impact on the church would prove to be significant. The name "Black Death" came from a blackening of the skin, which occurred by the fourth or fifth day of infection. It was also known as the "bubonic plague," the name deriving from the Greek word for groin (boubon), the lymph nodes of which were usually the first areas to be affected.

The Black Death began in Sicily in 1347 and quickly spread. The panic throughout Europe was intense because people had no idea what was causing the disease and its spread: fleas on rats. Some people died within a day. The best estimates are that one-third of Europe's population died—about 20 million people. The cities were especially hard hit. In Paris 50,000 people (one-half of the population) died at a rate of nearly 800 a day. In Florence, one-half of the population died. In Venice, two-thirds of the population died—about 600 a day.

The significance of this for the church was two-fold. Numbers and the quality of clergy were reduced drastically as the best clergy died tending to the infected, and the church scrambled to replace them too quickly. But there was also an economic revolution which involved the church. Permanent retainers disappeared from farms, to be replaced by fewer people who leased the land. Much farmland was turned to pasture. As a result, fewer people owed their allegiance to the landowners, and the few that remained owed little more than the rent. Thus workers improved their lot financially and gradually lost their fidelity to landowners, thus weakening the power of the landed gentry, as well as the hold of the monasteries on the local people. These decentralizing forces (landed gentry and monasteries), in losing their power base, gave way to an emerging group of nobility, not tied to the land, who depended on the king and royal policy for their advancement. Thus the power of the king and state increased while the power of his traditional rivals decreased. The results of this would become evident during the Reformation as kings tested the people's loyalty to the church.

The Papal (Great) Schism

The return of the pope to Rome in 1377 did not guarantee a restoration of papal power. Pope Gregory XI died in Rome only a year after returning, and all the talk was of returning to Avignon. The election, however, would take place in Rome. The Roman crowds made no secret of their desire to see a Roman pope back on the throne of Peter. As a result, some cardinals feared for their lives. One cardinal wore a coat of mail to the conclave; one dictated his will; the French cardinals moved their valuables to the safety of Castel Sant'Angelo. So afraid were they that, after the election, they dressed up the ancient Cardinal Tebaldeschi (a Roman) in a miter and cope to be shown on the balcony of St. Peter's as the new pope, while they made their escape.

The next day they announced that Urban VI, the Archbishop of Bari, had really been the one elected. He was an Italian, not a Roman, and he was thought to be very pro-French and in favor of the move back to Avignon. But Urban VI shocked everyone by announcing that he was staying in Rome. The cardinals promptly assembled and declared the election invalid because they had been under duress, and thought Urban VI would capitulate. That they *actually* believed he was invalidly elected is unlikely since they did not complain during the election (electing the man they wanted), and accepted benefices from him. They sought the approval for their nullifying action from the University of Paris, which they did not get, and in September 1378 proceeded to elect a new pope anyway (Clement VII, the Bishop of Geneva).

Urban responded by appointing his own college of cardinals (twenty-nine of them), hired an army, and defeated the forces under Clement and caused the cardinals to flee to Avignon in April 1379. The schism was now a fact: There were two popes. Governments would now take sides along political lines and further complicate matters. The French king and his allies (Scotland, Spain, and Naples) recognized Clement VII in Avignon as the legitimate pope. Countries opposed to France (England, Germany) supported the Roman pope. Religious orders split accordingly. The Dominican Catherine of Siena supported Urban, while her Dominican brother Vincent Ferrer in Spain backed Clement. The Dominicans ended up with two masters-general as a result.

Urban grew more irascible. He promoted worthless people and antagonized people unnecessarily. In fact, he seems to have come unhinged after his election. Defections among his newly chosen cardinals began, and Urban countered this by executing five of them for conspiracy. Then each pope excommunicated the others' followers. The cardinals from both parties knew that this situation could not go on. Together they met in Pisa in 1409, deposed both popes and elected a third—Alexander V. Unfortunately, the other two popes refused to step down, so now the world had three popes. Alexander was a good man, but died on his way to Rome, forcing yet another election. The combined colleges of cardinals immediately elected a man who took the name John XXIII. But the number of popes remained at three.

ROME	AVIGNON	PISA
Urban VI (1378–89)	Clement VII (1378–94)	
Boniface IX (1389–1404)	Benedict XIII (1394–1423)	
Innocent VII (1404–06) *(elected by 8 cardinals)*		
Gregory XII (1406–15)		Alexander V (1409–10)

ROME	AVIGNON	PISA
		John XXIII
		(1410–15)

Clement VIII
(1423–29)

*(resigned in 1429 and
was given diocese of
Majorca. Alfonso de Borgia,
who arranged this, was later
elected Pope Callistus III)*

The Emperor Sigismond had had enough and summoned a council to meet in Constance in 1415. Even the convoking of this council reveals the intricacies of negotiating a peace. John XXIII originally opened the council, was formally deposed, and then Gregory XII, now the Roman pope, agreed to come and reconvene the council, thus rendering its acts valid, then resigned. John XXIII fled, was arrested, and later reconciled to the new pope, Martin V. Clement VII had already fled to Spain and obstinately refused to be reconciled. Eventually, his successor, Clement VIII, abdicated in 1429. Despite the prolongation of papal claimants in Spain, the election of Martin V ended the Papal Schism.

The cost to the church was high. It had thrown people into confusion and cynicism, and they learned that they could live without popes. Excommunication had become a joke since everyone in Europe had been excommunicated by one pope or the other. But

---

Pope John XXIII

One question lingered: "Who *was* the pope in the line of Peter?" The Roman pope has always been regarded as the legitimate pope, though there remained a doubt about the Pisan pope. This was not resolved (in favor of the Roman line) until 1958, when Angelo Roncalli took the name John XXIII.

---

possibly even more important, councils of the church began to be regarded as superior in authority to any individual pope.

Conciliarism

The papacy had been seriously damaged by groups of cardinals, then put back together by a council. And these groups intended to hold on to their new-found power and keep the papacy weak. They did so by looking to democracy, a concept which was already being practiced in the orders of friars and in guilds. In cities like Florence democracy was being considered— with the head of government answerable to the people. There was also a social argument in favor of conciliarism. Many cardinals and bishops argued that councils were visible manifestations of the invisible essence of the church and that the church as a whole was prior to any of its parts. A council, according to this theory, was prior to any pope. In organic terms, they explained, the whole body can perform acts no single member can do.

The problems with conciliar theory were many. Secular rulers, who favored councils over popes because it would weaken the papacy, were not interested in applying conciliar theory to their own governments. So while they regarded themselves as above the law and representative government, they wanted to make the pope answerable to a council. But, even more, the problems of applying what was, up till then, very small-scale democracy to a large heterogeneous society had not been considered.

Two variations of conciliar theory emerged which sought to solve the dilemma. Moderate conciliar theorists regarded church councils as occasional legislatures and as an emergency power superior to the pope when he might be incapable of ruling because of illness or incompetence. These councils would meet rarely and only as circumstances dictated. Radical conciliarists, on the other hand, saw councils as the normal judicial sovereign in the church. They would meet on a frequent and regular basis. Four councils met within thirty years as the radical conciliarists attempted to determine policy. They were the Council of Pisa (1409); the Council of Constance (1414–17); the Council of Basle in 1431 and following; and, finally, the Council of Florence (1438–45).

Conciliarism failed as meteorically as it had risen. Pisa had elected a third pope who was never universally regarded as pope; Constance resolved the schism and is regarded as the high point of conciliarism, but failed to enforce its injunction that councils were superior to popes; Basle turned into a fiasco as the radical conciliarists clung pathetically to their claims despite being disbanded by the pope; and Florence was similarly ineffective, agreeing (sensibly) with the Greek Church to a unity of belief and diversity of ritual, but finding their decision overturned by the Greeks once they had arrived home from the council.

Following the Council of Florence, a succession of popes effectively dismantled the power of the cardinals and bishops. Only three councils would be called in the next 450 years.

John Wycliffe (1330–84) and Jan Hus (1372–1415)

During the Avignon papacy and subsequent papal schism, grievances against the papacy and church began to surface. The Englishman John Wycliffe became a spokesman for many of these grievances—150 years before they would emerge again remarkably the same at the Reformation. Wycliffe denied the supremacy of the papacy and the divine authority of the church. The only certain rule of faith, he claimed, was Scripture, which everyone must interpret for himself, and which must be made available in the vernacular. Furthermore, transubstantiation and the Mass were not scriptural. Wycliffe was also radically opposed to the ownership of property by the church. He maintained that the state had the right to take over the church's possessions and correct her misdeeds. John of Gaunt, the Duke of Lancaster and the virtual ruler of England at the time, protected Wycliffe from ecclesiastical censure. Wycliffe was condemned several times and by the time of his death he had completely broken with the church.

Jan Hus caught this spirit and introduced it to Prague. His particular rallying cry was that the Eucharist must be received under both species of bread and wine. In 1415 he appealed to the Council of Constance, was promised safe conduct, and was then burned as a heretic when he got there. The Czechs still regard him as a martyr.

The End of the Fourth Age

The unity which the church experienced in the 1200s, the theological heights, the architectural triumphs, the political dominance, all seemed to be waning in the late 1300s. The papacy had been weakened by division. With Wycliffe and Hus the unity of western Christendom was broken by a movement which was both religious and national. It was a prelude of things to come. Pope Martin V returned from Constance to Rome in 1420. Rome was a shambles, owing the neglect of papal governments absent for seventy years, and then mired in controversy for forty more years. The daunting task ahead was to rebuild Rome and get the papacy on better footing.

Recommended Readings

(B) Henri Chenu, *The Scope of the Summa* (Washington, DC, 1958). A highly readable introduction to St. Thomas's *Summa Theologiae*, describing how to read it, why Thomas wrote it in the manner he did, etc.

(B) G. K. Chesterton, *Saint Thomas Aquinas* (New York, 1933). Etienne Gilson, the noted Thomist scholar, said this was the best book ever written on St. Thomas.

(B) G. K. Chesterton, *St. Francis of Assisi* (New York, 1924). Another insightful look at the great medieval saint. Chesterton's books tend to be occasionally inaccurate factually, but his insights are so striking that the errors become relatively unimportant.

(B) Herbert Grundmann, *Religious Movements in the Middle Ages* (Notre Dame, 1995). A classic, recently translated into English.

(B) Bede Jarrett, *The Life of St. Dominic* (London, 1934). The biography which captures the spirit of Dominic better than any other.

(B) Henry Kamen, *The Spanish Inquisition: A Historical Revision* (New Haven, 1998). The best and most readable account available.

(B) Thomas Madden, *A Concise History of the Crusades* (New York, 1999).

(C) T. C. O'Brien, "Faith," in the Appendix to Aquinas's *Summa Theologiae* (McGraw Hill Summa, New York, 1974), Vol. 31, pp. 178–215.

(B) Zoé Oldenbourg, *The Crusades* (New York, 1966). Concerns the first three crusades.

(B) Edwards Peters, *Inquisition* (New York, 1988).

(C) Brian Shanley, OP, *The Thomist Tradition* (Boston, 2002).

(B) Barbara Tuchmann, *A Distant Mirror: The Calamitous 14th Century* (New York, 1978). Interesting essays on the Black Death, Papal Schism, a crusade, etc.

AUDIO-VISUALS:

Civilisation, by Kenneth Clark, Episode 4. BBC, 1969.

The Myth of the Spanish Inquisition, BBC Video, 1994.

Notes

1. See Edward Rothstein, "Was the Islam of Old Spain Truly Tolerant?" *New York Times*, 27 Sept 2003, pp. A15, 17.
2. Their names were Raymond of St. Giles, Robert of Normandy, Robert of Flanders, Baldwin, Godfrey of Bouillon, Stephen of Blois, and Bohemond from Vodena.
3. There are different theories as to why the Greeks did not continue to Jerusalem. Daniel-Rops says the Greeks feared the western armies far more than Islam and had made a peace treaty with Egypt (the Muslims who would be fighting in Jerusalem), and refused to fight. Zoé Oldenbourg suggests that the Greeks offered to help, but that such help would have meant further delay, and the western leaders were not in a waiting mood.
4. Zoé Oldenbourg, *The Crusades* (New York, 1966), p. 133.
5. Not all crusades were directed against Muslims. Occasionally a crusade was directed against heretical groups such as the Albigensians in southern France or against pagan Slavs.
6. See Barbara Tuchmann, *A Distant Mirror* (New York, 1978), pp. 538–63.
7. It is said that Viennese bakers, in honor of the victory over Islam, invented the crescent roll (the crescent being the symbol of Islam) as a token of victory.
8. Thomas Madden, *A Concise History of the Crusades* (New York, 1999), pp. 213–15.

9. Daniel-Rops, *Cathedral and Crusade* (London, 1957), p. 436.

10. Madden, *Crusades*, p. 213.

11. Kenneth Clark, *Civilisation* (New York, 1970), p. 42.

12. This rebellion is recounted in Oldenbourg, p. 127.

13. A further reform of this order saw a split into two groups: the Cistercians of Common Observance and those of Strict Observance. The latter are commonly known to us today as Trappists.

14. They are also known as Norbertines.

15. The word "Dominican" was both a reference to the founder, and to a pun on the name: *Domini Canes* (Dogs of the Lord), and hence the Dominican symbol of the dog was quickly adopted.

16. To get some idea of this form of prayer, it would be best to consult Thomas Merton's *Seeds of Contemplation* (Westport, CT, 1979) and Jean Baptiste Chautard's *The Soul of the Apostolate* (Garden City, NJ, 1961).

17. John O'Brien, *The Inquisition* (New York, 1973), p. 63.

18. Karen Armstrong, *Holy War* (New York), 1988.

19. Marvin Lunenfeld, *The Inquisition*, The History Channel, 1996.

20. In the History Channel's presentation, after the assertion is made that torture very rarely took place in the Spanish Inquisition, ten grueling minutes are then given to what those tortures *would* have been.

21. Edwards Peters, *Inquisition* (New York, 1988), p. 57.

22. Ibid., p. 58.

23. Henry Kamen, *The Spanish Inquisition: A Historical Revision* (New Haven, 1998) and Benzion Netanyahu, *The Origins of the Inquisition in Fifteenth-Century Spain* (New York, 1995).

24. See "The Myth of the Spanish Inquisition" (BBC/A&E Production), 1994, for an excellent summary.

25. Of the 134 cardinals created by the Avignon popes, 112 were French. Seventy percent of all the curial officials were French.

THE FIFTH AGE OF THE CHURCH (1450–1789)

Protestant and Catholic Reformations

The 1400s were a century of transition for the church. On the one hand, it was trying to recover from the losses of the Black Death, the cynicism caused by the Papal Schism, the criticism of Rome caused by the Avignon papacy, and conciliarism. The pope was returning to Rome and needed to overcome these setbacks, but he also needed to rebuild a neglected city. Unfortunately, the next century saw a succession of popes more bent on rebuilding the city of Rome than on repairing the fabric of the Roman Church itself. This is not to say that the Renaissance popes neglected the church altogether, but their focus tended to be more material than spiritual. We need to look at who these popes were and the age they lived in, to understand better what was to follow in the form of the Reformation.

The Renaissance

The Renaissance really had roots far back into the Middle Ages, beginning with William of Ockham (d. 1347), whose philosophy of nominalism would eventually lead to an emphasis on the importance of the individual. In the Middle Ages, almost everyone fit into a niche. If your father was a soldier or a craftsman or a butcher or a farmer, *you* would most likely follow in his footsteps. Only the church provided a way out. The son of a farmer might become the bishop of a diocese or the abbot of an important abbey. With the Renaissance, this began to change. A new educated class of lay people was emerging, which enjoyed a

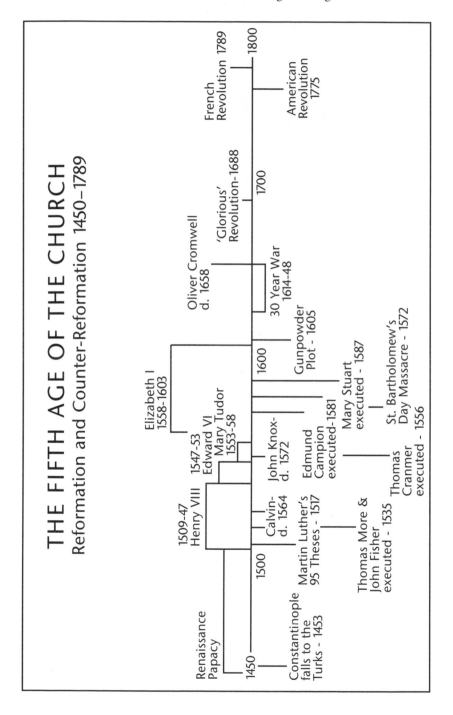

THE FIFTH AGE OF THE CHURCH
Reformation and Counter-Reformation 1450–1789

Renaissance Papacy

Constantinople falls to the Turks - 1453

1450

1500

1509-47 Henry VIII

Martin Luther's 95 Theses - 1517

Calvin- d. 1564

Thomas More & John Fisher executed - 1535

1547-53 Edward VI
Mary Tudor 1553-58

John Knox- d. 1572

Edmund Campion executed-1581

Thomas Cranmer executed - 1556

Elizabeth I 1558-1603

Mary Stuart executed - 1587

St. Bartholomew's Day Massacre - 1572

1600

Gunpowder Plot - 1605

Oliver Cromwell d. 1658

30 Year War 1614-48

'Glorious' Revolution-1688

1700

French Revolution 1789

1800

American Revolution 1775

freedom and an opportunity that had previously been enjoyed only by clerics or academics. Thus, while we see a cleric like St. Thomas Aquinas teaching in Bologna, Naples, and Paris in the 1200s, by the time of the Renaissance we see merchants, artists, and musicians with comparable mobility. In the early 1500s, Michelangelo created sculptures and frescoes for patrons in both Florence and Rome.

In the Renaissance, human activity became primary. The stage for this had been set not only by William of Ockham, but also by St. Thomas Aquinas (1225–74), who saw human activity as a means to salvation. By the time of the Renaissance two hundred years later, this same human activity had become an end in itself. The idea was that one should develop one's abilities and gifts to the utmost. Thus emerged the "Renaissance Man," as he has been called, the amateur who engaged and modestly excelled in a variety of human activities, from being an artist, to being a poet, a soldier, a scientist, an athlete, a dancer, a musician, and a theologian. Life was conceived as a fine art, as Christopher Dawson wrote, "in which no opportunity for knowledge and enjoyment is to be neglected."[1] Leonardo da Vinci personified this by being an artist, an architect, an inventor, a geologist, an anatomist, and a botanist, among other things. But perhaps even more typical was someone like King Henry VIII of England, who prided himself on a number of very different skills—from dancing to writing theology and music, to knowing Latin, political theory, and military tactics. It is no coincidence that René Descartes' statement, "I think, therefore I am," would be written in the 1600s.

The Europe of the 1400s was divided roughly between north and south. In the south, mainly in Italy, a great rebirth of the arts was taking place. Artists, sculptors, and architects looked to classical antiquity for their model. Michelangelo's *David* resembled far more the sculptures of ancient Rome and Greece than it did the elongated column-like statues of the Middle Ages. The Gothic was being replaced by a revival of Greek forms. The north was not without its Renaissance, but it emphasized the written word rather than the art found to the south. Printing had been invented in 1465 and was quickly being used to disseminate ideas about all sorts of things, but mostly about religion. The very first book to be printed by Gutenberg was, not surprisingly, the Bible. The Northern Renaissance, in fact, *is* the Reformation.

The Northern Renaissance

In northern Europe, civilization was not as advanced as in the south. Cities were very small and isolated and did not dominate as they did in Italy. If a student wanted to study classical languages, law, or medicine, he would most likely have gone to Italy. Northern universities were only lesser imitations of their formidable southern counterparts. But in the north the industrial arts flourished, especially printing. At first this might not seem to be important, since only works copied by monks (usually scriptures) were being reproduced in print. But as a result, the principal topics of discussion in the north focused on religion. While the south sought to return to *classical* antiquity, the north sought to return to *Christian* antiquity. In the south were found Alberti, Michelangelo, da Vinci, Raphael; in the north were found Thomas More, Erasmus, and Martin Luther.

The Southern Renaissance

Italy was a disorganized collection of city-states—Florence, Venice, Genoa, Naples, Rome, etc.—states that were eagerly engaged in commerce and were prospering by it. Each had its own colonies with which it traded and which had ready markets for its goods. Each formed alliances with certain other city-states when convenience or war dictated, then broke them when conditions changed. The city-states were always wary about the prospects even of their allies, and nervously watched for any shift in fortune. They were also reluctant to help each other in time of crisis. When the Turks threatened the Balkan Peninsula, where Venice had its colonies and markets, few cities were interested in coming to the aid of the Venetians, who called frantically for help. Such rivalry made it extremely difficult to fight the Turks effectively, and the 1400s was a century of frustration on the part of the popes, who continually and with only modest success called on these city-states to put aside their differences and come to the aid of Christianity. Only one pope, Sixtus IV (1471–84) was able to organize successful crusades, one a naval victory off the coast of Asia Minor and the other a successful siege of the Italian town of Otranto, which had been occupied by the Turks. Otranto, on the heel of the boot of Italy, was a little too close for comfort, and so an allied navy was formed by Naples, Venice, and the Papal States and, led by Cardinal Carafa, laid siege to the town. The Turks, who had reportedly captured the aged archbishop and mayor and had them sawed in half, and put to death 12,000 of the 22,000 people of the town (the remainder being sent into slavery), were soundly defeated. But even here, the allied navy would go no further, as the pope encouraged them to do, because of their bickering. The Venetian navy was the first to return, followed shortly by the Neapolitan navy. But popes would try again, and the great sea battle of Lepanto was fought against the Turkish navy in 1571 with ships from Spain, Genoa, Venice, and the Papal States taking part. Still, as spectacular as these victories could be, they did little else than prevent the Turks from advancing further into Europe. They did nothing to recover the lands lost to the Muslims in the Middle Ages.

The Renaissance Popes

1447–55	Nicholas V	1484–92	Innocent VIII
1455–58	Callistus III	1492–1503	Alexander VI
1458–64	Pius II	1503	Pius III
1464–71	Paul II	1503–13	Julius II
1471–84	Sixtus IV	1513–21	Leo X

The popes who held office during the early Renaissance (1450–1520) have been generally blamed for the corruption within the church, or are held up as examples of how bad things had gotten. This criticism is both deserved and unfair—deserved because these popes were concerned with the wrong things and could live scandalous lives, but unfair because the Reformation was a much bigger event than can be reduced to a reform of corruption. Much of the criticism of these popes was written by 1) talented propagandists who were hired by political enemies of the popes, 2) courtiers who were piqued at having lost papal patronage or who were excluded from the papal court, 3) preachers (especially Protestant preachers) anxious to justify their break with Rome. Furthermore, much of the corruption in the church was beyond the control of the popes.

Nonetheless, the Renaissance popes have something to answer for. Most of them were too intent on restoring the splendor and prestige of the papacy without restoring its moral force. Most of these popes, while able administrators, lacked holiness and were overly concerned with temporal matters such as organizing crusades and defending the Papal States from the incursions of Naples.

Popes knew that, in order to increase their own political power, they were going to have to limit the power of the bishops and (especially) the College of Cardinals. The fight was over what kind of government would control the church—a monarchy led by the pope or an oligarchy led by the cardinals, the latter a modified form of conciliarism. In 1415, when the cardinals ended the papal schism by electing a pope they could all recognize, the oligarchic power was supreme, but it had built-in flaws that the popes were quick to exploit. For one thing there was no limit to the number of cardinals in the college, so that the pope could (and did) appoint larger numbers and thus diffuse their strength. In less than one hundred years their numbers more than doubled from twenty (under Martin V) to more than forty by 1500.

Popes also undermined the cardinals' power by appointing relatives. This is known as *nepotism*, from the Latin word *nepotus* or "nephew." All of the Renaissance popes except Nicholas V appointed relatives, usually nephews, to the College of Cardinals. One pope (Alexander VI) appointed at least eight relatives. The extent of the abuse was such that five of the Renaissance popes were relatives of previous popes and by 1492, nine of the twenty-three cardinals at the conclave were relatives of previous popes.

Nepotism, while appearing to be not much more than a sophisticated form of tribalism, must be understood in the light of family rivalries at the time and the fact that, often enough, a pope or secular ruler could only trust members of his own family—either to get things done or to keep confidences. Popes also saw to it that their relatives were married into other Italian noble families, both for the diplomatic reasons of advancing the papacy, and the dynastic reasons of advancing the pope's family and ensuring that its gains would be permanent. Thus Pope Innocent VIII had his illegitimate son married to the daughter of Lorenzo de Medici, the first time a pope ever publicly acknowledged the existence of offspring. Popes also chipped away at the cardinals' power by making the College of Cardinals more Italian and thus more politically pliable. In 1455, seven of the fifteen cardinals at the conclave were Italians; in 1492, Italian cardinals numbered twenty-one out of twenty-three. This Italian dominance of the papacy would last for the next 450 years.

Finally, popes weakened the power of the cardinals by handing out gifts such as bishoprics (dioceses) and minor benefices in order to distract them from the business of the papacy. The cardinals began to build grand palaces—Palazzo San Marco is probably the most famous. It was begun by Cardinal Barbo (Bishop of Venice and later Paul II), and became known as Palazzo Venezia, with its famous piazza, which can still be seen in the center of Rome today.

While it is argued that the first Renaissance pope was Martin V, whose election ended the Papal Schism and who began the process of aggrandizing power once more in a centralized and strong papacy, it is not until we come to the reign of Nicholas V (1447–53) that we see significant efforts being made to reshape Rome. Nicholas V wanted a magnificent Rome and justified his building program by thinking that majestic buildings would lead people to believe in the authority of the papacy. So he restored buildings and erected new ones, including the first Trevi Fountain. His greatest contribution in hindsight is the foundation of the Vatican Library.

In the short reign of the next pope, Callistus III, the first pope to come from the Borgia family of Spain, we see two characteristics which will be repeated in successive papacies. The first was nepotism, which we have discussed above. Two nephews were made cardinals by Callistus and it is said that everyone in the family got something. The second feature, which would appear again, was the canonization of a fellow countryman or religious ally. In 1455 the Spanish Callistus canonized the Spanish Dominican Vincent Ferrer (d. 1419). Despite the reputation of the Borgias for luxury, Callistus apparently lived poorly. He gave his entire fortune to the fighting of the Turks, replaced the silver candle-sticks in the chapel with leaden ones, and had plain furniture made of wood and iron.

Pius II (Piccolomini) was Sienese and promptly canonized Catherine of Siena. He was possibly the greatest humanist among the Renaissance popes—being made poet-laureate by the Holy Roman Emperor (Frederick III) and writing several novels, some of which were bawdy. He was continually frustrated in his attempt to call a crusade, calling for one at a congress in Mantua in 1459, to which not one invited envoy came! Finally, he issued the encyclical *Execrabilis*, which forbade appeals from a papal decision to a future general council.

The idea of appealing to councils was never far from the minds of the cardinals. Despite Pius II's encyclical, the cardinals tried gaining the upper hand yet again by imposing a *capitulum* during the next conclave, whereby conditions were imposed on the future pope, whoever he might be, requiring that he:

1) continue to organize war against the Turks

2) reform the curia (church bureaucracy)

3) summon a general council

4) accelerate the process of reform throughout the church

5) ensure that fees charged for clerical services be proportionate to the function performed.

This *capitulum* was not new. It had been tried before, in 1352, when Innocent VI was elected. It was, even then, partly an attempt by the cardinals to control the papacy, and partly to reform it. Within three days of election he was to publish a bull accepting the *capitulum* and spell out the terms of the agreement. Instead, once elected, Innocent VI said that he had agreed to this arrangement *before* he was pope, so it was not binding on him. Not surprisingly, Paul II used the same excuse in 1464. Amazingly, the cardinals tried this again twenty years later, and the pope reacted the same way. It does not seem to have occurred to them that the election of a good pope would have been far more helpful than the most detailed *capitulum*. Paul II might best be remembered as the pope who first dressed the cardinals in scarlet. And while he tended not to approve of humanism and Renaissance studies, he restored several Roman monuments (including the arches of Titus and Septimus Severus), collected Roman art treasures, and allowed some humanists to print several Vatican manuscripts.

In Sixtus IV, we find the flourishing of the Renaissance papacy. He patronized the artists Perugino, Botticelli, Ghirlandaio, Pinturicchio, and Fillippino. He paved the Campo dei Fiore and Piazza Navona. He was minister general of the Franciscan Order before his election and made the feast of St. Francis (4 October) a holy day. He also canonized Bonaventure (a Franciscan) and instituted a special office for the Immaculate Conception on 8 December. This was a characteristically Franciscan feast and was generally opposed by the Dominicans, one of whom went so far as to say that anyone who believed in it was guilty of mortal sin.[2] Despite this, Sixtus tried to end the feuding between Franciscans and Dominicans, which could be ferocious and occasionally violent. Members of one order sometimes used their position as inquisitors to prosecute members of rival religious orders. Sixtus ordered this practice stopped.[3]

With Alexander VI (Rodrigo Borgia) we reach what has been widely regarded as the low point of the papacy, at least in the sphere of morality. Even so, the most serious charges against Alexander VI must be taken with a grain of salt. Immediately upon election to the papacy, Alexander was accused of having bought the election. Von Pastor's *History of the Popes* is explicit in charging Alexander VI and the preceding pope with simony. The conclaves of 1484 and 1492, writes von Pastor, "are among the most deplorable in the annals of church history."[4]

Twenty-three cardinals met in 1492 and Rodrigo Borgia was running fourth in the polling. The third place prospect (Ascanio Sforza) perceived he could not win and swung his votes to Borgia, who promised him several rich benefices. Other cardinals received other offers, leading one contemporary commentator to remark, "Judas sold Christ for thirty denarii; this man would sell him for twenty-nine."[5] Did he buy the election? Probably not. Michael Mallett, in a critical study of the Borgias, points out several factors which temper the charge of simony:

1) Borgia was a very good choice to be pope—at least in the political domain. He was a popular and experienced diplomat and was known for compromise and patience. In fact, many votes came to Borgia because the cardinals did not want to elect Julian della Rovere, who was known as, and would prove to be, intolerant and a militant.

2) His supposed simony was practiced on men hardly in need of money. All of the cardinals were independently wealthy and quite capable of offering similar rewards to their supporters.

3) Borgia, or any pope, had benefices in his possession which he had to relinquish on becoming pope—so why not at least give them to his friends?

Savonarola

As the Reformation neared, the voices of reform became more impatient. Reforms were attempted by most religious orders. The Franciscans were especially active and produced one of the great moral preachers of the fifteenth century, Bernadine of Siena. The Dominican Savonarola was similarly blessed as a great preacher. In 1490 Lorenzo de Medici insisted that he be recalled to Florence. In 1491 he was elected prior of the prestigious San Marco convent, where Fra Angelico's frescoes can be seen today. Savonarola showed immediately how troublesome he could be by slighting the Medicis and not paying them the customary visit after an election.

Savonarola then predicted the overthrow of the Medicis, a prediction which came to pass as the French approached Florence on their way to Naples in 1494. The Medici fled and Savonarola, whose star had risen rapidly, was now regarded as the virtual mayor of Florence, a position he decided to keep because it was "necessary for the good of souls." He promptly initiated several civic reforms (more equitable taxes, an elected city council), but began to run afoul of the populace with

---

his insistence on moral rigor. Gambling was outlawed, his punishments were too severe, and a system of child spies was used to detect moral infractions.

He also ran afoul of Pope Alexander VI, who did not appreciate Savonarola's charge that the papal election had been bought. Neither did this endear him to the cardinals who had been "bought." But what Alexander really did not like about Savonarola was his meddling in politics, in arranging an alliance between Florence and the French. This would de-stabilize northern Italy and threaten to turn Italy into a French peninsula. After being silenced by the pope, Savonarola defied him by writing to the heads of nations asking for a council to elect another pope, claiming "This Alexander is no pope.... I solemnly declare that he is no Christian and believes in no God." He was excommunicated shortly after and declared that anyone who honored the excommunication was a heretic.

But his end was not the pope's doing. Several of Savonarola's more enthusiastic followers had challenged the Franciscans to a trial by fire, which became the talk of Florence until it was called off—terms could not be agreed upon. The outraged populace stormed San Marco and Savonarola was tried by the Council, and executed in 1498.

Despite attempts to canonize Savonarola as a saint, his besetting faults were a sense of superiority and of exclusivity. He attempted to detach his own convent and the city of Florence from the greater church. It was an attempt we will see repeated in the Reformation as Calvin, Zwingli, and the Anabaptists all attempted to turn their respective cities of Geneva, Zurich, and Münster into a New Jerusalem. He entered a world of politics and was not a politician. His defiance of the pope was unseemly and unnecessary. Yet he was a sincere reformer, the likes of which would emerge more successfully very soon.

Mallett maintains convincingly that Borgia was not as bad a pope as history paints him. He was a very capable administrator. Even his notorious penchant for lavish spending must be tempered by the fact that he, like his uncle Callistus III, kept a frugal table—so much so that Bocaccio, the great humanist and ambassador to the Vatican from Ferrara, reported that the cardinals avoided Borgia's table because they could fare better elsewhere.

But this is not to excuse Alexander VI. He was excessive in his ambition to advance his family, and seemed oblivious to the scandal of sexual sins. While these would not have excited much comment in a secular ruler, it was shocking in a pope—especially to the more scrupulous northern Europeans. He had an acknowledged mistress (his second) and had fathered eight or nine children between them. It would be the focal point of criticism of the papacy in years to come.

One event mentioned by von Pastor is especially illustrative of the times. Cesare Borgia, the pope's son, probably had another son (Juan) murdered. The Tiber was dragged and the body was eventually found. A nearby fisherman was then asked if he had seen a body dumped into the Tiber and he said yes. When it was demanded why he had not told the police, he responded that if he reported *every* body that he saw being dumped into the Tiber he would be spending all his time at the police station and none in fishing.

A big thorn in Alexander VI's side was the Dominican preacher Savonarola, who called for his ouster. Savonarola issued the last great clarion call for reform before Martin Luther and was separated from the Reformation by only two popes, one of whom (Pius III) died of natural causes after only twenty-six days in office. The other was the formidable Julius II. As pope he was worldly, despite being a Franciscan, and a political schemer. Erasmus wrote a famous book denouncing him entitled *Julius Exclusus*—Julius, excluded from heaven. He was a great patron of the arts and hired Michelangelo to paint the Sistine Chapel, Rafael to paint the papal rooms *(Stanze)*, and Bramante to design a new St. Peter's.

The next pope, Leo X, saw the advent of the Reformation. When he took office he put on a great festive display which took the form of a Corpus Christi procession, though it featured him and his court instead of the Eucharist. One placard was carried which read, "Once Venus (Alexander VI) reigned, then Mars (Julius II), and now Pallas Athene takes the scepter." His knowledge of the classics was far better than his knowledge of the church, for Leo was the one who called Luther's problem "a squabble between monks." To be fair, the "monks" were always squabbling. How was Leo X to know this would be different?

The Reformation on the Continent

Any movement as large and all encompassing as the Reformation will have many and complex causes. It is not sufficient to say that the Roman Church was corrupt and that the Reformation was a necessary corrective. Many contributing factors spawned the Reformation and then gave it the direction it took, and they could simply be listed as

1. *Political factors:* the nations were gaining power and wanted the church to have less.

2. *Philosophical factors:* individualism was on the rise and sought expression in religious spheres.

3. *Religious factors:* the church was increasingly regarded as corrupt or outdated or simply wrong about theological issues.

1. **Political Factors.** Two items need to be mentioned here. First, the Reformation was either begun or fueled by politics. While theology gave the Reformation a direction, politics provided a base of operations, a shelter, and an alternative government. Luther, for example, was supported by Frederick of Saxony because his rebellion made the church less unified and powerful. Bishops and church (canon) law were replaced in Switzerland by city councils, who made canonical and liturgical decisions. Henry VIII made himself head of the Church of England because he needed to be the head of the Church of England to get his divorce, and not for any theological reason. He destroyed the monasteries, not because he was against the contemplative form of life and not because he wanted to reform the monasteries, but because he needed their money and wanted to silence their oppo-

Martin Luther (1483–1546), Augustinian monk, set into motion the Reformation through his strong opposition to the sale of indulgences and his espousal of the doctrine of justification by faith alone. A prolific author of hymn texts as well as of theological works, Luther never intended to break from the Catholic Church. He derived his inspiration from St. Paul's writings on the place of works relative to faith.

sition to his divorce. He married Anne of Cleves, not because he liked Lutherans, but because he needed political allies. The English supported the Reformation in Scotland, not because they approved of John Knox (Queen Elizabeth, in fact, did not like him), but because acceptance of the Reformation in Scotland would have the effect of getting rid of French influence there and thus remove an enemy from their back yard. Denmark and Norway, ruled for many years by King Christian III, who was a convinced Lutheran, became Lutheran, though the senior clergy in Norway resisted this. Sweden became Lutheran because King Gustav Vasa, like Queen Elizabeth in England, wanted to avoid the evangelical enthusiasm of the monarch who had preceded him (and been deposed!) and maintain the high ceremony of the traditional religion.

Secondly, the success or lack of success of the Reformation in a particular country depended directly on the interest of the ruling monarch or ruler. In almost every case, if the ruler was in favor of the Reformation, then the Reformation took permanent hold. Likewise, as in France or Spain, if the ruler was against the Reformation, it did not take hold. In Scotland, Parliament was in favor, and the legitimate monarch (Mary Queen of Scots) had to be replaced by her more manageable infant son.

2. **Philosophical Factors.** The individualist philosophy of William of Ockham had come of age and would be a keynote of Reformation theology. Scriptures were to be read and interpreted by individuals, not by the church. Jesus became one's personal

Lord and Savior. Jesus had saved *me*. Religion became, with the Reformation, a personal matter between the believer and God.

3. **Religious Factors.** Theology, to some extent, took over where politics left off. What was done in England for political reasons under Henry VIII would be continued under the boy-king Edward VI for theological reasons. His theologians, under the guidance of Archbishop Thomas Cranmer, took over the direction of the Reformation. Their reasons were both negative and positive. Negatively, the reformers wanted to purify the clergy of its immorality. The openly sexual relationships of some high-placed clerics (including the pope) became a flash point of discontent. Along this same line, they wanted to rid the church of many rituals and customs they regarded as being outdated, superstitious, and unscriptural. Some of this reform was driven by a desire to simplify worship, but also resulted from a "fear of the physical." This meant the destruction of a tremendous amount of art: sacred vessels, statues, stained glass, and pictures. The usual course for the Reformation was to destroy as much of the old as was possible. What survived was preserved out of necessity, such as cathedral churches in England, which served as seats of Anglican bishops, or the sections of monastic churches which became parish churches. The remainder was vulnerable. In the whole of Scotland, all that remains of medieval stained glass is four tiny coats of arms in a family chapel in Edinburgh. Celtic art survived because its crosses had no body on them, and because its artwork in books surrounded the Scriptures. Iconoclasm was the symbol, sometimes called the "sacrament," of the Reformation, the one physical act which reformers could carry out to affirm their commitment to the elimination of superstition.

But iconoclasm also had a deeper theological significance. Sacraments were physical: every sacrament consists of a physical sign (water, bread, wine, oil, even sexual intercourse), and then there were other signs such as ashes on Ash Wednesday, candles on Candlemas Day, palms on Palm Sunday, the Easter fire and water, processions, bell-ringing, etc. The reformers generally regarded these symbols as superstitious and a distraction from the Gospel, and so they had to be gotten rid of. How, as one modern evangelist would ask, can you possibly believe that this wafer could become the Body and Blood of Christ?

Positively, the reformers wanted to make Sunday worship more accessible to the faithful through the use of vernacular languages, and emphasize the reading of Scripture. Calvin would stress moral improvement.

The Corruption of the Catholic Church

We know that the church was in need of serious reform because of the disciplinary reforms passed by the Council of Trent, which was the Catholic Church's way of cleaning up its own act. Absenteeism, concubinage, luxury, a lack of clerical training, the lax spiritual life of the clergy, etc., were all addressed by Trent because they were serious problems. Did they *cause* the Reformation? They certainly helped to bring it about. In the popular mind, even today, they were the issues which made the Reformation necessary. But did the Reformation seek to get rid of abuses, or did it regard abuses as part and parcel of a corrupt Roman theology? Ulrich Zwingli instructed his preachers to concentrate on the negative aspects of Rome rather than on the positive aspects of his own program, which might prove to be unpopular or difficult for the common person to comprehend.

What were the abuses to which these reformers, both Catholic and Protestant, so easily pointed?

1. **Finances.** Because of the increased splendor of the papal courts, going back to the 1300s in Avignon, more revenue was required. Building projects were going forward, the Papal States had to be maintained, crusades had to be funded.

The money for these projects came in several forms—some of them quite legitimate and still in use today, but some of them were open to abuse.

The forms of generating revenue included:

- the taxing of dioceses

- revenues from the Papal States: cities sending in taxes

- appointment fees (pallium money), which were paid by newly appointed bishops and abbots

- annates, one-half of the first year's income from any papal appointment

- "Peter's Pence," the contributions of the laity through an annual collection for the pope

- dispensations—authorized exemptions from the law, including permission to hold more than one benefice

As legitimate as these revenues were, even *they* could lead to trouble, as when Albrecht was appointed to be the Archbishop of Mainz. Only the year before he had been appointed Bishop of Magdeburg, at the tender age of twenty-three. This meant he paid to Rome the appointment fee for Magdeburg, then one-half of his income for that year, then his appointment fee for Mainz, and one-half of his first year's income again, plus a dispensation fee for holding two dioceses at the same time. Added to his predicament was the fact that Mainz had seen three bishops in ten years, so the diocese was out of money—to what end we shall see.

More dubious forms of making money included *spolia*, the total personal assets of a deceased prelate, and revenues from vacant benefices. These two forms of revenue, while designed with the best of intentions, led to a desire to keep benefices vacant for longer than necessary. Local churchmen or politicians would, in many cases, confiscate the money or a large percentage of it before it ever got to the pope. Cardinal Wolsey used such income to support himself in England, and King Henry VIII, having got rid of Wolsey, followed Wolsey's example.

Finally and most famously, there was the sale of indulgences. An indulgence is the remission of the temporal punishment due to a forgiven sin, granted by the church, and effective before God. With each act of confession and absolution, a penance was (and is) attached which requires the penitent to make some sort of "atonement" for his sins. In the early church and right up to the late Middle Ages, these penances could be physical and public: e.g., standing outside a church each Sunday for a number of weeks or years, having certain privileges and rights revoked, going on pilgrimage (to local shrines for lesser sins, or distant and more prestigious shrines for greater sins). Increasingly, as these penances disappeared, the notion of getting souls out of purgatory gained ground. And this could be done by donating money to charity, and for Masses to be said on behalf of the deceased. Chantry chapels appeared, at which priests did nothing more than say Masses all day for various intentions. One papal official wrote: "The Lord desireth not the death of a sinner, but rather that he should pay and live."[6]

Some preachers used indulgences as part of their act. The most notorious of these preachers was the German Dominican Johannes Tetzel. Most bishops in Germany did not permit him to come into their dioceses, such was his reputation for an almost circus-like performance. But Albrecht and the diocese of Mainz were out of money, and so Tetzel was invited to preach a new indulgence—for the building of the new St. Peter's in Rome on the condition that half the money went to the diocese of Mainz. This drove Luther over the edge.

2. **The Multiplication of Benefices.** Other abuses were not financial. A benefice is an ecclesiastical position that carries with it a salary. Sometimes the same person could hold more than one benefice. This was a widespread problem. In the Netherlands, the "vicars" who served in place of a nonresident benefice holder as canon, curial official, professor, or administrator of a monastery, has been estimated at thirty to fifty percent. Other, more spectacular examples can be found. The Reformation historian A. G. Dickens notes one such:

> Cardinal John of Lorraine was appointed coadjutor of Metz at the tender age of three, his nephew Charles of Guise received the archbishopric of Rheims at fourteen, and later became bishop of Metz, administrator of the bishopric of Verdun, abbot of ten abbeys and Cardinal of Lorraine…. Cardinal d'Estouteville had in France one archbishopric, three bishoprics, four abbeys and three priories, but they did not prevent him from spending most of his time in Italy, where he had a further bishopric.[7]

Even as late as 1556, Cardinal Alessandro Farnese, grandson of Paul III, possessed ten episcopal sees, twenty-six monasteries, 133 other benefices (canonries, parishes, and chaplancies)! Wolsey drew revenues from his archbishopric of York, from never less than one other see, the wealthy abbey of St. Albans, and never visited *any* of his dioceses until he fell from power.

3. **Absenteeism.** This was an abuse directly, but not necessarily, connected to the multiplication of benefices. One French bishop entered his cathedral for the first time at his funeral. There were twenty-two bishops in the area of France known as Languedoc; only six lived there. Priests who were poor often sought refuge in cities, effectively abandoning their parishes.

4. **Diplomatic Overkill.** When King Louis XII entered Italy in 1509 he was accompanied by three cardinals, two archbishops, five bishops, and one abbot. This was mostly for show. But churchmen could hold important diplomatic jobs as well, and were brought in by kings in the Middle Ages in order to improve the reliability and efficiency of the court. Problems could arise if things pertaining to the state went badly. If the economy was weak, a battle was lost, or an alliance went bad, and if the person responsible (even remotely) was a churchman, then the church would or could be blamed.

5. **Nepotism.** In Germany, where the practice of nepotism was widespread, eighteen dioceses were occupied by sons of princes. Many of the episcopal sees and most abbacies were only open to members of the nobility. Even if a bishop wanted to improve the inner state of his diocese, it was nearly impossible because he did not control the area.

Martin Luther (1483–1546)

Martin Luther was an Augustinian friar, a priest, and a Scripture scholar. He seems to have been strictly raised, but disobeyed his father's wishes by refusing to go into the legal profession and entering a monastery instead. He had a strong sense of fear and, in the beginning of his life, an extraordinary terror of sin and judgment. There was an incident during a particularly violent storm when Luther prayed: "Help me Saint Anne, and I will become a monk." She did, apparently, and he kept his promise. He was overcome by a spiritual crisis during his first Mass and almost had to leave before he completed it.

He had humor, not wit, and could be crude and vulgar. He wrote a diatribe against Henry VIII calling him a pig, dolt, and liar, who deserved to be covered in his own excrement.[8] One English author called him "that spleeny Luther." This was not entirely out of character with the times. Thomas More, a much steadier personality, called Luther "an ape, ass, drunkard, a lousy little friar, a piece of scurf, a pestilential buffoon, a dishonest liar."[9] He was energetic, robust, and creative. G. K. Chesterton called him "one of those great elemental barbarians."[10] Scholars debate whether he was a genius or not, but he certainly had an active intellect.

The Ninety-Five Theses

His difficulties with Tetzel and indulgences caused him to write the now-famous Ninety-five Theses to the bishops concerned in 1517. When they did not respond, or responded unsatisfactorily, he sent the theses to theologians who also, it seems, ignored him. He most likely never nailed them on the door of the castle church in Wittenberg on 31 October 1517. Only his disciple Philip Melancthon mentioned this after Luther was dead, in attempt to create a legend of the defiant Luther, in a work which has been shown to be unreliable in other factual matters. But Luther probably did post them in some fashion at the University of Wittenberg in the custom of the time—on a kind of academic bulletin board. He was thirty-four years old at the time.

The Ninety-five Theses contained some very good criticism of the indulgence system, complaining of its tendency to mislead people into thinking that salvation can be bought. But Luther's problems with indulgences went deeper than mere abuses and contained a theology which goes to the heart of his understanding of sacraments. He separated the action of God from the action of man to such an extent that he rendered the hierarchical priesthood unnecessary, or at least something which is not divine. In 1520 he would write that anyone (even a woman or a child) could absolve from sins. Sacramental absolution, therefore, does not cancel guilt and punishment, but only indicates that a cancellation has already taken place. By this way of thinking, God accepts the actions of the church only as an occasion for his own saving action, without actually entering into it. Thus, modern-day evangelists do not emphasize *baptism*, but personal *conversion*. Baptism may take place later, but only as a public witness that conversion has occurred.

Luther had touched a nerve, however, and even scholars who were later to be his bitter enemies, hailed the theses—partly because of their popular tone. He knew that the theses contained some questionable propositions, and did not really intend them to be digested by common people. He honestly wanted a discussion with the authorities—and humbly committed himself to the pope "with all that I am and have."

Luther can be difficult to categorize. Much like St. Augustine, he was not writing a systematic theology, but rather taking on problems as they arose. Consequently, his writing is not always consistent. There are times when Luther seemed only to want to correct abuses, but then there are other passages which point to deeper doctrinal issues. It might be said that Luther eventually realized that some doctrinal beliefs underpinned the abuses. And so Luther slipped rather easily from a concern for correcting abuses, which even Erasmus and Thomas More welcomed, into the changing of more substantive matters. People who wanted to correct abuses did not want to discard the pope, only to improve him. They did not want to abolish the church, only correct the distortions and aberrations. They wanted to reform morality within the ranks of the clergy and the efficiency of ecclesiastical administration. Many reformers such as Thomas More, Bishop John Fisher, and Erasmus stopped here.

But other reformers such as Luther, Zwingli, and Calvin increasingly saw abuses as resulting from flawed beliefs and structures. "I would have little against the papists," Luther wrote, "if they taught true doctrine. Their evil life would not do great harm." Luther's reform program emerged gradually. It began by focusing on the Mass, then moved to other sacraments. At the root of all of his reforms was his philosophic background as a *nominalist*. Nominalism was the philosophy begun by William of Ockham, which denied that there were such things as universals. Every reality, in this way of thinking, is an individual entity. The only real unity is a numerical unity of individual things. This means that the object of knowledge is not a common nature, but an individual. Thus, we cannot talk about a community of human beings who share a human nature, but rather a collection of individual human beings.

This has all kinds of repercussions from the moral sphere to the liturgical—and here we are getting close to the mind of Luther and Protestantism. The radical difference between the reformers of the sixteenth century and traditional Catholic teaching can be highlighted by contrasting Luther's moral outlook with that of St. Thomas Aquinas. Aquinas saw moral life as a coexistence with God. God is good, and therefore we are good insofar as we share in his goodness, which we do imperfectly. Morality, in other words, is part of our *being*. Since God made us in his image, the more "human" we are, the closer we are to being Godlike.

Ockham (and Luther after him) held that morality is not the perfection of human nature (which has no reality), but conformity on the part of an individual to God's law, which is external to us and arbitrarily laid down by him. Goodness, therefore, is not a property of being, but something as it ought to be, just as knife is a good knife if it does what it is supposed to do. Since God's will determines what a thing ought to be, or do, thus the notion of goodness is tied up with that of will. We are good, therefore, if we conform to God's will. We are good if we do what we are supposed to do, and God decides what we are supposed to do. Human action is good not because it is in conformity with our nature, but because it is in conformity with God's will.

God's law is not determined by any eternal law; he can change laws as he likes, because in a philosophy so dominated by will, God's greatest attribute is that he is all-powerful. Theoretically, at least, God could make adultery a good thing, and we would be obliged to practice it, just as now we are obliged to avoid it. And thus God is a "mighty fortress," as he is called by Luther in the famous hymn.

Justification by Faith

One of the keys to understanding Luther is to realize he was trying to combat the idea that we could save ourselves. The sale of indulgences was symbolic of this mistaken notion. We cannot earn or buy our way into heaven. We cannot bribe God into letting us in, or demand that certain actions on our part will necessarily result in salvation. But then, how are we saved? This is where Luther thought he had struck on something new and liberating, namely that the justice of God is the justice by which God makes us just.

Before Luther discovered this, he had believed the justice of God to be a frightening thing. It was a punitive justice. Our actions, he had thought, are good only if God looks on them as good. Nature is unknowable, a world of confusion and riddles. God is hidden and the only way to salvation is blind obedience and faith. Every movement of the appetite seemed to him sinful, even if unwilling. If faith or love did not impel a man, then even his good actions are sinful. This led Luther to the haunting fear that he would not be chosen. He thought he was full of sin, and saw no way out. He wrote:

> When I heard them [the words just and justice] I was horrified. If God is just, he will punish. However, thanks be to God, when I was once meditating in this tower and in my study over the words "the just man lives by faith" and "the justice of God," I thereupon thought: If we, as just, must live by faith and if the justice of God must bring about salvation in everyone who believes, then it must be not our merit but the mercy of God.[11]

Justification, or the means by which we are saved, became for Luther an external relationship. One graphic example will show how this differed from the thought of Aquinas. Luther felt that the human being was a pile of manure (he used a more graphic word) which was then covered over by the snow of grace. They are two separate things. The human is corrupt and dirty, the divine is pure and snowy. Aquinas, on the contrary, would say that the human being is a pile of *snow* that becomes, after a time, dirty. Grace comes like a new snowfall and renews the original pile. They are, in some very real sense, the same thing.

Justification came for Luther in two stages. The first and more important is an external justification; through the merits of

Christ our sins are forgiven. The second is an internal conversion, a rebirth in the Holy Spirit. The second does not cause the first, but flows from it. God wants to save us through a justice or wisdom which does not come from us, but rather from God himself. But, more than anything else, Luther wanted to *feel* as if he had been saved or was in a state of grace.[12]

Two problems that Luther (and even more, Calvin) faced were: 1) how to get people to behave religiously and morally while preaching that good works were worthless for salvation; and 2) how to convey a fear of sin while preaching that God's mercy did not result from any good works we might perform. Luther would answer that good works show that our faith is genuine. Calvin would say that good works show the glory of God.

Luther's Progress

After writing the Ninety-five Theses, Luther found himself suspect by the Roman authorities. Cajetan, the Dominican Master General and a formidable theologian in his own right, feared that Luther was not merely opposed to the abuses surrounding indulgences, but had deeper issues in mind, such as the efficacy of the sacraments and the authority of the pope. Cajetan met with Luther in Augsburg in 1518 and said that Luther must submit to Roman demands; he refused, and was whisked out of town that night, lest the same thing happen to him as had happened to Jan Hus 100 years before.

Luther appealed to the pope for a clarification of indulgences. This was given, but Luther was now at the point where he said the doctrine had to be shown clearly to exist in Scripture. So he appealed to a general church council for a hearing. This council would have resulted in the discussion he was asking for, but first Luther needed to demonstrate why councils were any more authoritative than the pope, and this Luther was unable to do. In the summer of 1519, he had a debate with Johannes Eck (called "the Leipzig Disputations"), who forced Luther to concede that the Council of Constance of 1415 had condemned Jan Hus unjustly. This made an appeal to a general council worthless, since general councils were no more infallible than the pope. So Luther was left with an authority crisis. Who is the ultimate authority in the church? His answer was really twofold: "Scripture Alone" and "the Princes," or the secular authority. Since there was no longer a supreme ecclesiastical teaching authority which could render a binding interpretation on Scripture, Luther needed a body which could at least enforce the mandates of Scripture.

Scripture Alone

Scripture would not merely replace the church and the pope as authorities, it would also displace the "philosophers" who enabled so many theologians to carry on in their work. He called Aristotle, on whom Thomas Aquinas depended, "that rancid philosopher." Luther was a Scripture scholar who felt that Scripture was the answer to everything, so he began to attack philosophy. Jacques Maritain, the twentieth-century philosopher, took particular exception to Luther's assault on reason, and maintained that Luther failed to see the difference between an individual and a person. "As individuals," Maritain wrote, "we are subject to the stars. As persons, we rule them." But Luther did not see the distinction, which highlighted the use of reason. Instead, he maintained that reason was contrary to faith, saying "Reason is directly opposed to faith, and one ought to let it be; in believers it should be killed and buried."[13] As opposed to all this philosophy, Luther developed the idealistic view that Scripture was the answer, and

---

Desiderius Erasmus (1469–1536)

Erasmus of Rotterdam was the most renowned scholar of Northern Europe, whose achievements are found principally in translations and new editions of the Scriptures and the fathers of the church. His blistering attacks on the church (especially in *The Praise of Folly*) gave great impetus to the Reformation movement, but he himself remained a Roman Catholic to the end, and scolded Luther pointedly for going too far in his protest.

---

that it only had to be read to be understood. People needed to be educated and the Bible taught in the language they could understand. So he translated the New Testament in 1521, but he was neither the first to translate it into German (fourteen High German and four Low German editions had appeared between 1461 and 1522), nor did he translate entirely from the original languages. He had only begun studying Greek seriously in 1518, so he depended heavily on the Vulgate translation of St. Jerome and the newer Latin and Greek texts of Erasmus.

His translation, powerful though it was, posed problems. He was not alone among the reformers in going beyond the bounds of faithful translation. For example, he translated "the justice of God" into the "justice valid before God," and more famously St. Paul's text, "the just shall live by faith" (Romans 3:26, 28), into "the just shall live by faith *alone*." Luther defended this by claiming that it may not have been what Paul wrote, but it was what Paul meant. This practice would come back to bite Luther in his debate with Zwingli over the Eucharist, which we will discuss later. Also, Luther did not accept the entire Bible as the word of God, and laid aside whole books, calling the Letter of James an "epistle of straw" because it emphasized good works.

This selectivity would lead to problems down the road, because there was no longer any authority to decide which interpretations were valid.

"The Princes"

In the summer of 1520, Luther wrote a pamphlet entitled *To the Christian Nobility of the German Nation* and sold 4,000 copies. It was a blockbuster, calling on lay princes to take the reform of the church into their own hands. He wrote:

> When necessity requires and the pope is vexatious to Christendom, the first person who is able should, as a true member of the entire body, do what he can so that a legitimate and free council take place. None can do this better than the secular sword, especially since they are now also fellow-Christians, fellow-priests, equally spiritual, equally powerful in all things.[14]

It is difficult to underestimate the confidence the reformers had in the secular authority. Not only did Luther appeal to it. Zwingli appealed to the secular authority and used the city council of Zurich to enforce his reformation. Calvin used the city council of Geneva to enforce his reformation. John Knox used the Scottish Parliament to enforce his reformation. The Tudors in England looked to the Parliament to enforce their reformation. When Archbishop Cranmer was pressed on this issue by Queen Mary's Catholic bishops, he said the prince was *always* in authority over the church. When asked if this was always true, he said yes. When asked if this meant that Nero was superior in authority to Peter over the church, Cranmer hesitated, and then said Yes! He had to; any acknowledgement of any pope's legal superiority over a secular ruler, even if it was Peter over Nero, would have ruined his entire argument.

"The Babylonian Captivity of the Church"

Three months after the *Christian Nobility* was written in 1520, Luther produced another pamphlet putting forth his reform program. This is what finally lost him the sympathy of Erasmus and others like Thomas More, who thought Luther had gone too far. Luther wanted the Mass simplified and celebrated only on Sundays and holy days in a language the people could understand. Private Masses, which priests said by themselves for a particular intention, were to be abolished. Luther also removed the sacrificial language from the Mass, and with it the offertory, which was the presentation of gifts to be sacrificed, and soon his followers were celebrating Mass without vestments, which were also sacrificial. Nominalism, once again, played a role here. If, as Scripture says, there is only one sacrifice, how then can a Mass be regarded as a sacrifice as well? Is not the church multiplying sacrifices? His philosophy could not encompass a sacramental "sharing" in the one sacrifice of Calvary. But Luther remained steadfast in the traditional belief that the Eucharist was really the Body and Blood of Christ. While he dismissed "transubstantiation" as a late and irrational doctrine, not warranted by Scripture, yet Scripture demanded a belief in the Real Presence, though Luther thought it best to avoid further elaboration. His own attempt at explanation of communion was called "consubstantiation," by which he meant that the substances of bread and wine remained present alongside the new substances of Christ's Body and Blood. Going along with this was Luther's teaching on the priesthood. To him, there was no ordained priesthood in the traditional sense—he recognized only a "priesthood of the faithful"—and thus the only thing to distinguish a priest from the laity was work and not station. Nomenclature soon changed from talk of priest to talk of "ministers." If the sole authority was to be the Scriptures, then a hierarchy had only a utilitarian purpose.

Luther also reduced the sacraments to two—baptism and eucharist—as these were the only two clearly warranted in Scripture. Private confession was a distant third owing to Luther's understanding that confession did not involve absolution so much as signified that absolution had already taken place. (Catholics believe that a person can be forgiven without absolution, but only in an emergency, and only with the assumption that sacramental absolution will be forthcoming. They also believe that absolution can be given in an emergency without a confession of sins, as in the case of soldiers going into battle, though with the assumption that the penitent will confess his sins to a priest at the first opportunity. When the World Trade Center was attacked on 11 September 2001, firemen were seen asking priests for absolution—and receiving it—before heading into the buildings.) Later reformers would similarly "downsize" baptism by stressing the importance of being "born again" or "accepting Christ as your personal Lord and Savior." Baptism would merely signify that a conversion had taken place. The key to Luther's understanding of the sacraments is this acceptance on the part of the believer—the belief that one is born again, or saved, or forgiven—was necessary in order for the sacrament to take effect. A sacrament produces its sanctifying effect only if it is believed by the recipient.

In 1520, the pope issued *Exsurge Domine*, which condemned forty-one propositions of Luther's, demanded that his books be burnt, and gave Luther two months to recant. Luther burnt the bull on 10 December 1520 and was excommunicated on 3 January 1521.

Luther's Followers

Luther's followers would quickly outdistance him in radical ideas and actions. They often did not share his respect for the past, such as it was. Two mob scenes occurred in Wittenberg, when armed students and townspeople invaded the parish church and Franciscan friary, and carried away the missals. Luther approved of their fervor, but the atmosphere of revolt disturbed him. Gabriel Zwilling (1522) wanted all side altars and images destroyed. Andreas Karlstadt (d. 1541) said Mass on Christmas in 1521 in German, omitting the elevation and the canon except for the words of institution. He was dressed with lay clothes, and offered the cup to everyone. He denied that Christ meant the bread and wine to become his Body and Blood. The Lord, Karlstadt claimed, pointed to himself when he said the words "This is my body." Luther ridiculed the exegetical license—saying that he (Luther) was also tempted to deny that Christ was in the elements of bread and wine, since such a denial would have dealt the pope a great blow, "but the text is too powerfully present... and the words should be taken simply as they are."

With Thomas Muntzer (1490–1525) we see what Luther had unleashed and what he was up against in his own camp. Muntzer saw himself as God's chosen instrument in bringing about a new, apostolic church. Scripture, he claimed was not historically important, but important only because of what it says to us today. It was also overrated. He emphasized the gifts of the Holy Spirit, and the Church of the Elect, which would begin in Bohemia, and then spread. He believed in revelation through dreams and visions, and that the Holy Spirit communicated directly with the elect. Baptism is a movement of the Spirit and, thus, external baptism is not important. After all, neither Mary nor the apostles were baptized in the Scriptures. He called himself a "destroyer of unbelievers" and Luther "Doctor Liar...with your rotten humility." He was a social revolutionary who called on the elect to turn on the "ungodly" with violence. When the Peasant's Revolt broke out, Muntzer joined in and said it was a fight between God's rule and everyone else's. He was captured within three weeks and executed. Luther called him a "murderous and bloodthirsty prophet" and an "archdevil." Luther was always combating these extremists. He had an affection for music and art and certain traditions, and wanted priestly vestments and the elevation kept, and provided a Latin Mass minus the allusions to sacrifice. Karlstadt called him a "neopapist."

Even in the sphere of religious life—where monks and nuns were to be freed from vows and celibacy lifted—Luther bemoaned the number of people leaving religious life. He himself married a Cistercian nun, Katherina von Bora, and defended himself by saying that vows could be broken if they could not be followed. A vow should read, "I vow chastity as long as it shall be possible for me, but I can marry if I cannot preserve it," and justified this by saying the commandments took precedence over vows, and that if one of them had to go, it should be the vows.

Undoubtedly the best of Luther's immediate followers was Philip Melanchthon (1497–1560), who is called "The Theologian of the Reformation." He created the legend of the defiant Luther, but also salvaged and softened much of Luther's thought. He wrote a theology which was not complete, but focused on themes in Paul's Letter to the Romans: sin, grace, and law. He originally sided with Luther's radical anthropology—no free will and one's inability to know God by natural means—but later modified this, and in some ways combined humanism with the Reformation. So great was his influence that later historians have suggested that Luther would be little known today but for Melancthon.

The Peasants' War (May 1524–30 July 1525)

Luther had appealed to the people, and was popular. The Bible was to be given to everyone, for whom it was to be a rule of spiritual life for all, but a rule of political and social life as well. Princes would be bound to it as much as the rank-and-file. But Luther had said some menacing things about political change:

> The secular lords could no longer flay and scrape, impose a toll on some, a tax on others…and act as though they were rather brigands and knaves and their secular government was as much neglect as the rule of the spiritual tyrants.

Usually they [secular princes] are the greatest fools or the worst knaves on earth.

People will not, cannot, do not intend to endure your tyranny and wantonness for long.[15]

Muntzer and Zwingli were not slow to take up the challenge and supported active resistance and set about changing the social order. The people who began the revolt, however, were prosperous and respected farmers trying to gain an equal footing in their civil rights (e.g., hunting and fishing rights) previously limited to the nobility. Peasants and poor city folk, who were feeling a widespread resentment of their social betters, joined in.

The Peasants' Revolt was a combination of social and economic demands, fused with religious demands, and was often justified by references to the Gospel. The peasants looked to Luther for moral support, which he was loathe to give. At first he condemned both sides for their violence (in the case of the rebels) and oppression (in the case of the princes), but once he saw the widespread chaos and "misuse of the Gospel" caused by leaders like Muntzer, he asked the princes to put down the rebellion in typically direct language:

> A rebel is outlawed by God and the emperor, so that the first one who can and will slay him does what is right....Whoever can should here slam, choke, stab, secretly or publicly, and bear in mind that there can be nothing more venomous, more pernicious, more diabolical than a rebel. It is just as though one had to kill a mad dog....And so, dear lords, save, rescue, help there. Have pity on the poor people. Stab, strike, slay here, whoever can. If you should perish in this, know that you can never die a more blessed death. For you will die obedience to the divine word and command (Romans 13) and in the service of love, in order to rescue our neighbor from hell and from the devil's bonds.[16]

The princes did not need to be asked. A little more than a year after it began, the Peasants' Revolt was over. One hundred thousand peasants are estimated to have perished in battle or were executed. The popularity of Luther's Reformation ended with the Peasants' Revolt.

Pontificate of Hadrian (1522–23—13 months)

Just prior to the Peasants' Revolt, thirty-five cardinals (of whom only three were non-Italian) elected a Dutchman who was absent from the conclave. The Roman cardinals were furious, and said they had elected a "barbarian." But Hadrian was a true reformer—with the idea that he would reduce the amount of taxation which was inciting so much rebellion. But this did not impress Luther, who had fought too many battles with Rome, and so he refused to acknowledge Hadrian's attempt at reform. He said Hadrian was a graduate of Louvain, where "such jackasses are crowned." The Reformation had come to stay.

Ulrich Zwingli (1484–1531)

The Reformation south of Germany was independent of Luther, and took on a form of its own. It could be compared to isolated thunderstorms in the summer—popping up in different places. In Switzerland, in fact, the Reformation was different from canton to canton. Zwingli supported what he called "the freedom of the Christian." This, as in the case of Luther, had something to do with celibacy. Zwingli was known not to take the vow of celibacy seriously, and had seduced a woman in Einsiedeln—which he admitted, though adding that she was not a virgin at the time. He was voted in as the pastor of Zurich Cathedral seventeen to seven, even though this behavior was widely known. In 1522 he petitioned with ten other priests (all of them, including Zwingli, probably already married secretly) for the abolition of celibacy. In October 1522, he resigned his priestly office.

In order to bring about this freedom—mainly from the hierarchy—he taught the absolute authority of Scripture—free from all interpretation by any church. In 1523, the city council of Zurich took unto itself the running of church matters and issued a new order: Christ alone is the authority, and the Bible is his word, and it is sufficient unto itself. (This, of course, leads to the question: Where in the Bible does it say this?) The papacy, Mass (as a sacrifice), the intercession of saints, fast laws, holy seasons and places, religious orders, celibacy were all repudiated. Soon the radicals came to the fore and wrecked altar images, statues, crucifixes, sanctuary lamps.

What was crucial in all this is that the *city council* was making the decisions. The city council became the ecclesiastical authority, and later decided on marriage cases, canon law, property, etc. This caused the more radical elements (who did not believe in the intrusion of a secular authority) to leave and form the Anabaptists. Freedom, even for Zwingli, had its limits. When this Anabaptist trouble arose, he called on the arm of secular authority to impose the Gospel and curb them. In 1526 the city council had tired of the Anabaptists and declared that rebaptizing and attending Anabaptist meetings was punishable by drowning. So much for the freedom of the believer.

In 1525, the city council voted out the Mass and substituted an evangelical Last Supper—to be celebrated four times a year:

The Numbering of the Ten Commandments

In 1527, one of Zwingli's followers (Leo Jud), publicized a different numbering for the Ten Commandments. In the early and medieval western church, the command not to worship graven images was regarded as a later and secondary addition to the command to have no other Gods but the one God. Another tradition (Jewish and patristic) treated the commands separately. The Zwinglians thought that a renumbering would reinforce their distaste for images, so they separated the First Commandment into two, making sure to combine them in the end by fusing the commandments about coveting one's neighbor and goods into one. Rome and Luther were both against this change, but it caught on in England, where Cranmer was probably responsible for introducing it and thus giving the English Reformation its characteristic iconoclast direction. Thus the numberings are different.

Easter, Pentecost, the Dedication, and Christmas. On Sundays only a service of the Word (readings from Scripture, sermons, and some psalm-singing) was to be used. The new order for this Lord's Supper was completely different from the medieval liturgy: after a sermon and prayers, unleavened bread and wine were placed on a table in the middle of the nave, surrounded by the people. Ministers faced the people, wore lay clothes, and carried bread in wooden baskets to people seated in pews.

Thus Zwingli radically minimized the theology of the Eucharist. He not only eliminated sacrificial language but also held that the Eucharist was only a symbol, shrinking from the idea that physical objects could be vehicles of spiritual gifts. Thus, when Christ said, "This is my body," he meant it in the same way he meant "I am the vine," etc. Martin Bucer, an ex-Dominican and an unflappable peacemaker among the warring tribes of new Reformation sects, saw the Eucharist as a very real source of division, and sought to bring Zwingli and Martin Luther to some agreement. At this famous (and apparently brief) meeting, Zwingli stated his position, and Luther wrote on the desk *"Hoc est Corpus Meum,"* the ancient words of the liturgy which stated that "This is my body." Zwingli countered that the Latin should read *"Hoc significat Corpus Meum,"* or "This symbolizes my body." Bucer attempted desperately to arrive at the compromise that the Eucharist would be whatever the receiver wanted it to be, the ultimate in individualism, but both Zwingli and Luther had too much integrity to settle for such a position. The meeting ended without any agreement.

Zwingli had the idea that anything not expressly permitted by Scripture was sinful. Hence hymns and pipe organs were unscriptural. For modern Zwinglians—namely the Amish in the United States—the logical consequence of this is that electricity, the internal combustion engine, or modern medicine, are not in Scripture, and are therefore to be avoided. Luther differed from this radical position completely. He thought that whatever Scripture did not forbid was permissible. Consequently, he was far more flexible (and traditional) than other reformers—allowing vestments, stained glass, organ-playing, and hymn-singing.

Zwingli's Contribution

Zwingli's contribution to the Reformation was mainly liturgical. His Sunday word service and "evangelical Last Supper" became the principal ways of worship for most mainline Protestant churches: Presbyterians, Congregationalists, Methodists, Baptists, Evangelicals. In Presbyterian churches, this led to a two-tiered congregation: an elite few who were "practicing" Presbyterians, and the rest. So, if communion is given, only a few receive. Protestant liturgical art would also follow Zwingli's lead: simple churches unadorned with statues, stained glass, candles, or altars. Most often, a small table stands at the head of the congregation with a Bible on it. An even more extreme form of this would be the modern-day auditorium—e.g., the Crystal Cathedral. Because of the loss of Roman sacrificial vestments and a corresponding dependence on knowledge of Scripture, ministers soon began to wear academic garb to demonstrate their theological credentials.

John Calvin (1509–64)

John Calvin's father, who had been a sexton in the parish church, died excommunicated in 1531. This, no doubt, influenced his children. John Calvin's conversion to the emerging Reformation probably came in the same year. Calvin did not come to the Reformation like Luther did, by lengthy grappling with Scripture, but rather saw a need for more order and organization. He first attempted to reform the city of Geneva, which was a mess at the time (1532–36), owing to religious and political turmoil. His first visit to Geneva resulted in his being asked to stay by the primary reformer (Farel), and then in his eventual eviction in 1538 because of the severity of his proposals. Many Genevans adopted the Reformation only as a way of throwing off the yoke of their bishop and the Duke of Savoy.

Calvin wanted much more than this. He proposed communion once a week and men to be appointed to watch over the morals of the populace—including visiting people in their homes. Offenses would be mentioned to the appropriate pastor. He also recommended congregational psalmody (not hymn-singing) and a catechism for the young. All of this, he claimed, was based on Scripture alone, "without the addition of any human ideas whatsoever." He shared the reformers' general optimism about the transparent truth of the Bible, saying it "bears its proof within itself." Without the Bible, he claimed, what we have to say about God is folly. Consequently, a significant part of his program was directed against philosophy and the possibilities of human reason. A creed was drawn up to which everyone had to submit, or lose citizenship and be exiled.

As in Zurich, the city council became the ecclesiastical court. Opposition grew as pressure was applied. The pillory was used, and the people were being forced to accept the creed. The city council, seeing Calvin's unpopularity, compromised on a few issues: everyone could come to communion; and some Catholic practices which had been retained at Bern would be reintroduced, such as baptismal fonts and holy days. Calvin and Farel refused to comply and defied the council by refusing to give anyone communion on Easter (1538), and were promptly expelled.

After a brief stay in Basel, Calvin went to Strasbourg at the insistence of Martin Bucer, and learned about Protestant liturgy and about how to get things done. In 1541 he was recalled to Geneva (the pastors were no match for the Roman Catholic cardinal who was urging a return to the church). He persuaded city council to pass a series of laws, known as *Ecclesiastical Ordinances*, which ran along the same lines as his previous ordinances. He was opposed this time by the mayor, whose family had run afoul of the reformers. Among other things, the mayor's wife had been rebuked for dancing at a wedding. But the mayor was soundly defeated at the next election, and Calvin's party was victorious.

Calvin's Theology

Calvin was probably the most profound of all the Reformers. He resembled St. Augustine in two ways: He concentrated on morality, and he had a rather grim view of the number of the saved. While Luther's line was "the just shall live by faith," Calvin's was, "Thy will be done." God was all-powerful and willed every event. "No wind ever blows," Calvin wrote, "unless God has specially commanded." God moves men to walk in the way he directs, and so the ultimate religious act is to assent to his will.

Furthermore, Calvin tended toward an Old Testament notion of God—giving to those who follow his law, taking away from those who disobey him in order to chastise them. Some see in this the theological justification for wealth and prosperity. Calvinism's attraction was primarily its moral rigor and personal discipline, not its theological content or doctrine. It is important to keep in mind that the reformers did not see their restructuring of the church as a "break" from the church. Rather, they thought that the Roman church had become so laden with externals and unscriptural beliefs and practices, that *it* had fallen away from the primitive church. The job of the reformers, as they saw it, was to restore this church to its ancient simplicity. In most cases, this meant a rejection of any physical connection to the early church *via* apostolic succession.

This also meant a rejection of Eucharistic practices that reached back at least one thousand years. While Luther maintained a high regard for the Eucharist as the Body and Blood of Christ if not as a sacrifice, and Zwingli downplayed any physical presence of Christ, Calvin sought a middle ground. He disagreed with the Catholic Church and with Luther over the physical presence of Christ in the elements of bread and wine, and agreed with

---

Predestination

Calvin believed in "double-predestination." God, by this way of thinking, has chosen some to be saved, some to die unredeemed. Calvin wrote, "To some eternal life is assigned; to others, eternal damnation." The Catholic notion of predestination is different: God chooses that all should be saved; some do not accept this or do not cooperate. Some have claimed that the Calvinist notion of predestination remains the stumbling-block of Calvinism, because it makes God into a tyrant.

Zwingli in saying that Christ was not locally present in the Eucharist, since Christ is in heaven and not in the bread and wine. But Calvin thought we "really participate" in his Body and Blood through the strength of "fellowship." Christ's power can unite us to himself without a physical union, and thus makes the elements of bread and wine more than a mere symbol. Still, anyone who adores the host is an idolater. Finally, Calvin insisted that a communion service be held every Sunday because it had been the practice of the early church. However, his city council permitted it only four times a year—as was the Zwinglian practice.

Critique of Calvin

Calvin accepted the moral rigor of St. Augustine, but he failed to incorporate Augustine's sacramentality, which softened much that was harsh about Augustine's theology. As a result, Calvin was grim, and could get ferocious about even minor offences. When several distinguished citizens were imprisoned for holding a dance in a private house, Calvin declared he would get to the bottom of it, "even at the cost of my life." Taverns in Geneva were abolished and cafes substituted; bawdy conversations or songs were banned, the saying of grace mandatory, a French translation of the Bible was required to be present on each table, etc. People who did not adhere to his rules were to be driven from the city. In the 1560s, five people a *week* were being excommunicated by the city council.

As a result, he was not popular. He identified opposition to himself as opposition to Scripture. He had either devoted disciples or bitter enemies, mostly the latter. But he stamped the Reformation with a morality which, at least in the English-speaking world, endures today. The cycle which we can trace in the church's history of a Manichean view of the physical world, running from the Montanists to the Manicheans to the Albigensians, would be renewed by Calvin. His notion that the physical pleasures of smoking, drinking alcohol, game-playing, dancing, and sexual activity are sinful or tainted took hold in parts of France, and would influence John Knox in Scotland, the Puritans in England, and eventually Protestantism in the United States.

Anabaptists

The Anabaptists began in Zwingli's Zurich, but were unhappy about the slow pace of the Zwinglian reform. In 1523 they began to question the appropriateness of infant baptism. They ran afoul of the city council in Zurich when it began to legislate and enforce reformed practices in Zurich. Their overriding principle was that people should be free to search the Bible for the truth. After being expelled from Zurich, they constructed a Confession in 1527 that set out the principles and organization of a pacifist sectarian creed which was to avoid civil oaths, public office, and bloodshed. The Anabaptists are a difficult group to categorize, because they believed many different things in different places, depending on who their leaders were. However, there are common threads which allow us to identify Anabaptist sects to some degree. They generally held the following notions in common: 1) a desire to establish the primitive community of Jerusalem; 2) only the elect could belong to it and be saved; 3) the life of the congregation and individual must be oriented to the Scriptures, and preferably the New Testament; 4) the Spirit of God guarantees the correct understanding of the Scriptures (i.e., not the church and not any civil government); 5) a denial of the Real Presence and the corresponding belief in the Lord's Supper as a memorial feast; 6) excommunication was to be applied liberally; 7) the pursuit of a bustling missionary movement, spurred on by proximity of Second Coming; 8) a rejection of military service, the taking of oaths, the death penalty, the acceptance of any civil position of authority; 9) the allowance of private property. (Related groups like the Moravian [Hutterites] regarded private property as sinful—saying "Those who have it have no Father in heaven.")

Such religious determination could, and did, lead to extremes, the most sensational of which was the episode of the Anabaptists in the northwestern German city of Münster. There Melchior Hofmann (1500–43) preached that the Bible was a secret revelation, which only those spirit-filled few could interpret correctly. Of course, he was one of them. He believed that the world was going to end soon, and he thought he was one of the final witnesses announced in Revelations 11:3—the new Elijah. When the Reformation became established in Münster in the early 1530s, the town became crowded with Anabaptists, much like San Francisco became crowded with hippies in the 1960s. All who opposed them were expelled. The town council became completely Anabaptist in 1534. John von Leiden soon took over and dissolved the council and appointed twelve elders in its place—as rulers of the twelve tribes of Israel. In reality, he did the ruling. After a failed military coup against him, he executed the opposing leaders (1534). He also executed one of his wives (polygamy had been introduced in 1534). After this military success, he declared himself king of the world.

With friends like him, the Anabaptists did not have to look far to find enemies. Luther and Roman Catholics were both appalled at what was happening in Münster and agreed that military action was necessary. The bishop of Münster raised an army, someone inside the city opened the gates, and von Leiden's coup was put down in June 1535. Von Leiden and his close associates were examined under torture for seven months until they died. The cages where their corpses were hung can still be seen hanging from a church tower in Münster. Religious toleration thus became a dirty word and would not be tried again for another century (in Maryland).

The English Reformation

The Reformation scene soon shifted to England. The state of the Roman Catholic Church in England prior to the Reformation has been shown recently to have been very healthy. Eamon Duffy, in his *The Stripping of the Altars* (1995), has demonstrated that Catholicism was popular among rich and poor alike, and could be both intellectually aware and yet accessible to the illiterate. It was also very much the same as it is today. Catholics venerated the saints and their relics, said prayers for the dead, believed in transubstantiation and the Mass as a sacrifice, wore vestments, practiced devotions, went on pilgrimages, lit candles, and held parish festivals. In 1530 Richard Whitford wrote a handbook for laity on how to be a Christian. It ran to thirty-two editions. Whitford was not alone. The Catholic Church in England was healthy. So why did the Reformation happen there, and what form did it take?

The English monasteries were in good shape. The Benedictine historian of the monasteries, Dom David Knowles, estimated that one-third of the English monasteries were very observant—in fact, the very models of religious observance in Europe; one-third were acceptably observant; and one-third either very lax, corrupt, or simply understaffed. However, monasteries owned a vast amount of land: nearly one-fifth of the land of England. And they did not have the mechanism to divest themselves of such land, had they been so inclined. When benefactors donated land or valuables to a monastery, they did not take well to seeing it sold off or given away. Only an outside agency could bring such a transfer about, and that agency would have to be the king.

In addition, the bishops of England were good people and well educated, but were (like the popes of the time) chosen because of their administrative rather than spiritual skills. They were also chosen by the king and were the king's men. When the king changed his mind, they tended to change theirs.

The state of the clergy was nothing unusual, except that there were probably too many priests and not enough jobs for them. The best estimate suggests that there were 30,000 diocesan priests and 30,000 religious, of which only 2,000 were nuns. This was not an insignificant problem. Clerical privilege could be, as it always is, annoying. Sanctuary was abused. It was an act of mercy designed to give those pursued by the law either time to think about their plight or to gather witnesses in their defense, but could become a haven for criminals. Even more annoying was exemption, whereby anyone who had received the tonsure was considered a cleric and was entitled to certain privileges. Any such cleric charged with a felony could appeal to a church court, which put them effectively out of grasp of the local magistrate and population. Church courts could also be annoying. The church had complete control over marriages and probate of wills, and these sometimes involved long journeys or long drawn-out legal fights.

But these problems did not cause the English Reformation. What caused it—at least to happen when it did—was Henry VIII and his marriage problems. As a young king he was a staunch defender of the faith. He did not like Martin Luther and prided himself on writing a tract against Luther's theology, called *In Defense of the Seven Sacraments*. Some of his administrators were among the foremost humanists and reformers of the age (Thomas More, John Fisher, John Colet). But he needed a male heir, and he needed money.

Henry VIII's family, the Tudors, were new to the throne. The War of the Roses unseated the Plantagenets (the final battle, Bosworth Field, was fought in 1485) and put Henry VIII's father on the throne. Even though Henry VII reigned for twenty-four years, the Yorkists (the losing side in the war) were always present and waiting for an opportunity to strike. This had the understandable effect of making the Tudors nervous about the line of succession.

Add to this the fact that England was a second-rate power. The great powers of Europe were France and Spain. Scotland, a separate country at that time, was allied with France in the Auld Alliance. Ireland was also hostile to England. The Tudors felt surrounded and their only hope was Spain. So they arranged a marriage between Henry VII's oldest son Arthur and the Spanish Crown in the person of Catherine of Aragon, the niece of the Spanish king Charles V.

The Divorce

Arthur died when he was sixteen years old. Henry VII tried to use this as a bargaining chip, and spent a lot of time deciding whether his next son (Henry) would take up where the dead Arthur had left off. He did this in hopes of extracting even more dowry money from Spain's King Charles V, but also to look over other prospects.

Catherine and Henry were eventually married, but she bore several stillborn children, and only a girl (Mary Tudor) survived. For disputed reasons, Henry began courting Anne Boleyn, the relative of an important family (the Howards, from which came the Dukes of Norfolk). Some have claimed that Henry was worried about the validity of his marriage and had genuine scruples—

which was *his* story. Others have claimed that he was worried about the male line; others that he was bored with Catherine; others that he was a victim of lust.

Even Protestants do not believe the conscience theory anymore; there are simply too many holes in it. Henry's later life certainly did not bespeak a timorous conscience. Rather, Henry was becoming desperate. This can be seen in his maneuvering for a divorce. Any excuse would do. Sacred Scripture was searched and was found to be ambiguous: Leviticus forbade marrying a wife of a deceased brother, but Deuteronomy encouraged it. The original dispensation was searched to see if there were loopholes. What emerged was a strange combination on Henry's part of doubting the pope's authority (i.e., to grant a dispensation) on the one hand, and desiring (if necessary) to grant the pope even more power on the other.

There is a stipulation in canon law that allows a married couple, if they both agree, to separate and enter religious life. So Henry sent two agents to Rome to ask whether Catherine could take a vow of chastity and enter a convent, while Henry would be dispensed from a similar vow; or whether Henry might actually enter a monastery, his wife a convent, and then have himself released from vows. Failing either of these, Henry wondered whether the pope could allow him (like the ancient patriarchs) to have two wives, of whom only one would be publicly acknowledged.

The opinions of the great universities were solicited, and those that found in Henry's favor did so only under duress. Catherine was then put under house arrest and separated from her daughter, whom she never saw again, in an attempt to break her resolve. What was wanted from her was a confession that her marriage with Arthur had been consummated, and this she repeatedly refused to give.

The Chancellor, Cardinal Thomas Wolsey, made constant efforts to obtain the divorce, without success. He stood to lose either way: If he did not obtain the divorce, he would fall into disgrace for incompetence and lack of loyalty; if he obtained it, the Boleyns would come to power and they were determined to get rid of Wolsey. We cannot underestimate the importance of this divorce. When Thomas More was talking to his son-in-law (William Roper) about three things he would be willing to be put in a sack and thrown in the river to achieve, he said a) that warring peoples would be at peace, b) that the church would be unified, and c) that the marriage question would be "brought to a good conclusion." A show trial (at the Dominican house in London) in May and June 1529 found in Henry's favor. This might be seen as the beginning of the English Reformation.

In September 1530, lawyers produced a brief which showed that the English Church was independent from Rome and that the divorce could be settled in England. At the same time Cardinal Wolsey had to be eliminated. He had been chaplain to Henry VII, was appointed Bishop of Lincoln (1514) and York (1514), and made cardinal in 1515. Wolsey was very unpopular with priests and laity, rich and poor. He could be tactless in Parliament, where he made great financial demands; he was ineffective in foreign policy; he repressed the nobility who resented his low birth as a butcher's son; he was voracious of other cleric's privileges; and he exhibited a personal arrogance and splendid ostentation. When such a man begins to fall, there are not many who want to help him.

Wolsey was charged with violating *Praemunire* in 1529. *Praemunire* was the practice of appealing outside the country to another prince, or allowing foreign intervention in England's affairs. It enjoyed a very wide interpretation under Henry VIII and was eventually applied to anyone who looked to the pope as the head of the church. Wolsey was forced to resign and returned to his see of York. Henry was vindictive and took over all of Wolsey's property—Hampton Court, Whitehall (which was known then as York Place)—suppressed Wolsey's college at Ipswich, and changed the name of Cardinal College at Oxford to "Christ Church."[17] Shortly after, Wolsey was arrested in 1530, and on his way to London for trial, died from exposure, uttering his famous line, "Would that I had served my God as faithfully as I had served my king." Thomas More replaced him.

Things began to move quickly now. In May 1532, Parliament passed an act entitled "Submission of the Clergy." It was the English version of what was happening in Switzerland, where city councils took over the running of the church. It meant that all ecclesiastical appointments had to be approved by the king retroactively. Any cleric who had received an appointment from the pope had now to resign and be reappointed by the king. The next day Thomas More resigned as Chancellor, because he saw where this legislation was headed.

William Warham, the Archbishop of Canterbury, died that same summer of 1532 and handed Henry his chance to wipe the slate clean. Henry appointed Thomas Cranmer, chaplain to the Boleyns, as the next Archbishop of Canterbury. Cranmer swore allegiance to the Holy See, then secretly disavowed it and annulled the marriage. Anne Boleyn was married to Henry in secret a week before Parliament opened in 1533. She was already pregnant and time was now of the essence, since illegitimate children could not assume the throne. (There may have been a private ceremony earlier in mid-November.) She was made queen on 12 April 1533.

Thomas More refused to go to the coronation despite the urging of three conservative bishops, among them Cuthbert Tunstall, the Bishop of London. More responded by telling them a story about the Roman Emperor Tiberius, who enacted a law that exacted death for a certain crime, unless the offender be a virgin. When presented with a virgin on such a charge, he did not know what to do. One of his councils said, "Why make you so much ado, my lords, about so small a matter? Let her first be deflowered and then after may she be devoured."

Thomas More commented,

> And so though your Lordships have in the matter of the matrimony kept yourselves pure virgins, yet take good heed, my lords, that you keep your virginity still. For some there be that by procuring your lordships first at the coronation to be present, and next to preach for the setting forth of it, and finally to write books...in defense thereof, are desirous to deflower you; and when they have deflowered you, then will they not fail soon after to devour you. Now, my lords, it lieth not in my power but that they may devour me. But God, being my good Lord, I will provide that they shall never deflower me.[18]

It was not a happy marriage; Anne produced no son—only Elizabeth. On the day Catherine of Aragon was buried (29 January 1536), Anne Boleyn miscarried a son. Soon after Anne was beheaded on the charges that she had committed indiscretions with court personnel, including her brother. Soon after, Henry was married to Jane Seymour.

Thomas Cromwell (1485–1540)

With the demise of Thomas More, Henry appointed Thomas Cromwell as Chief Minister, a post equivalent to a Chief of Staff today. Cromwell gradually built up the legislation which gave the king and Parliament more power, the nobles and church less. In 1534 Parliament passed the Act of Supremacy, whereby the king was not only a secular protector, but a religious reformer. He now had power to correct opinions of preachers, to supervise the formulation of doctrine, to reform canon law, to visit and discipline regular and secular clergy, and to try heretics in person. All of this was what Thomas More had feared when he resigned.

In 1535 Cromwell was made Henry's "vicar," which gave him power over the church no person, lay or cleric, had held before. Soon an act was passed, the Act of First Fruits and Tenths, which took the first fruits of *all* ecclesiastical positions (half of one's year salary), and one-tenth of all income. Previously this had been restricted to bishops.

The Dissolution of the Monasteries

Even more heavy-handed was the dissolution of the English monasteries. In 1535 there were 825 religious houses of monks, friars, and nuns. Five years later, in 1540, there were none. Monasteries were problematic for the king in that they were more independent than bishops and diocesan clergy (also known as secular clergy). A religious house was often an entity unto itself or, in the case of the friars, it might have as an overall superior someone from a foreign country holding an office in Rome. Monks and friars were therefore more prone to independence and could speak out on issues of the day more freely than their diocesan counterparts.

The best of them were the first ones to be targeted by Cromwell because they had publicly questioned the right of the king to marry Anne Boleyn. The Franciscan Observants, a very strict, dynamic group, had served Queen Catherine and her daughter Mary as their confessors from their house at Greenwich. In 1532 Henry's divorce plan and the submission of the clergy were both denounced from the pulpit by the Franciscan provincial, William Peto, who was confessor to Mary. Members of the court were present. Peto was summoned to the king, where he was asked to explain himself. He repeated what he had said in the sermon. In his absence the king appointed one of his own chaplains, Dr. Curwen, to preach at Greenwich against Peto. Early in the sermon he wished out loud that Peto was there to answer him, at which point from the rood loft came the voice of Fr. Elstow, the warden, who said he would be glad to answer any charges on behalf of the provincial. Several unpleasant exchanges took place before Curwen was finished, and Peto was ordered to deprive Elstow of office. Peto refused, and both were imprisoned, then exiled to the continent. They were the lucky ones. Elstow was succeeded by John Forrest, Catherine's confessor. Franciscan superiors were instructed by the crown (there were seven houses with 200 monks) to impose conformity or silence, and they uniformly refused. In addition, they all now had to sign an oath acknowledging the king's supremacy, deny that of the pope, and swear allegiance to Henry, Anne, and their issue. The Observants did not yield. In June 1532 cartloads of friars were taken to the Tower. By the middle of August, all seven houses were emptied, and many of the friars put in prison. Most were never heard from again.

The Bridgettine nuns in Syon abbey were one of the most observant, most educated, sophisticated communities in the country. They were the tenth wealthiest as well. They were cared for by the most informed and observant clergy in the country. Cromwell went after them with a vengeance, and they did not break. Neither did the Carthusians. With them began the executions.

In the spring of 1535 (More and Bishop Fisher of Rochester had been in jail for almost a year at this point), three Carthusian

211

The Bodies of More and Fisher

More's head was placed on a pole on London Bridge, removed by his daughter, and taken to the Roper Chapel in Canterbury. His body was buried underneath the floor of the Tower chapel and reburied in a room adjoining the chapel in the twentieth century. The tomb can be seen by asking the guide just after the tour is completed. Fisher's tomb is in this room as well.

---

priors and Fr. Richard Reynolds of Syon ("the most learned monk in England") were brought to trial for treason—for denying the Royal Supremacy. In May 1535 they were put to death at Tyburn in their habits, against all precedent. The king himself may have been present at the execution in disguise. Three weeks later, three more Carthusians were sent to prison, tortured by being bolted upright for seventeen days, then executed on 19 June. John Fisher was the only bishop to defy the king on the divorce, and he was beheaded on 22 June. Nine days later Thomas More was similarly executed. The monasteries would begin to be visited by Cromwell's agents in July.

Cromwell had learned how a "visitation" was carried out while he worked under Wolsey. Visitations were formal ecclesiastical visits conducted by a bishop or superior of a religious order both on a regular basis and as a result of some serious conflict within a particular house. On occasion a house would be suppressed (closed down) as a result of the visit. But far more normally a report was issued, recommendations were made for the house to address, a few corrections were given, and life in the monastic house carried on.

Suppressing a monastery was a big deal. Monasteries had been dissolved in the past because they were "alien monasteries"—i.e., their revenues went back to motherhouses outside the country—or because they had ridiculously few numbers. Houses built for 250 men might contain two, in which case they should be sent elsewhere to join a larger community. But semi-autonomous houses did not do this easily, and it often took a heavier hand to effect any change. Wolsey had dissolved a few religious houses in his early years as chancellor. Two houses were suppressed in 1521 with the approval of Bishop Fisher. But even here there was an ominous note to the suppression, as the king wrote to the Bishop of Salisbury (where the suppressions would take place) that the "enormities, misgovernances, and slanderous living" of the convents would come to an end. The king seemed to be exaggerating, but to what end? Even as early as 1521 the king seems to have had more extensive dissolutions in mind. His attention had been caught.

Wolsey also sought to suppress twenty-nine religious houses in order to build colleges at Oxford (Cardinal College) and Ipswich. While Wolsey never conceived of suppressing all the monasteries, he did create a mechanism by which their destruction could come about. Cromwell and all the visitors had been Wolsey's men. Cromwell was in charge of Wolsey's dissolutions, and learned how they were done.

Cromwell wanted to create the impression that he was only carrying out a similar visitation in order to assess the state of religious life in England. So his visitors fanned out in the summer of 1535. What they found they wrote back in letters to Cromwell, who compiled them in a book called the *Comperta*. It is uniformly damning of the monasteries, so much so that, as late as the 1880s, even Roman Catholic historians would not try to defend the monks. David Knowles, writing in the latter half of the twentieth century, admitted that the first time he read the *Comperta*, he was quite prepared to believe that the monks were guilty and that the monasteries should have all been dissolved. He would change his mind when he looked at the evidence and gave it careful evaluation.

Cromwell's strategy for dissolving the monasteries was to do it gradually and to make it appear to be a reform. While his visitors were gathering information from all the monasteries, he initially proposed only dissolving those monasteries which were deemed "lesser"—those producing less than 200 pounds annually or containing less than twelve religious. This would seem a modest reform. There were 304 monastic houses in this category, and

Sts. Thomas More (1478–1535) and John Fisher (1460–1535), one a lawyer, husband, and father and the other the Bishop of Rochester in England, both lost their lives rather than approve Henry VIII's plan to divorce Catherine of Aragon and break with the pope. More and Fisher, who was named cardinal while imprisoned in the Tower of London, were beheaded within a few days of each other.

their income amounted to less than one-fifth of the total monastic income. Even so, it took intimidation to convince Parliament to pass the Act of Suppression in 1536.

The *Comperta* has long been regarded as the argument in favor of dissolving the monasteries. But there are serious problems with this argument. Logical flaws abounded. For one thing, the *Comperta* was never seen by Parliament, so their Act of Dissolution was more the result of bullying than an action based on solid information. Secondly, while calling the dissolution a "reform," Cromwell dissolved the best monasteries first. Thirdly, he moved monks (from Chertsey Abbey) who had been charged with incontinence with women and with unnatural vice to staff the king's new abbey at Bisham, and the abbot was mitered by Henry himself.

Other than the illogic of calling it a reform, the visitation was carried out too quickly to be a serious attempt at reformation. The monasteries were dissolved before they had any time to put reforms into effect. One visitor, Richard Layton, was severely rebuked by Cromwell because he praised the abbot of Glastonbury and the house as observant and the model of religious life. He wrote to Cromwell that all was in good order at Glastonbury, and Abbot Whiting, a virtuous man, then groveled when Cromwell told him his job was not to find virtue, but vice. He wrote back to Cromwell, "He [Whiting] appeareth not, neither then nor now, to have known God, nor his prince, nor any part of a good Christian man's religion, (his monks) were false, feigned, flattering hypocritical knaves."[19] The visitor's reports focused on the sensational—nuns getting pregnant, monks having mistresses, sodomy, even "solitary sin." Some accusations concerned the tyranny of a superior, laxity in prayer, poor upkeep of the house and grounds, high living, superstition, and treason.

The *Comperta* was assembled by threatening the religious. One visitor (Ap Rice) complained to Cromwell that another visitor was bullying the monks. Commonly, monks were told that their monastery would be closed down, they would be tried for treason, and they would be left without a penny, if they did not give damning evidence. This evidence was never evaluated. The most disgruntled monk was given credence. Neighbors who had a feud with the monastery would give evidence. Every negative accusation was taken at face value as a conviction. Nor were cases necessarily recent. Those listed as bearing children could have done so in the distant past, before they were nuns. (Some may have been put in convents *because* they were pregnant.) Cromwell was in a hurry and did not have time to bring people to trial, or at least a fair trial.

Other contemporary reports support the religious. Officials from the Court of Augmentations, taxmen who worked for the government and were unlikely to criticize the visitors' reports, were also visiting the monasteries at the same time as Cromwell's visitors and found the monasteries to be in good condition and the monks to be of high moral repute.

Bishops also visited monasteries on a fairly regular basis and some of their reports have survived, most of them in direct conflict with the *Comperta*. Often an abbot (sometimes a layman!) would be appointed by Cromwell so that when the time came to dissolve the monastery, the abbot would willingly cooperate and be rewarded with some of his own monastery's land.

Cromwell had devised the means by which he could eliminate opposition to the king's divorce and royal supremacy, but also establish a permanent source of revenue for the crown. Some monastic property would be sold immediately in order to raise necessary cash, some would be given away as gifts, but the bulk of the property would be leased and serve as a steady source of income. Unfortunately, the plan did not work. By 1580 almost all of the land had been sold.

Dissolution of the Lesser Houses

When a house was suppressed, the monks or nuns were first sent away, some with pensions, some to other houses, some with nothing but their families to fall back on. There was no rhyme or reason to pensioning. Cromwell was in a hurry and did what he had to do in order to shut down a monastery. The valuables were carried back to London to be melted down and sold, or reshaped. Then a small army descended and began removing the bells and leaden roofs, and melted them on the site using the wood from the choir stalls, rood screens, and statues. Altars, stained glass windows, and all other images were usually smashed. Some things were hidden by the monks or locals. Other items were used for other purposes for centuries before being discovered.[20] Once the roof was removed, the building quickly deteriorated. Local people often took the bricks and stones for building material; sometimes, as at Lindisfarne, the bricks were used to build a castle or manor house. Rarely (as at Fountains Abbey) do the buildings remain almost intact.

Pilgrimage of Grace (August 1536–February 1537)

There was one significant reaction to the dissolution of the monasteries. In the autumn of 1536, there occurred simultaneous

THE WIVES OF HENRY VIII
(see Strickland: *The Queens of England*, Vol. II
and Antonia Fraser: *The Wives of Henry VIII*)

1) **Catherine of Aragon** Married Henry on 11 June 1509
"Divorced" in 1532
Gave birth to Mary Tudor

2) **Anne Boleyn** Married 25 January 1533
The niece of the Duke of Norfolk, crowned queen 1 June
1533 at Westminster (she used Catherine of Aragon's barge)
She also ordered, to be embroidered on her liveried ser-
vants, the phrase *Ainsi sera, groigne qui groigne:* "It will
happen, no matter who grumbles."
Gave birth to Elizabeth
Executed 19 May 1536

3) **Jane Seymour** Married 29 May 1536
Died two weeks after bearing Edward VI

4) **Anne of Cleves** Married 6 January 1540
Marriage nullified on 7 July 1540 by convocation of York
and Canterbury on the grounds that Anne was betrothed
to another at the time of the wedding, and because Henry
had not assented.

5) **Catherine Howard** Married 8 August 1540 (she was 19,
Henry 49)
Executed 15 months later for adultery. She was also the
niece of Norfolk.

6) **Catherine Parr** Married 12 July 1543
Henry was her third husband.
(She would have one more [Thomas Seymour] who
would be executed.)
She outlived Henry by a year, dying in 1548.

"Seldom has marital career been so productive of ecclesiastical change" (Martin Marty).

risings in the northern countries of Lincolnshire and Yorkshire. What moved the people to revolt was a mix of economic and religious grievances. Yet the glue that held this revolt together was religion. The "pilgrims," as they called themselves, demanded the restoration of closed monasteries, saints' days, and all of the sacraments.

It was one of the most remarkable revolts in history for it included a cross section of every English class. Those monks in monasteries that still survived were caught in the middle. Abbots knew that these revolts usually did not succeed and that reprisals could follow. So, sympathetic though they might be to the cause of the pilgrims, they did not want to antagonize the government further. Some southern monasteries (Glastonbury) even gave money to defeat the pilgrims, as evidence of their loyalty to the king. Some monasteries (the larger ones were still unsuppressed) on the path of the pilgrims, were forced to give physical aid; some supplied monks. The abbot of St. Mary's of York was made to lead the procession with the abbey's best cross, and he excused himself at the first opportunity. The bishops, to a man, refused to support the revolt.

The pilgrimage, which took over the towns of Durham and York, was met by a small army raised by the Duke of Norfolk, a Catholic, at the request of the king. Norfolk met the pilgrim

A Shrine Survives

In one interesting episode, the Benedictine monks at Durham moved St. Cuthbert's body from the shrine and buried him in a pillar of the cathedral, replacing his body with another deceased brother. In the 1830s, during a restoration of the cathedral, a body was found in the pillar which was almost certainly Cuthbert—episcopal vestments and furnishings could be seen—and he was reinterred at the original site. Ironically, or perharps significantly, the only thing left of the old shrine in Durham is the money chest.

army at Doncaster and played for time by negotiating. Robert Aske, the leader of the pilgrimage, was permitted to make his demands known to the king in person, and was promised quick compliance. Satisfied with the king's promises, he disbanded the army, which was a very serious mistake. Norfolk proceeded to round up the ringleaders and 200 participants, including Aske, and hung them all.

Dissolution of the Greater Monasteries

It is difficult to say when the greater monasteries began to be closed down. Lewes fell in 1537, and the greater monasteries began being closed one by one. Early in 1538, Cromwell's visitors, Layton and Legh, were on the road again. Shrines were included in this dissolution: St. Edmund's shrine at Bury St. Edmunds, Becket's shrine in Canterbury Cathedral, St. Swithun's shrine in Winchester, St. Cuthbert's shrine in Durham, and the Marian shrine at Walsingham. Not only were the jewels and money taken and the shrine dismantled, but the bones of the shrine's patron saint were burned or thrown away, to eliminate possibility of a revival. At Walsingham the miraculous wooden statue of Mary was burned.

Motives for this varied. Money was uppermost in the king's mind. But in some cases (e.g., Canterbury) he wanted to erase famous precedents for resistance to royal power. In other cases, such as Walsingham, reformers like Hugh Latimer wanted to erase all possibility of "image worship" and superstition, so crosses or statues were destroyed.

The larger monasteries disappeared gradually through a variety of threats, bribes, and evictions. The threats could be dramatic. Cromwell called a meeting of the abbots of Yorkshire just after the Pilgrimage of Grace, and they had to walk through the gate of Fountains Abbey, from which swung the bodies of the abbots of Fountains and Jervaulx. In another episode, Abbot Richard Whiting of Glastonbury was arrested. Glastonbury was the richest monastic house in England. Whiting was respected, though he was a typical politician. He had been against the king's divorce, but took no stand against it; he even signed the petition to Rome and all the oaths connected with it and the oath of Royal Supremacy. He was taken to the Tower on the scant grounds that a book against the divorce was found in his coffers. Cromwell wrote a note saying, "The abbot of Glaston to be sent down to be tried and executed at Glaston." The trial took place at Wells (the only charge they could convict him for was "robbery") in November 1539. The next day Whiting was taken to his abbey, put on a hurdle, and dragged through the town and up Tor Hill, where he was hung, drawn, and quartered. His head was set up over the gateway. He was seventy-five years old.

Suppression of the Friars

Suppressing the friars was a mopping-up operation. The friars—Dominicans, Franciscans, Augustinians—were poor, observant, but weakened by the Reformation. Many of their best minds had been attracted to Germany, to service with Cromwell, or had been executed or were in flight for resistance. Cromwell used former and current provincials to close down the friaries, beginning in 1538. One thousand friars were sent home. The last house fell in 1540, the same year Cromwell himself would be executed.

The Henrician Reformation was over. Henry, seeing how far Cranmer had tried to take him in making the land Lutheran or Calvinist, pulled the plug in September of 1538 and passed Six Articles, which tried to restore the ancient faith, including the practice of celibacy for the clergy. By 1543 most of the Reformation legislation was reversed. One man, John Lambert, was made an example in November of 1538. He was burned by being dragged in and out of the fire for holding the very same beliefs about the Eucharist that Cranmer held. Cranmer was made to watch the whole brutal event. He also had to send his wife back to Germany.

But Henry, try as he might to apply brakes to the Reformation in England by restricting it and (toward the end) reversing it, had set in motion a formidable machine. When Henry died in 1547, all of the monasteries, friaries, convents of nuns, and shrines were gone. Because his fifth wife, Catherine Howard, had come from the family of the Duke of Norfolk and had embarrassed him by her sexual excesses, Henry brought in Protestants along with his very Protestant sixth wife, Catherine Parr. When he died, they were the ones in place to take over the government of his ten-year-old son, Edward.

The Reign of Edward VI

When Henry died in 1547 his ten-year-old son, Edward VI, became king. Because he was a minor, he would not be able to rule England until he came of age. The first "Protector" was the Duke of Somerset, Edward Seymour (also Earl of Hertford), who was also Edward VI's uncle. He was overthrown in 1550 and executed by his own brother, Thomas Seymour, Duke of Northumberland (Earl of Warwick). During this unsettled period, Cranmer passed a series of ecclesiastical laws, which he had long wanted to do under Henry. This could be called the "Protestantizing" of the English Reformation. In 1547, all pictures and all candles were condemned except for two before the Blessed Sacrament; a copy of the Great Bible (by Coverdale) and a paraphrase of Erasmus were provided in every church; the reading in English of the Epistle and Gospel at High Mass was enforced.

Also in 1547 Parliament imposed communion under species of both bread and wine, and repealed Henry's Six Articles, which included celibacy for the clergy. By 1548 priests and bishops were now free to marry. In January of 1548 Cranmer announced to the bishops that candles on Christmas, ashes on Ash Wednesday, and palms on Palm Sunday would all be banned. Before Holy Week of that year, he also banned the use of Easter fire and water.

Cranmer was just getting started. In 1549 the Act of Uniformity imposed *The Book of Common Prayer*, which both put into English a Communion service, but also eliminated almost all variety within the church's calendar. Every day was more or less the same. Gone were most saints' and Marian feasts, penitential seasons such as Advent and Lent, rogation and ember days.

In 1550 a new Rite of Ordination was approved, eliminating all mention of sacrifice. In the same year, altars were destroyed, to be replaced by wooden tables, thus emphasizing the "Lord's Supper" rather than the Sacrifice of Calvary. (Cranmer had the same problems with "sacrifice" as did Luther.) A second *Book of Common Prayer* was printed in 1552, eliminating all ambiguity about the first. In 1553 Forty-two Articles of Religion were added to the *Book of Common Prayer*, a sort of confession of belief. (In 1563 these were pared to the present Thirty-nine). They, like the Westminster and Augsburg Confessions (and most conciliar documents), are largely stated in the negative:

> #19 As the Church of Jerusalem, Alexandria, and Antioch have erred; so also the Church of Rome hath erred, not only their living and manner of Ceremonies, but also in matters of Faith.

> #22 The Romish Doctrine concerning Purgatory, Pardons, Worshipping and Adoration, as well of Images as of Reliques, and also invocation of Saints is a fond thing vainly invented, and grounded upon no warranty of Scripture, but rather repugnant to the Word of God.

> #25 There are two Sacraments ordained of Christ, or Lord in the Gospel, that is to say, Baptism and the Supper of the Lord....The Sacraments were ordained of Christ not to be gazed upon, or carried about, but that we should duly use them.

> #28 The Body of Christ is given, taken, and eaten, in the Supper, only after a heavenly and spiritual manner....The Sacrament of the Lord's Supper was not by Christ's ordinance reserved, carried about, lifted up, or worshipped.

The keynote of Edwardian Reformation was that many of the changes begun by Henry for financial or political reasons (assigning all chantries, guilds, free chapels, colleges, hospitals to the crown, dissolving the monasteries) became under Somerset and Warwick *doctrinal* changes.

The main question is: What did the *Book of Common Prayer* do? Was it an invention by Cranmer, albeit a linguistically brilliant invention, or was it a reform of the church's prayer? Edmund Bishop and Aidan Gasquet (*Edward VI and the Book of Common Prayer*) attacked it in the late nineteenth century as an innovation, claiming that Cranmer had changed the nature of the Mass deliberately, deceitfully, and progressively. All notion of sacrifice was swept away, transubstantiation was disavowed, and a Zwinglian interpretation of Eucharist was substituted.

Archbishop Thomas Cranmer would not long survive. In 1553 the sickly Edward died. The Protector Warwick attempted to keep control by having Lady Jane Grey (her great uncle was Henry VIII) marry his son. Princess Mary Tudor (Henry's daughter by his first wife Catherine of Aragon) escaped from house arrest, however, and ruined the plans. She imprisoned Cranmer for treason and he was executed in 1556.

Evaluating Archbishop Cranmer

What are we to make of Cranmer? Roman Catholic historians over the centuries, whether of liberal or conservative bent, all agree that Cranmer was a dissembler, a coward, and a man who would (and did) do anything to survive, including condemn his friends to death for believing in exactly the things he believed in. In order to be made Archbishop of Canterbury, he took an oath pledging obedience to the pope, then immediately took another oath swearing he did not mean any of it. He benefited from papal bulls while formally rejecting their authority. While in prison under Mary, he swore several times that he believed in transubstantiation and the authority of the pope and, when this was not enough to save him, gave a speech from the scaffold defending his previous positions. He, who had always defended his king as the head of the church in England, now found himself in particular straits when his new monarch, Mary, professed her adherence to the pope.

But there is more to Cranmer than these cowardly traits. He was often out of the political loop. He had virtually nothing to do with the dissolution of the monasteries, except to benefit by receiving a few properties. Rather, he was an artistic genius fully committed to the Reformation. When the monarch (or protectors) gave him license to promote the Reformation, he did so enthusiastically and almost ruthlessly, using his powers as Archbishop of Canterbury to the fullest.

Cranmer followed Luther in separating Holy Thursday from Good Friday, distinguishing between the "remembrance" of

223

the Last Supper on Holy Thursday and the sacrifice of Calvary, which happened once on the first Good Friday. According to Cranmer, the two had nothing to do with each other. The latter is over and done with, and the former we do once a week, or as often as we like. Cranmer went further than Luther on the Eucharist, thinking it to be only a symbol.

Yet he could tolerate compromise. Cranmer insisted on vestments. When John Hooper, soon to be consecrated bishop of Gloucester, refused to be ordained in episcopal vestments, Cranmer had him imprisoned until he submitted—a submission that the historian Diarmaid MacCollough claims led to the "peculiar hybrid" known as Anglicanism.[21] We might say of Cranmer that he was a convinced reformer who was also a survivor in the old sense, as Wolsey was a survivor. Both prelates knew when to compromise, when to lie, and yet they also knew when to push their own programs and be ruthless in getting rid of opponents. And yet, neither Cranmer nor Wolsey survived. Events carried them both away.

The hybrid, Anglicanism, did not have a certain future in England. The new queen Mary was a determined Roman Catholic and would attempt to restore the old religion.

Mary Tudor and the Catholic Reaction (1553–58)

When Mary escaped from house arrest as Edward VI was dying in 1553, the countryside rose in her cause, and Warwick was defeated and executed. Mary then imprisoned Jane Grey and Cranmer for treason; adding the reformers Latimer, Ridley, Hooper, and Coverdale for heresy. "Catholic" bishops (including Bonner and Gardiner) were released from prison. Mary was declared queen in July, and in August she attended an "illegal" Mass in the Tower of London. This was a sign to the people that the Mass could be restored. It was done immediately and everywhere. Festivals, processions, and jollification returned. Married bishops were deprived of their sees. Foreign Protestants were allowed to leave the country.

Mary's reign began calmly enough—she even spared her half-sister Elizabeth, who was involved in the Jane Grey matter—

but as resistance stiffened Mary became more violent. She made two serious mistakes: She married Philip II of Spain, which was not at this time a popular ally, and she tried people for heresy.[22] She seemed oblivious to public opinion. She eventually put 282 people to death, burning them for heresy, and earned herself the name "Bloody Mary."

English Protestant historians have exaggerated these burnings, since their scale was not unknown at the time and had been surpassed by Henry (his executions during the marriage controversy and after the Pilgrimage of Grace) and would be surpassed by Elizabeth, who executed 800 at one time after a minor rebellion. But Mary ignored the advice of her chaplain and her Spanish husband, both of whom advised her not to burn people for heresy.

She restored some religious houses, made no attempt to restore their stolen property (Rome agreed with this) as a conciliatory gesture, and brought in her cousin Cardinal Reginald Pole to be the new Archbishop of Canterbury. He was one of the great Catholic reformers of his day. But this all came undone when Mary and Cardinal Pole died on the same day, 17 November 1558, both of natural causes. Elizabeth was now the Queen of England.

Elizabeth and the Anglican Settlement

One of Elizabeth's primary goals was to restore order to her kingdom. It had gone through tremendous religious upheaval in a very short period of time. The religious issue, if left alone, would only divide the nation further, so some compromise had to be reached. The Anglican Settlement was that compromise. In it, Elizabeth attempted to produce a religion so vague that it could include both Catholic and Protestant factions within one church. It had never been done before. As we will see, it never really worked. Catholics loyal to the pope never accepted it, and divisions soon surfaced among those who accepted it, once Elizabeth was gone.

The Mass was outlawed and Catholics were forced underground, or abroad, and could be ruthlessly hunted. Those who remained Catholic were called *recusants*. The government policy was to fine people who did not attend the Anglican service until they conformed, and place disabilities on them and their families which could be crippling. Penal laws, applied to those who refused to take an oath denouncing the pope, prevented Catholics from becoming members of the professions, from holding political office, voting, and educating their children. Travel restrictions were also quite severe. Such harassment would prove quite effective. By 1780, only one percent of the population of England was Roman Catholic.

But even though the laws were on the books, Elizabeth held off enforcing them until several events forced her hand. In 1570 Pope Pius V excommunicated her, thinking (along with the recently completed Council of Trent) that it would clear the air and hopefully unify the opposition. Some clarification was necessary. People in England were still wondering if they were Catholic or not, and there are examples of parishioners attending the Anglican service in the morning and a Roman Catholic Mass in the afternoon to ensure that they had fulfilled their Sunday obligation. But the papal excommunication also managed to give the Queen and her counselors a pretext for persecuting Catholics—for treason instead of heresy—because part of excommunication entailed removing subjects from their fealty to the excommunicated prince.

Defiance of Elizabeth was on the increase. In 1579 the Desmond Rebellion broke out in Ireland and was aided by Spain. The Jesuits then complicated things by arriving in England in 1580. The Jesuit priests, Robert Persons and Edmund Campion, were both Oxford graduates who had converted to Catholicism, were trained in Rome, and returned to England in disguise. The combination of these activities frightened Elizabeth into action. Campion was captured and martyred in 1581, and Persons fled back to the Continent. In all, 180 Catholics were executed: 123 were priests, fifty-four of whom were converts and nine former Protestant ministers. The usual punishment for treason was hanging, drawing, and quartering.

The difficulties for the Church of England would not end with the elimination of Roman Catholicism. Internal feuds were about to erupt once Elizabeth died in 1603. She never married and left no children, thus the succession went to the Stuarts, the rulers of Scotland. James VI of Scotland, son of Mary Queen of Scots, would now take the throne of England and assume the name James I. Catholics thought this spelled the return of Roman Catholicism, but James, tolerant as he was of Catholics, would not restore the old religion. Disappointed, a small group led by Guy Fawkes tried to blow up the opening of Parliament in 1605, when James and his young son would have been present. The plot, known as the Gunpowder Plot, was discovered by a Catholic peer, who reported the whole thing to the authorities, who then arrested Fawkes and averted disaster.

Nonetheless, the Stuarts promoted a very High Church interpretation of Anglicanism, leading to the ascendancy of William Laud as Archbishop of Canterbury. This provoked the Puritans into action and in 1642 Oliver Cromwell defeated the forces of King Charles I in the English Civil War, and took over the government for the next sixteen years, until he died in 1658. In the Restoration of 1660, the Stuarts were returned to the throne, there to remain under Charles II and James II until 1688, when the "Glorious Revolution" placed William of Orange on the throne.[23] Anglicanism, as a unique mix of high ceremony and Low Church belief, had come to stay.

The Reformation in Scotland

In Scotland, the church had the same problems it had everywhere: pluralities of benefices, concubinage, extravagance, a too-political church, etc. There was also a strong reforming party. Complicating this was the political situation. There existed a strong pro-French party (the Auld Alliance), backed by the royalty—the Stuarts (there is some question whether Mary Queen of Scots could even speak English!)—and a strong English party that sided with the reformers.

England (under the Tudors, especially Elizabeth) supported the reformers, not because their religion was so correct, but because they threatened to weaken the Scottish crown, and consequently the French connection and the Scottish threat to its northern borders. The result for the Scots was the acceptance of the English Bible, which destroyed the Scots language and went a long way to destroying Scottish culture.

A related problem was the weakness of the Scottish throne. A series of "minorities" had put the government into the hands of people who were bent on maintaining their own power at all costs; and who, as a result, were amazingly fickle and unpredictable, changing their loyalties several times in the course of the next few years. These people were also bent on keeping the royalty in its place. In 1542 James V died in battle against the English. His daughter Mary succeeded him. She was one week old. There was an immediate struggle over the regency between the Protestant, pro-English party and the Roman Catholic, pro-French party. Mary was sent to France for her education, and returned in 1560, after her husband, the King of France (Francis I) died. She was eighteen years old.

Mary was immediately embroiled in several crises: in religion she desired people to be left alone to worship as they wished, while John Knox and the Scottish Parliament wanted the Catholic faith outlawed. Then she united herself in marriage to Lord Darnley in 1565. The rest is an amazing story of intrigue and betrayal. No wonder the Tudors were worried about having a daughter ascend the throne. Soon after the wedding, a group of nobility killed her Italian secretary, Riccio, as he dined with her one night. They disliked him because, among other reasons, he was a direct connection to Rome. That same night, a Dominican priest with similar strong ties to Rome and the queen was also murdered on Edinburgh's High Street. Darnley was himself murdered by the same group of nobility in 1567. This was the famous Kirk-o-Field (on the grounds of the present Old College of the University of Edinburgh), when the castle was supposed to have been blown up with Darnley in it. But Darnley got suspicious, tried to escape, was caught and strangled, and then the house was blown up as a cover.

Bothwell, the mastermind behind Darnley's assassination, then took Mary in marriage. It seems she had little choice. Debates still continue as to whether this was rape or whether Mary saw the wisdom of the arrangement and went along with it. Whatever the case, the combination of events tied Mary in with the murder of Darnley and ruined her name, making her a harlot in the minds of the common people. These same nobles who had killed Riccio and Darnley now turned on Bothwell, just as they turned on Darnley, forced him out of the country, and then blamed Mary for the very marriage which they had arranged and advised her to accept.

Mary was imprisoned in Lochleven Castle in 1567 and was forced to abdicate the throne to her infant son James. However, she escaped in 1568 and managed to raise an army. After a disastrous battle near Glasgow, where one of the lords she was counting on for support went to the English side, she fled to England, where she placed herself at the mercy of her cousin Elizabeth, the Queen of England. She was disappointed in this. Instead of meeting the Queen as she had hoped, she was imprisoned for nineteen years and eventually executed by Elizabeth's order in 1587. The Spanish, outraged by this regicide, attempted to invade England in 1588, only to have its famous Armada destroyed in a sea battle.

John Knox (1513–1572)

John Knox was in minor orders and possibly a priest when he embraced the principles of the Reformation in 1544, under the spell of the magnetic George Wishart. Wishart was captured by Bothwell in 1546, and was burnt that same year by Cardinal Beaton in St. Andrews. Shortly after, Beaton himself was assassinated by a party of reformers, and his dead body hung out of his palace naked. In 1547 Knox could be found preaching in St. Andrews, but he was captured in the castle of St. Andrews by the French, exiled to France, and released in 1549. In 1551 he was made chaplain to Edward VI, and assisted in the final stages of the revision of the second *Book of Common Prayer*. Between the years 1553 and 1555, he sought shelter on the continent when Mary Tudor became queen. He met Calvin there, but was expelled from Frankfurt after a dispute over worship and returned to Scotland. In 1536 we find him again in Geneva, where he wrote *That Monstrous Regiment of Women*, an attack on Mary of Guise (mother of the Queen of Scots), saying political rule by women is forbidden by natural law and the law of God. This was taken personally by Queen Elizabeth, who never liked Knox, but could use him for her own purposes.

In 1560 he drew up the Scottish Confession and formed a commission that abolished the authority of the pope, "idolatry," and both the celebration of and attendance at Mass, for which punishment was death. The Scottish monasteries were to be abolished. Ordination by laying on of hands was repudiated. The congregation would elect its own clergy. Interestingly, the Scottish Confession, in addition to assuming the doctrine of justification by faith, affirmed the Calvinist notion of predestination. It also emphasized a Calvinist notion of Eucharist, and condemned the Zwinglian notion that the elements are bare signs, while at the same time condemning transubstantiation. Thus the Presbyterian Church, as it came to be known, combined Calvinist Eucharist theology with Zwinglian liturgical practices.

John Knox is not remembered for his theology or his moderation. Most Presbyterians are embarrassed by his teachings today and his gravesite is not known precisely, though he is thought to be buried somewhere near the present High Street in Edinburgh. But he was an inspiration. He was driven, and he drove the Scottish Reformation. Gone were the monks, priests, bishops, statues, bells, and stained glass. Knox's cleansing of the old religion was thorough and was particularly vicious when directed against monasteries and churches. He led an assault against one monastery (Balmerino) on Christmas Day. The extent of the damage done to Scottish artwork can only be estimated by what little survives: a few items from St. Andrew's Cathedral moved to France just prior to Knox's destruction of that building. Four little stained glass coats-of-arms in an Edinburgh chapel (ironically, one of them is Mary of Guise's) are all that remains of Scottish medieval glass. Feast days were abolished, including Christmas, which was not made a public holiday again until the 1960s!

Finally, he was, in some ways, the most international of the famous reformers. His Scottish kirk was not the product of nationalism or provincialism. He courted the English because he needed them, but he could not brook the liturgical compromises made by Cranmer. He may very well have been a sixteenth-century version of the abolitionist John Brown.

Protestantism

The Protestant world, having established the precedent of breaking away from Rome, began to fracture itself into many different "denominations," or interpretations of how the message of the Gospel should be lived and governed. One major division occurred between the radicals (Puritans, Evangelicals, later Fundamentalists) and those who wanted to retain some practices of the old religion. There was a sense among the latter that too much had been lost. Both the Anglican and Lutheran churches eventually divided into two major parties, a low church and a high church. The low church wanted little or nothing to do with hierarchy, sacraments, or ceremony. The high church advocates wanted to retain as much as they could while eliminating the authority of the pope.

In the early 1620s, the English high church party was in charge. Puritans, who were now persecuted, began to make their way to the American colonies, arriving in Massachusetts on the *Mayflower* in 1620. Others made their way to Virginia, founded in 1608. Baptists appeared for the first time in Amsterdam in 1609 under a leader named John Smith, stressing the baptism of conscious believers (i.e., adults). In 1639, the first Baptist church was founded in the American colony of Rhode Island, in Providence, by Roger Williams, who had grown weary of the Puritan intolerance in Massachusetts. These churches and the Congregational Church in Massachusetts were Presbyterian in structure—each church was independent—and this made them well suited to the American frontier. They stressed more or less the same things: the priesthood of the faithful, adherence to scripture, and strict morality.

With the ascendancy of the Puritan Oliver Cromwell, matters reached a crisis in the English Civil War of 1642–46, ending in the defeat of the king. Archbishop Laud was executed in 1645 and the king in 1649. The great rift, which Elizabeth had tried so hard to avoid, was now a fact. After the death of Cromwell, the Stuart kings were returned to the throne in the "Restoration" of 1660. A strict Anglicanism was enforced again. Separatists like the Puritans or Baptists or Quakers (lumped together under the name "nonconformists") were threatened and looked to the colonies again. In 1656, Quakers arrived in the American colonies, eventually settling in Pennsylvania. William Penn arrived in 1682. Methodism began in 1729 with the Anglicans John and Charles Wesley—stressing evangelization and social justice—and found fertile ground in the American colonies. This was also Presbyterian in structure.

Ireland

Ireland was difficult to convert to the Reformation because it was an island. Scotland, especially in the south, and Wales were closer and more vulnerable to English influence. Ireland was also poorer. Penal laws and fines, so devastating to the Catholic nobility of England, had less effect in Ireland. The pope was also more interested in Ireland. While Henry VIII claimed to be king of Ireland in 1541, and appointed bishops, the popes appointed rival bishops and these, in some cases, managed to depose the king's appointments. Finally, Catholicism became increasingly associated with nationhood and national identity.

Oliver Cromwell intensified the process of suppressing Catholicism in Ireland, both by law (priests and Mass were forbidden) and by the displacement of planters, especially in the east and north. But once he was gone, Catholicism quickly resurfaced, so much so that Bishop Oliver Plunkett, by the late 1600s, complained about the high number of religious order priests who had nothing to do but beg.

France

France remained Catholic because the Crown remained Catholic (unlike England and the principalities of Germany), and defeated the opposition (unlike Scotland). Protestantism in France was centered in the east, along the Swiss and German borders. It bore a particularly Puritan stamp. French Protestants were known as Huguenots, after a medieval King Hugo.

Religious tensions rose in France and resulted in one very ugly event, the St. Bartholomew's Day Massacre in 1572, where Protestants were attacked by Catholics. The massacre is still debated today—was it a spontaneous act of violence, or was it planned by the Catholic government? The best answer seems to be that it was mostly spontaneous, but that the government did little to prevent it from happening, once it had begun. In some places, the government seems to have openly encouraged the violence. Religious tension remained until Henry IV (of Navarre) took over and enacted the Edict of Nantes in 1598, which granted religious toleration. But the Reformation would really come to France with the French Revolution, which was both the end of the Reformation period and the beginning of the modern age.

Germany

In Germany, so divided was the country that wars of religion dragged on in the Thirty Years War (1618–48). This finally ended in a compromise solution, called the Treaty of Westphalia, in which the phrase *cujus regio ejus religio* became the working arrangement whereby Germans determined their religion. If the ruling prince was of a particular religion, be it Lutheran or Roman Catholic, everyone in his region would belong to that religion. One either conformed or moved to another area.

The Catholic Response

How was the Roman Church to react to all of the above? It had been decimated in the Scandinavian countries, in Germany, in Switzerland, in England, Scotland, and Wales. Monasteries and dioceses and wealth and power simply ceased to exist in vast areas of Western Europe. Some considerable reaction was necessary if the Roman Church was to survive.

Pope Paul III (Alexander Farnese, 1534–49) led the way. He was not the likeliest candidate, but provided a real look at what the papacy would go through in one generation. He was not known to be a holy man himself and had a mistress who bore him four children before he was ordained to the priesthood, yet while he was holding several important church positions. He had risen to be treasurer of the local church in Rome, was made a cardinal-deacon by Pope Alexander VI, and was known as "Cardinal

Petticoat" because his sister Giulia was the pope's mistress. But, having been made bishop of Parma, he underwent a remarkable conversion, ending his relationship with his mistress and joining the reform party. He maintained a strange combination of reforming instincts with Renaissance display—building the Farnese Palace, hiring Michelangelo to paint the Last Judgment in the Sistine Chapel, funding lavish festivals in the city, and giving the red hat to two of his grandchildren. But he had a sense of what was wrong with the Catholic Church and the desire to do something about it.

First of all, Paul III confirmed several new religious orders. The Capuchins were already in place, having been founded in 1529.[24] He confirmed the first order of teaching women known as the Ursulines in 1544. They had been founded by Angela Merici a few years earlier and would soon have some 500 religious houses and tens of thousands of professed women.[25]

St. Ignatius Loyola and the Society of Jesus

The other significant religious order approved by Paul was the Society of Jesus, founded by Ignatius of Loyola (1491–1556) in 1540. Ignatius was a soldier when he was injured in 1521. While recuperating, he read a *Life of Christ* and the *Lives of the Saints* and then decided to give up everything to the service of the church. He was strongly influenced by the *Imitation of Christ*, and began to write his *Spiritual Exercises*. The aim of the *Exercises* was strictly practical: to strip the mind of all distractions, place it face-to-face with the ultimate issues of Christian life, to arrive at a decision, and then to choose a way of life best suited to fitting that response. The whole orientation of the *Exercises* is directed toward a personal decision and dedication to the service of God. The *Exercises* begin with the individual. In some ways, they were a response to Protestantism's emphasis on the individual, on being saved, or on making Christ one's personal Lord and Savior. Anyone who played an important role in the Catholic Reformation made these *Exercises*.

Ignatius supported this with a commitment of his own. In founding the Society of Jesus, he desired it to be adaptable to new challenges in the missions and in education. This was a revolution in religious life: there was to be no habit, no choral office, and no common life. Ignatius regarded these as impediments to the demands of the post-Reformation church, tying one down to communities, and limiting one's mobility and adaptability. By the time Ignatius died in 1556, the Society had 1000 members and twelve provinces, and would be the most influential religious order for the church's reform in the next 400 years.

Council of Trent (1545–63)

Paul III brought several influential Catholic reformers to Rome and made them cardinals: Reginald Pole, Marcello Cervini, Giovanni Carafa, and Gasparo Contarini, among others. They issued a report in 1537 that became the foundation for the work of the Council of Trent. Paul then convoked a council in June of 1536. There were two immediate problems: No one thought Paul III was serious; and the kings of England, France, and Spain did not want such a council to take place because they did not want a well-organized church that was not under their strict control.

Getting the council started was no small feat. Mantua was finally agreed on as a site. It was outside the Papal States, which meant that Protestant reformers (who were invited) would feel safe to come. The King of France, Francis I, backed out, because it was in an area under the control of Charles V, the Emperor of Germany (and coincidentally the King of Spain). Vicenza was substituted, but no one came except the pope's three legates. In May 1539 it was prorogued to an unspecified date. In September 1541 the Emperor proposed Trent. In November 1542 it was supposed to begin, but war broke out again between France and Spain. In March 1545 it was scheduled to open for the second time, but again, no one showed up except the papal legates. All obstacles were finally overcome and the Council opened on 13 December 1545.

The first problem was to establish an agenda. There was no order of business. The hoped-for participation of Protestants delayed all debates on doctrine. But work was soon underway. All bishops could vote, as well as all heads of mendicant orders, and two abbots from monastic congregations. These voting numbers

Sts. Ignatius Loyola (1491–1556) and Teresa of Avila (1515–1582) made significant contributions during the Catholic Reformation. Ignatius, a former soldier, founded the Society of Jesus (Jesuits), which became a great force for Catholic education, and Teresa, a Carmelite nun and one of the great mystics, brought about badly needed reforms in her religious order.

kept changing. At the beginning of December, there were only twenty-nine bishops and five heads of orders. By mid-June the numbers were up to sixty-six, but down to fifty in the autumn. By the following January, the number of bishops was up to almost seventy.[26] The idea of a council was catching on.

The method of the Council of Trent was to establish "particular" congregations, where theologians debated the issues before the bishops (which served to educate the bishops), and "general" congregations, where bishops met alone and approved final texts. The two main issues disputed were discipline and doctrine. Under discipline, the bishop attempted to correct the abuses so publicized by reformers such as Erasmus. They even wanted to underline this by making Erasmus a cardinal, but he declined. One pressing issue was the plurality of benefices. This abuse was a great scandal and a serious problem. Those with more than one benefice had to resign them.[27] A related issue was residency, which would now be enforced. Money issues were also addressed. Bishops could no longer tax a parish for visitation; this was part of their job. They were forbidden to receive gifts. The clergy could no longer provide for family out of church funds. Indulgences could not be purchased. Excommunication was to be used less frequently and not at the request of princes.

The priesthood was of particular concern to the council. It was especially forthright here, calling the clergy "the dregs," which, if true, was mostly the fault of the bishops themselves. They sought to ensure the education of their clergy by establishing special colleges, which would be close to the bishop, where it was his responsibility to educate his priests. The recruitment of future priests was now to concentrate on poor boys who would then be assigned to take care of the poor. They should be at least twelve years old, literate, and legitimate. This last proscription was to prevent priests from sending their illegitimate sons into seminaries and thus to address the issue of concubinage at the same time. The spiritual life of the clergy was legislated: priests were to celebrate Mass every day, go to confession every month, and to assist at the cathedral on major feasts. Mass (chantry) priests were discouraged by limiting the number of Masses a priest could say each day to one. Problem priests were to be dismissed.

The Council of Trent took place over eighteen years, and the increased attendance of bishops indicates that it was producing results even as it was going on. At Sessions 1–10 (December 1545 to June 1547), 29–68 bishops were in attendance. In Sessions 11–17 (May 1551 to May 1552), there were 44–51 bishops, and in Sessions 18–25 (1562–63), 105–228 bishops!

Under doctrine, the council's aim was to clear the air and end a period of uncertainty. Canon I read:

> If anyone shall deny that the body and blood, together with the soul and divinity of Christ, are truly, really, and substantially in the Eucharist; and shall say that He is only in it as a sign, or symbol—let him be anathema.

You might disagree with that, but at least you knew where you stood. The whole Catholic world was now united. French Jesuits working in the St. Lawrence River basin and Spanish Dominicans working in the Baja Peninsula were teaching the same things.

By 1600 the state of the clergy had improved noticeably. Even by the end of the third session, the type of bishop had altered as well, as can be seen by the numbers attending. Trent had no effect in Protestant countries. Division had come to stay. The best the council could do was clean its own house. In some ways, it had little effect in France and Spain, because their respective governments had much control over the church. Spain, under Cardinal Ximenes, was carrying out its own reform independent of (and prior to) Trent. France never promulgated the decrees of Trent, which effectively meant that the Council of Trent never happened for the French.

Cultural Directions Resulting from the Reformation

In the world of art, the Protestant Reformation was catastrophic. A staggering amount of medieval art was destroyed. One art historian recently remarked that art history can best be defined as "Jewish professors teaching Protestant students about Roman Catholicism." Nor did the Protestant world recover. Kenneth Clark, a Protestant at the time and curator of the National Gallery in London, claimed in his *Civilisation* series that he had never found a single piece of art inspired by the Protestant Reformation. In fact, art became more secular. The household themes of Vermeer began to supplant religious and scriptural themes of medieval and Renaissance artists. Many artists in Protestant countries (e.g., Rubens) would travel to Catholic countries for work.

Architecturally, this was not the case. While Protestants did not need to build new structures—they simply took over existing Catholic churches and converted them for Protestant service—there did appear the "Quaker meeting house" and the more important New England Congregational church, a white clapboard structure with a modest belfry, plain glass, and simple furnishings. Catholics went to other extremes. Renaissance art exploded into the magnificent baroque and its extreme, the rococo. Furnishings became spectacular and proportions became immense. The interior of St. Peter's Basilica in Rome is a good example.

Music was a different matter. Protestants, because of their insistence on the vernacular, created psalm-singing in local languages and wrote hymns based on the psalms. Hymnbooks were now called the *Geneva Psalter* and the *Scottish Psalter*. Some composers wrote for *both* Protestant and Catholic patrons—depending on who paid them. Thomas Tallis made the transition from being an organist in a monastery to being the organist at the Royal Chapel, writing in both Latin and English. His brilliant student, William Byrd, remained a devout Roman Catholic and yet wrote extensively for Queen Elizabeth in English. Heinrich Schütz and, later, the great Johann Sebastian Bach, wrote sacred music in both Latin and German. Bach's cantatas and Passions in German broke new ground.

Catholic music in the post-Reformation period tended to focus on the Latin texts of the liturgy, often expanding on plainchant melodies. Palestrina is regarded as the high point of this kind of music. Gabrieli, Monteverdi, Boccherini, and Pergolesi were giants in this as well. Because Protestants did not pray for the dead—Brahms, in the nineteenth century, wrote a brilliant "requiem" of sorts, in German, but it is simply a collection of consoling biblical texts put to music and not a requiem in the strict sense—requiem music was usually written for the Latin Mass. Thus, Catholics in the Classical and Romantic periods, such as Mozart, Fauré, and eventually Verdi, wrote Requiem Masses, although they did not restrict their sacred music to Latin.

Conclusions

Protestantism

Protestant reformers shook the Christian world from its complacency. They focused on the word of Scripture and on morality. Christianity became for them something very literary. Reading from Scripture, especially Paul, became central. Beautiful translations of the Bible, especially that of Luther in

German and of the King James Version in English, set the standard for language for centuries to come. So ingrained has the King James Version become in the English-speaking world that, when one Iowa town had a debate about introducing foreign language studies into the local high school curriculum, one angry parent rose up and said, "If English was good enough for Jesus Christ, it should be good enough for my children." Sermons were indispensable to the Protestant minister, and could no longer be ignored or fobbed off on preaching friars.

Protestants gave up a lot in doing this. Some of them may have claimed the fathers of the church as theirs, but they needed to be selective. Calvin looked to Augustine as his model, but he needed to ignore Augustine's sacramental theology and practice, as well as Augustine's exaltation of the priesthood. Protestant reformers literally closed their eyes to roughly 1400 years of rich Christian (and human) tradition. The Middle Ages became denigrated as a time of superstition and ignorance, where they were anything but. Protestants also gave up a religious unity that was impressive and important. From now on Protestant denominations would multiply and split. Some progress has been recently made toward unification—some denominations have signed agreements over intercommunion—but these agreements tend to stress the importance of fellowship and sharing rather than clarity in definitions about doctrinal matters such as the Eucharist. Doctrine has been replaced by social action or togetherness. Other issues, such as homosexuality, threaten to cause even further divides.

Roman Catholicism

The Reformation affected the Roman Catholic Church in two ways. First, it forced the church to get serious about reform. There was now an urgency for action. With Trent and the foundation of new religious orders, the Roman Catholic Church experienced a tremendous revival in several significant areas: in spirituality, attention was now given to the individual and to a revival of mysticism (especially under the influence of two Carmelites, Teresa of Avila and John of the Cross, as well as

Francis de Sales); in education, clerics would now be better schooled and the education of the laity was also improved by the proliferation of secondary schools; higher studies (history, philosophy and theology) were reinvigorated. There emerged a unity which became evident especially in mission lands.

But secondly, the Catholic Church became somewhat defensive. Any reform movement that had been going forward before the Reformation became suspect. Cardinal Quinones had begun a revision of the breviary in Spain that would not really be completed until the 1970s! Scripture reading became suspect. Any proposals to put the Mass into vernacular translations would not be taken up again until the Second Vatican Council. In other words, if Protestants promoted something, Catholics tended to avoid doing it. This is understandable, but would delay the cause of some real reform for four centuries.

The Missions (1500–1800)

During the Renaissance mission activity was at an ebb, but with the discovery of the New World in 1492 and sea routes to the east, mission activity increased immediately and rather spectacularly. The Spanish, because they were the pioneers in most exploration, also saw their missionaries at work one hundred years before those of other countries. The first diocese in the west was founded at Santo Domingo (1511). In 1519 Cortez had made contact with the Aztecs, and had subdued them by 1521. In 1531 Pizarro entered Inca territory in Peru; in five years he was master of the whole area. In area, Spain controlled all of South America except Brazil (in the possession of Portugal) and Central America, and a significant portion of the North American southwest.

In the east, the Jesuit Francis Xavier was already in India (Goa) by 1542 and in Japan by 1549. Reports tell us that there were 200,000 Catholics in Japan less than forty years later. So great was the spread of Christianity and so threatening to the government of Japan that a persecution began in the late 1500s to reestablish the status quo. Several Christians were martyred in Nagasaki in 1597, and Japan would remain closed to the west for

Book by Bartolomé de las Casas. Bartolomé de las Casas (1484 – 1566), born in Spain and appointed first Bishop of Chiapas in Guatemala, campaigned fearlessly against the treatment of the native people by the Spanish colonists. His "Concerning the Only Way of Drawing All Peoples to the True Religion" was one of his several works insisting that the Indians be regarded and treated as rational human beings.

another two hundred years. Jesuits were successful (at least initially) in the east because they knew science and were willing to adapt to local customs. In Vietnam, the Jesuit De Rhodes showed the ruler a chime clock and gave a talk on mathematics and, as a result, was allowed to open a church in Hanoi.

Sometimes the Jesuits were too successful. When De Rhodes preached the necessity of monogamy, he angered Vietnamese concubines and multiple wives, and he was expelled. The willingness to adapt to local customs was also regarded with suspicion by a Tridentine Rome that was looking to ensure unity of worship. In China, the Jesuit Matteo Ricci attempted to integrate ancestor worship somewhere into the sphere of Catholic liturgy. He was reported to Rome in 1631 by a Franciscan and a Dominican, in a rare display of solidarity, and was told to stop. Essentially this meant that converts needed to become "European." It was not until 1939 that official permission was given to adapt local customs to Catholic worship. Vatican II's decision on the use of the vernacular in the liturgy made this adaptation into a positive policy.

Western nations had mixed reactions to missionaries working in their colonies. While the missionaries could help the parent country by teaching the mother tongue and "subduing" the natives, missionaries could also advocate better treatment of the native population. The colonizing countries did not want missionaries creating a separate society of natives. Spaniards and French wanted the natives to become good Spaniards and Frenchmen and willing allies in war while the missionaries increasingly sought to segregate the natives in order to preserve their cultures and protect them from the influence of alcohol and firearms.

The race was to grab as much land as possible, as many riches, and sometimes (in the case of Spain) as many converts. Spain, almost alone among the colonizing powers, was conscious of making converts to its religion. France did not care particularly what its missionaries did as long as they did not interfere with its policies of colonization. England wanted to make sure only that colonists did not become Roman Catholic. Anything else would do.

Spanish Colonization in the New World

Spain was united in its Catholicism and was at a religious peak. The Muslims had been finally defeated (1492) after more than 400 years of conflict, the Spanish Inquisition was attempting to enforce religious unity, the Holy See had granted the crown power of clerical appointment, and Spain was, unquestionably, the strongest Catholic country in Europe. Its close ties to the church led it to provide salaries, supplies, buildings, and protection in the colonies in exchange for the missionaries "civilizing" natives, making converts, and making conquest possible and permanent. Tensions arose over authority and slavery. The Spanish government looked on natives as less than human. Missionaries tended to differ, sometimes emphatically.

One Dominican, Bartolomeo de Las Casas (1474–1566), made a nuisance of himself by appealing to the crown to end the system of *encomienda* and slavery. *Encomienda* was a system of isolating the natives. While well-intentioned—the missionaries supported some isolation—the Spanish version amounted to communities of slaves. When the explorer Pizarro was asked to relieve this situation, he replied, "I have come to take away from them their gold." This system was ended by the king, largely through the intervention of Las Casas, who returned to Spain to plead the cause of the Indians in 1515.

The number of baptisms could be staggering—Peter of Ghent (a Franciscan) wrote:

> I and the brother who was with me baptized in this province of Mexico upwards of 200,000 persons—so many in fact that I cannot give an accurate estimate of the number. Often we baptized in a single day 14,000 people, sometimes 10,000, sometimes 8,000.[28]

Spain's colonization of North America can be easily divided around the year 1700. Its eastern colonies (West Indies, Florida) were developed before 1700 and its western colonies (now the U.S. Southwest and California) were developed after 1700. New Orleans was the hinge. Spain made four major attempts to settle in Florida from the West Indies—all were frustrated, either by the native Seminole Indians or by English incursions from Georgia. There were more than twenty-one mission stations in Florida, beginning with St Augustine in 1565, the first parish in what is now the United States. By 1769, Spain had given up on Florida.

The western colonies (in what is now Texas, New Mexico, Arizona, and California) differed from Florida in that they were settled from Mexico. New Mexico had forty-two missions, with Sante Fe founded in 1609, and Texas had twenty-one.[29] By 1682, El Paso had become the major mission and the safest, owing to its proximity to Mexico. San Antonio de Valero (The Alamo) was founded in 1718. The five Franciscan missions around San Antonio remain a living example of how these missions were built and functioned. With the exception of the Alamo, which is a government museum, they are still active Catholic parishes and still have many of the native population as their parishioners today.

In much of the American Southwest, major obstacles slowed the work of the missionaries. Languages were difficult to learn and the nomadic nature of many of the western tribes made them wary of attempts to settle them on missions. There was an unpredictability about native conversions. One day the natives would accept baptism, and the next day they would slay the entire mission. In 1680, Pueblo Indians in New Mexico rose up and killed 400 Spanish, twenty-one of whom were friars.

Another factor that impeded the missionaries, was the very nature of colonization. The mother country was usually more interested in political and material gain and used the missionaries to further these ends. Missions were sometimes opened in order to stop the spread of another country's influence. Thus the Spanish missions in East Texas were opened as the French began to explore the southern Mississippi. The California missions were begun only after the Russian explorer Vitus Bering showed an interest in what is now Sonoma County.[30] Once these threats were overcome, the missions could be neglected by the mother country. Clearly, their role was confused. A further complication was that the mother country could be harsh to the native population. Conversions in the southwest of North America could be regarded by the Indians as acquiescence to slavery, since many natives were sent south into slavery after baptism.

The missions declined as the Indian population declined and simultaneously as the Americans encroached, immigrating illegally after the purchase of the Louisiana Territory in 1803. By the time Mexico became independent in 1821, most of the missionaries were gone and the church had to be rebuilt.

The California Missions

California was not settled by Spain until Florida was abandoned in 1769. There were twenty-one missions in California altogether, and their founder was the Franciscan Junipero Serra. San Diego was the first mission established in 1769. Monterey was the second in 1770, and the others soon followed: San Antonio (1771), San Gabriel (1771), San Luis Obispo (1772), etc. In the next fifty years there would be sixteen more foundations. Serra died in Monterey (San Carlos) in 1784. These missions served as the economic center of California. At the mission school, Indians were taught to be ranchers, shepherds, carpenters, blacksmiths, masons, and weavers. But the Indians did not adapt well to the Spanish work ethic and way of life, and lost a lot of their freedom: They could not leave the mission once they were baptized and were flogged for infractions and for trying to escape. By 1832, the missions in California were dead. The Spanish tried to convert it to a penal colony, but by 1834, the long-awaited secularization was to take place, with the missionaries turning control of land to Indians. Instead, the politicians divided the land among themselves (some families gained as much as 300,000 acres), and the Indians were simply turned loose. By 1847, California belonged to the fledgling United States, and a year later gold was discovered in the Sacramento Valley.

Generally speaking, the Spanish missions were an effort to Christianize and civilize the natives, not to eliminate them. There is some controversy today about whether the missionaries enslaved the native populations or were attempting to save what they could of native culture and life. If the natives did not accommodate themselves to some degree to their conquerors, they were in danger of being eliminated. That would be left to the Americans.

French Missions

The French did not have religious unity at home. Huguenots (French Protestants) were at odds with the Catholic Church. Within the church itself there were three main factions: Gallicans, Jesuits, and Jansenists. In the early 1600s, the mathematician Blaise Pascal wrote his famous *Provincial Letters*, brilliantly denouncing the Jesuits as being "casuists." This meant that the Jesuits were lax and allowed "cases" or circumstances (or what we might call "situation ethics") to influence their moral theology. This feuding did not have an effect in French North America, where Jesuits were the principal missionaries, but did weaken the prestige of the Jesuits, making them popular targets and government scapegoats. They were eventually suppressed in France in 1764, and then by the pope in 1773 under pressure from the governments of France, Spain, and Portugal. The major complaints about the Jesuits were that they were powerful and rich, and that their system of education was too religious and antiquated. In fact, the Jesuits posed a serious threat to autocratic governments and, thus, had to go.[31]

France attempted to colonize North America first under Jacques Cartier, who was promised supplies and people for a permanent colony as early as 1541, the third time Cartier crossed the Atlantic. But hostilities between France and Spain ended any

The Acadians of Grand Pré

The French of Nova Scotia were expelled in 1755 by order of the military governor. His order read "That your lands & tennements Cattle of all Kinds and Live Stock of all Sortes are Forfitted to the Crown with all other your Effects Saving your Money & Household Goods and you your Selves to be removed from this his Province." The French moved to Maine and Louisiana, where they are known to us as "Cajuns," or back to France.

thought of a permanent colony until 1562, when a Huguenot leader, Admiral Gaspard de Coligny, attempted to settle Huguenots in Florida in response to Spain's encroachment there. This colony (Fort Caroline on the St. John's River) was destroyed by the Spanish within three years. Finally the explorer Samuel de Champlain founded Quebec in 1608. A few years before, several Jesuit missionaries had established a mission in Nova Scotia, but were killed or captured by the English on Mount Desert Island as they tried to relocate further south to what is now Bangor, Maine. This was an inauspicious start to the French colonial mission effort, and would prove typical.

Franciscans supplied the initial missionary thrust in Canada, saying the first Mass in Quebec on 24 June 1615, the feast of John the Baptist, which to this day is the patronal feast of French Canada. But the Franciscan effort failed due to lack of numbers on their part and a contemplative mode of life ill suited to missionary work. Jesuits were called in. France's colonies stretched from the St. Lawrence River Valley, through the Great Lakes, and across the Illinois country, eventually moving down the Mississippi. One of their great explorers was a Jesuit priest named Jacques Marquette.

Maine

In what is now Maine, the French missions were caught in the middle between an anticlerical French government and the hostile English. After the Peace of 1726, these missions never revived. Missionary fervor had passed, the French government had opposed segregating natives (something the missionaries saw as necessary to their survival as Christians), and the English had imposed anti-clerical laws. England claimed this area, which was peopled by Abenaki Indians and the French. The Jesuit Sebastien Râle, who had worked there, tried organizing the Indians, and a price was put on his head. In 1724, a combined Mohawk and New England raid attacked an Abenaki village, where Râle was killed. His scalp was soon paraded in Boston.

New York

In what is now New York State, the French were caught between the Hurons, whom they favored, and the Five Iroquois Nations. The Jesuit Fathers, Isaac Jogues, Jean de Brébeuf, and several others, were tortured and murdered in the 1640s. Their mission could be said to have been a failure, although it produced a remarkable correspondence between the missionaries and their superiors in Rome. Years later, the governor of New York, Thomas Dongan, despite being an Irish Catholic, worked actively to have the French and their missionaries leave the colony. The French missions failed because of the dependence of the church on the state, and the state was both incompetent and uninterested. In 1760, France surrendered to England on the St. Lawrence River.

English Missions

English Catholics came to North America in order to escape the penal laws. In England they could not vote nor hold public office; they could not worship in public or in private; they could not send their children to school either at home or abroad; they could not live within five miles of London, etc. Of the thirteen English colonies in North America, only Maryland and Pennsylvania had any appreciable numbers of Roman Catholics. They were greatly outnumbered even in those colonies. In Maryland in 1708, only one out of eleven people was a Catholic. In Pennsylvania in 1750, only one in two hundred was Catholic.

Martyrdom of Isaac Jogues. St. Isaac Jogues (1607–1646), a Jesuit priest, and his fellow missionaries endured fearful hardships in their endeavors to convert the native peoples of the wilderness in present-day northern New York State. The first white person to lay eyes on Lake George, Fr. Jogues was tortured and martyred by an Iroquois chief near Auriesville, N.Y.

By 1785, there were four million people in the United States; only 25,000 were Catholic.

Maryland

George Calvert had been a highly ranked official under the Stuart King James I. In 1624, however, he converted to Catholicism and resigned from his government post and his seat in Parliament. King James, to his credit, named Calvert Lord Baltimore and maintained him on his Privy Council. Calvert sought from the new king and his son, Charles I, a grant to begin a colony in what would be called Maryland, so named after the wife of Charles I, Henrietta Maria. He did not live to see his dream realized, but the grant passed to his son Cecil.

Two ships sailed amidst considerable drama in November 1633. Catholics boarded downriver to avoid detection. Then sailors attempted to report the presence of two Jesuit priests on board, when the captain ordered the passenger ship (the *Ark*) to cast off. The two ships (the supply ship was the *Dove*[32]) became separated almost immediately in a storm and did not see each other again until they arrived within days of each other in Barbados.

Calvert's attempt was aimed at religious toleration. Catholics, the minority of the two hundred to three hundred passengers, went out of their way to appease the Protestants. They were told to hold services in private and not to engage in conversations about religion. When the ships arrived on St. Clement's Island, both a Mass and a Protestant service were held in thanksgiving. Religious toleration was the practice of the colony from the start, some say from far-sightedness and a genius to avoid the mistakes of the past and provide Christians with a free atmosphere in which to practice their religion; others (e.g., Sydney Ahlstrom, the historian of American Protestantism) say from necessity: that it was the only way the colony could continue with crown approval, and attract new immigration.

No matter what the motives, many Catholics flocked to Maryland. But persecutions would dog them even there. The fortunes of their coreligionists in England were mirrored in the fortunes of the Maryland colony. In 1642, civil war in England brought Oliver Cromwell and the Puritan party to power. The Puritans, who had previously sought asylum in Maryland from the Virginia Anglicans, and who had taken shelter in Annapolis (then called Providence), took over the administration of the state. They did not wait long to renew the persecution of Catholics. Leonard Calvert, the first governor of Maryland, was forced to flee to Virginia, and in 1645 the Jesuit Fathers Andrew White and Copley were sent back to England in chains, there to be charged with entering England illegally because they were priests.

But an extraordinary thing happened. In 1646, Calvert fought his way back to power, but died soon after. His successor in England, Baron Baltimore, then sent an amazing document to the Maryland legislature, the majority of whom were Roman Catholics, which was passed on 21 April 1649: the "Act of Toleration," which granted religious toleration to all Christians. It read in part:

> Noe person or persons whatsoever within this Province…professing to believe in Jesus Christ, shall from henceforth bee any waies troubled, Molested or discountenanced for or in respect of his or her religion nor in the free exercise thereof…nor any way compelled to the belief or exercise of any other Religion against his or her consent.

It had never been tried before. Oliver Cromwell, however, had other ideas. In 1651 he appointed commissioners to implement his policy of forcing Chesapeake Bay settlements to comply with the new regime in England. In 1655 a Puritan victory in Maryland guaranteed a continuance of persecution for Catholics, but all was to change again in 1658, when Cromwell died and his ineffective son took over in England. In 1660 the Stuarts were back on the throne, Baron Baltimore was restored to his proprietary rights, and the Act of Toleration reinstated.

In 1688 the Stuarts were overthrown in the Glorious Revolution, which put William of Orange on the throne of England. Ripple effects were felt as always in the colonies, and Baltimore was replaced in 1691. In 1692 the Church of England was established as the official church of the colony and Catholic disabilities returned until the American Revolution. The capital was moved from St. Mary's City to the heavily Protestant Annapolis in 1696. Roughly speaking, what happened in England eventually happened in the American colonies. From 1718 to 1775, Catholics could not vote in Maryland. In 1715 a law was passed permitting children of a Protestant father and a Roman Catholic mother to be taken from their mother on the father's death. We will see later why this penal legislation ended as a result of the American Revolution.

The End of the Fifth Age

The Fifth Age of the Church was at an end. Events were taking place in France that would change the world forever. The Enlightenment was in full swing in the eighteenth century. It was the result of advances in science and mathematics, new ideas about liberty and democracy, and an overriding cynicism about organized religion. The pursuit of happiness would end with the French Revolution. From its ashes would arise the modern world, and a very different church.

Chronology of the Reformation

1509 Henry VIII becomes the King of England at age 18
1517 Luther posts his Ninety-Five Theses
1518 Cajetan interviews Luther at the Diet of Augsburg
1519 Johannes Eck debates Luther (the Leipzig Disputations)
1520 Luther writes "To the German Nobility" and "The Babylonian Captivity of the Church"
1521 Luther is excommunicated
1522 Zwingli resigns from the priesthood
1532 Cranmer appointed Archbishop of Canterbury
1532 Act of Submission of the Clergy (England)
1533 Cranmer grants a divorce to Henry VIII
       Five days later, on 28 May, Henry marries Anne Boleyn
1533 Elizabeth is born on 7 Sept
1534 Act of Supremacy (England)

1535 Thomas More and Bishop John Fisher executed
1536 Catherine of Aragon buried (29 Jan); Anne Boleyn miscarries a son on the same day
1536 Anne Boleyn executed (19 May)
1536 Act of Dissolution of the Smaller Monasteries (England)
1536 Calvin comes to Geneva
1539 Act of Dissolution of Greater Monasteries
1540 Thomas Cromwell executed
1540 Society of Jesus approved
1544 Ursulines approved (first order of teaching nuns)
1545 Council of Trent begins
1547 Henry dies, Edward VI is king
1548 (4 Feb) Act abolishing various sacramentals
      (21 Feb) Royal order for destruction of images and
         pictures
      (8 Mar) New rite for Holy Communion (in English,
         denies Real Presence)
1549 First Prayer Book
1550 All altars to be destroyed; tables to replace them
1553 Forty-two Articles (later the Thirty-Nine Articles)
1553 (6 July) Edward VI dies; Mary Tudor becomes Queen
1554 Mary married to King Philip II of Spain
1554 Papal obedience restored
1556 Cranmer burned for heresy
1558 (17 Nov) Mary and Cardinal Pole die on the same day;
         Elizabeth becomes queen
1559 Act of Supremacy, Act of Uniformity restored
1560 Scottish Parliament takes over running of the church
1560 Mary Stuart lands in Scotland at 18
1563 The Council of Trent ends
1568 Mary Queen of Scots flees Scotland, is imprisoned
1570 Elizabeth excommunicated by Pius V
1572 (23–24 Aug) St. Bartholomew's Day Massacre (France)
1580 The Jesuits Edmund Campion and Robert Persons arrive
1587 Mary Queen of Scots executed
1588 The Spanish Armada defeated
1603 Elizabeth dies, James I (Stuart) becomes king
1605 Gunpowder Plot

Recommended Readings

(B) Peter Ackroyd, *The Life of Sir Thomas More* (New York, 1998).

(A) Robert Hugh Benson, *Come Rack! Come Rope!* (New York, 1910). This is probably Benson's best book. It is a historical novel about the struggles of the missionary priests (and their families) in Elizabeth's England.

(A) Robert Hugh Benson, *The King's Achievement* (London, 1904). A historical novel about Henry VIII's dissolution of the English monasteries.

(A) Robert Hugh Benson, *The Queen's Tragedy* (London, 1906). A historical novel about Catholic life under Elizabeth.

(B) Christopher Dawson, *The Dividing of Christendom* (New York, 1965). A very good one-volume history of the Reformation as a whole.

(C) Eamon Duffy, *The Stripping of the Altars* (New Haven, 1992). A masterpiece detailing what was lost at the English Reformation.

(B) Eamon Duffy, *The Voices of Morebath: Reformation and Rebellion in an English Village* (New Haven, 2001). Explains how the Reformation affected a typical English village.

(B) John Tracy Ellis, *Catholics in Colonial America* (Baltimore, 1965). Great detail on the Spanish, French, and English missionary efforts in the Americas.

(B) Antonia Fraser, *Mary Queen of Scots* (New York, 1969). Still the most readable life of this troubled queen.

(B) Antonia Fraser, *Faith and Treason* (New York, 1996). The story of the Gunpowder Plot of 1605. Superbly done.

(B) Edwin Jones, *The English Nation: The Great Myth* (Thrupp, England, 1998). A new look at how English historical writing (especially about the Reformation) has perpetuated some very wrong ideas.

(C) David Knowles, *The Religious Orders in England*, Vol. III (Cambridge, 1959). Recounts the dissolution of the English monasteries. Superb.

(C) Diarmaid MacCulloch, *The Reformation: A History* (New York, 2004). This could be the standard work on the subject for many years.

(B) Michael Mallett, *The Borgias* (Chicago, 1987). The first half of the book—dealing with the Renaissance papacy and the Papal States—is especially interesting.

(C J. J. Scarisbrick, *Henry VIII* (Berkeley, 1968). Still considered to be the definitive biography.

(B) Evelyn Waugh, *Edmund Campion* (London, 1935). A biography of the foremost Jesuit in England during the Reformation by one of England's foremost Catholic novelists.

AUDIO-VISUALS:

Black Robe. A feature-length film about the Jesuit mission on the St. Lawrence River. Based on a novel of the same name by Brian Moore.

Civilisation, by Kenneth Clark, episodes 5–9. BBC, 1969.

Elizabeth R. BBC, 1975. A three-part series.

A Man for All Seasons. Oscar-winning film based on play by Robert Bolt.

The Mission. A feature-length film about the Jesuit mission in Paraguay. Screenplay by Robert Bolt.

The Wives of Henry VIII. BBC, 1970. A highly acclaimed series.

Notes

1. Christopher Dawson, *The Dividing of Christendom* (New York, 1965), p. 47.
2. St. Thomas Aquinas, for example, did not believe in the Immaculate Conception. His concern was that it made the Blessed Mother's salvation somewhat unnecessary.
3. 200 years *later* the primate of Ireland, Oliver Plunkett, found in favor of the Dominicans in a turf battle. The three chief witnesses against Plunkett at his trial for treason were Franciscan friars.
4. Ludwig von Pastor, *The History of the Popes from the Close of the Middle Ages*, vol. 5 (St. Louis, 1898), p. 233.
5. Michael Mallett, *The Borgias: The Rise and Fall of a Renaissance Dynasty* (Chicago, 1987), p. 4.
6. A. G. Dickens, *Reformation and Society in Sixteenth-Century Europe* (London, 1966), p. 37.
7. Ibid., p. 38.

8. In Peter Ackroyd, *The Life of St. Thomas More* (New York, 1998), p. 227.

9. Ibid., p. 230.

10. G. K. Chesterton, *Thomas Aquinas* (New York, 1933), p. 244.

11. Hubert Jedin and John Dolan, eds., *History of the Church*, vol. 5 (Reformation and Counter-Reformation), p. 34.

12. Jacques Maritain, *Three Reformers* (London, 1928), p. 6.

13. Maritain, p. 34. Maritain provides even more embarrassing quotes from Luther's *Table Talks*.

14. In Jedin and Dolan, p. 68.

15. Jedin and Dolan, p. 139.

16. Ibid., p. 142.

17. When Thomas More was jailed, his manors and estates went to the crown, and one estate (to rub salt in his wound) went to George Boleyn, the father of Anne.

18. Ackroyd, pp. 342–43.

19. Aidan Gasquet, *Henry VIII and the Dissolution of the English Monasteries* (London, 1888–89), vol. 2, pp. 43–44.

20. At Downside Abbey there is a pre-Reformation altar (a rare thing) found in someone's back yard and used for generations as part of a cattle trough.

21. Diarmaid MacCulloch, *Thomas Cranmer: A Life* (New Haven, 1996), p. 484.

22. Elizabeth learned from this and changed the issue to one of treason.

23. Oliver Cromwell's body, which had been buried in Westminster Abbey, was disinterred and hung at Tyburn.

24. The Franciscans split in 1517 into Observants and Conventuals, and the Capuchins split in 1529 from the Observants.

25. Religious orders are normally founded and functioning for a few years before Rome confirms them. Paul also approved the Barnabites and the Calmodolese.

26. Three-fourths of the bishops were Italian; the only other sizable group was Spanish.

27. This abuse was not completely wiped out until the 1960s, when Paul VI ordered Bishop O'Hara to choose between being apostolic delegate and Bishop of St Augustine, Florida.

28. Stephen Neill, *A History of Christian Missions* (New York, 1986), p. 168.

29. See Willa Cather, *Death Comes for the Archbishop* (New York, 1929) and Paul Horgan, *Lamy of Sante Fe, His Life and Times* (New York, 1975).

30. He was actually Danish, but was working for the Russians.

31. See Chapter 6 "The Fall of the Jesuits" in Owen Chadwick's *The Popes and European Revolution* (Oxford, 1981) for an excellent description of their demise.

32. A replica of the *Dove* can be seen today in St. Mary's City, Maryland.

THE SIXTH AGE OF THE CHURCH (1789–Present)

The Modern Age

The Enlightenment or the Age of Reason

Two great books heralded the Enlightenment or the Age of Reason. One was Isaac Newton's *Principia Mathematica* (1687), and the other was John Locke's *Essays on Human Understanding* (1690). Both authors thought that the world and humanity respectively could be explained by laws or mathematical formulations.

Galileo

Another mathematician who attracted attention was Galileo Galilei (1564–1642). He had the best telescope in the world and he supported Copernicus's theory that the earth moved around the sun. He was a good friend of the pope and used to let the pope look through his telescope. What got him into trouble was not his scientific study of the solar system, but rather his claim that the Bible might be wrong. Since Rome was paranoid about Protestantism and its claims that Rome was unscriptural, the pope was sensitive to any attacks on the Bible. And so Galileo was asked not to publish any more findings. He could not resist, and so was condemned. He was never imprisoned or tortured, but put under house arrest in Florence, where he died.

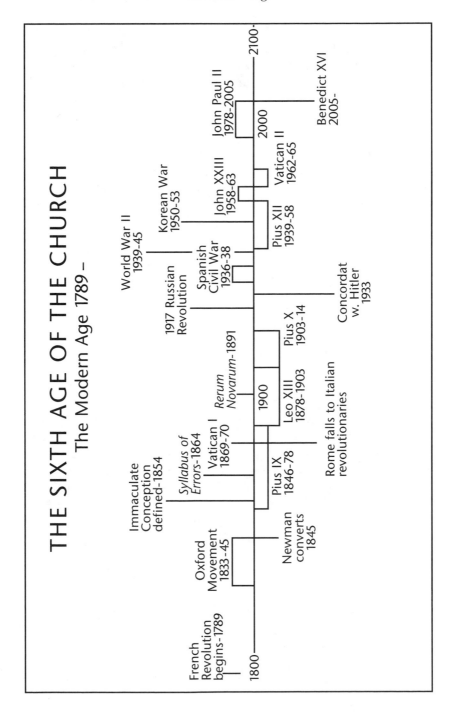

THE SIXTH AGE OF THE CHURCH
The Modern Age 1789 –

French Revolution begins -1789

Oxford Movement 1833-45

Newman converts 1845

Immaculate Conception defined -1854

Syllabus of Errors -1864

Vatican I 1869-70

Pius IX 1846-78

Rome falls to Italian revolutionaries

Rerum Novarum -1891

Leo XIII 1878-1903

Pius X 1903-14

1917 Russian Revolution

World War II 1939-45

Korean War 1950-53

Spanish Civil War 1936-38

Concordat w. Hitler 1933

Pius XII 1939-58

John XXIII 1958-63

Vatican II 1962-65

John Paul II 1978-2005

Benedict XVI 2005 –

1800

1900

2000

2100

259

Mathematics was on the rise. It was replacing philosophy, namely Aristotelianism, with its causes (final, efficient, material, and instrumental), matter-form, substance-accidents arguments, which was now giving way to experiment and observation, to that which could be measured and quantified. René Descartes and Blaise Pascal were both mathematicians and both had theories about how the world worked. So did Isaac Newton. Granted, how the world began and where it was going was still unknown in the late 1600s (as it is four hundred years later), but what it was *doing* could be known and measured. The mathematician, in other words, saw the world as a machine. And if it was a machine, it could not only be understood, but also improved. This was Newton's idea.

John Locke took this idea and applied it to the mind. He had the idea that he could explain thought as originating in sense experience. In doing this he wanted to combat the notion of "innate ideas," or intuition, or instinct. He saw the mind, rather, as a machine. The implication was the same as Newton's: If what went into the mind could be improved (via education), humanity would be more rational, happier, and better.

These theories led to optimism about the possibilities of improvement. If humans could understand how they and the world worked, they could control both. The human mind was sovereign. Kant said, "Dare to think." The mind had become a sophisticated computer that turned material into ideas. Mathematics (or the scientific method) was applied to ultimate questions. All aspects of reality that could not be reduced to mathematical formulations (e.g., religion) were treated as mere subjective impressions of the human mind and were written off as unsatisfactory. Religion thus became separated from science. Theology and philosophy (i.e., science) became two distinct, unrelated things. Protestant theology reinforced this, and may, in fact, have encouraged this way of thinking by its denigration of philosophy and its enthronement of Scripture Alone.

Christopher Dawson called the Enlightenment the "last of the great European heresies."[1] This was due to the fact that philosophers who followed Newton and Locke warred on anything that smacked of instinct, sentiment, feeling, intuition. They appealed to reason in such a way as to make the appeal to reason an act of faith, and they admitted of no criticism. Alfred North Whitehead, a twentieth-century mathematician and philosopher, noted, "While the Middles Ages were an age of faith based upon reason, the eighteenth century was an age of reason based upon faith." The Enlightenment retained some elements of Christianity—a belief in a beneficent creator, the idea of an over-ruling providence, chief precepts of moral law, a teleological con-ception of life (i.e., an afterlife), but they were coasting on Christianity and did not realize it. Progress became a mechanistic law of nature and, in some ways, a principal part of the new creed. If these *philosophes* had a religion, it would be called "deism." They believed in a God who created the universe and then sat back and has done nothing since—or what might be called natural religion, which was neither a formal nor very specific thing. Morality involved "the greatest good for the greatest number," and was not something based on divine law or on conformity to God's law or God's being. The economy was important in this. Adam Smith wrote *The Wealth of Nations* with the idea that free trade would eliminate nationalism and be productive of peace. Why should profits not be mutually beneficial, he asked. And how this all related to God was unimportant.

The *Philosophes*

There is no question that the *philosophes* were an extraordi-nary group of people. Despite the fact that they came from dif-ferent countries, they displayed an astonishing agreement about all sorts of topics. Their program was the freedom of people to make their own way in the world. They proposed "the pursuit of happiness," "liberty," and "equality" as ultimate ideals. They did not always mean what they said; when Thomas Jefferson died, he still owned 200 slaves.[2] But no matter what they thought or did, they knew what was right. In politics they sought to realize their ideals by advocating representative government with (white) male suffrage. They did not believe in original sin and thought it an invention by priests. People were essentially good and, if left to themselves, would be happy and virtuous. They detested asceti-cism with its self-denial and notions of making amends to God for sins committed. While they preached a libertinism, few of them led immoral lives. More characteristic of them was their commitment to work, to moderation, and to faithfulness. Their penchant for paganism stemmed from their affection for classical thought rather than classical sensuality.

The *philosophes* were descendants of Renaissance Men. They were popular and they were versatile. Adam Smith was an economist, moralist, and a political theorist. Diderot was a translator, editor, playwright, novelist, art critic, theorist, psychologist, classical scholar, and educational and ethical reformer. Thomas Jefferson was a political theorist, an amateur scientist, a remarkably accomplished architect, and an educational pioneer. While they were witty, they were humorless. They were driven, and did not tolerate jokes—especially about themselves. They could be extremely touchy, and when attacked from the outside, they closed ranks. While Voltaire could make enormous fun of the church and society in his *Candide*, he did not appreciate it when people made fun of him.

Possibly most important about these *philosophes* was their regard for the past. They saw it as divided into two periods, Classical and Medieval. The Classical period (Rome and Greece) supplied illustrious models and responsible ancestry, much like those cited in Machiavelli's *The Prince*. Jefferson, in fact, cited Machiavelli as a good model. The Classical period also represented reason. The Medieval period, on the other hand, was Christian and was associated with bigotry, superstition, and the Inquisition. Christianity became the adversary which had to be eliminated. History thus became a battle between reason, life, and philosophy against superstition and asceticism. One historian (Gilbert Burnet in 1693) boasted that he did not know anything about the Middle Ages because they were not worth knowing anything about! David Hume and Voltaire were no better. Edward Gibbon's magisterial *Decline and Fall of the Roman Empire* blamed Christians for the fall of the Empire. Classicism was taken for granted by the *philosophes*. If you were educated, you could read the classics, or fake it. You knew Latin and possibly Greek. Often enough, they looked to Epicurus—the master of the useful—or to the Stoics—self-reliant, contemptuous of death and superstition.

The Scottish city of Edinburgh, an amazingly prolific environment for the Enlightenment, was called the "Athens of the North." Scientific discoveries were made at its Royal Infirmary concerning blood serum and vaccinations, and industrial advances were proposed concerning steam. Even a reproduction of Athens's *Acropolis* was planned and begun on the hill overlooking Edinburgh's main street. Yet it remains unfinished today, for the *philosophes* had conveniently forgotten that Greece was built with slave labor.

What does all this have to do with the church? As it turns out, everything. One might say that the *philosophes* were smoking their pipes on the upper floors, and tossing matches out the windows, which then caught fire among the lower classes. Their musings would lead not only to modern thought, but also to the French Revolution, both of which would come in sharp conflict with, and help to change, the Catholic Church.

The Ancien Régime

In 1715 Louis XIV died in Versailles. He had ruled for fifty years. He represented the *ancien régime*, the old way of doing things. In France this meant the king was in charge and the church was his subject. He appointed bishops, who in turn wielded a lot of power. One of the old ways of doing things was privilege. The church got caught in this in two ways: 1) it was itself a stronghold of privilege (tax exemption, exemption from state law); and 2) it had within itself a feud between the privileged (episcopacy) and the unprivileged (lower clergy).

The Gallican Church

The Gallican Church was one in which the church and state were united. The state had considerable control over the church, but the church kept its independence from Rome. Every aspect of life was touched by the church: coronations, births, marriages, education, deaths. Despite the monopoly, some tolerance was practiced. While the seventeenth century had proclaimed the importance of authority, social distinctions, and coercion, the eighteenth proclaimed independence, equality, and tolerance. Jansenists were free to oppose their own church—in fact, their feud with the Jesuits, as carried out by Pascal in his *Provincial Letters*, provided great sport. The irreligious were free to show their feelings. Protestants were free to worship in fact, but not in law until 1787.

But these times were strange. Even Voltaire had a chaplain, built a chapel, and performed his Easter duties. There was something civilized about religion which the *philosophes* did not quite want to abandon. The difference, as they saw it, was that religion was made for the state, and not the state for religion. Rousseau substituted another religion for Christianity. His God's social maxims and articles of faith were the happiness of the just, the punishment of the wicked, and the sanctity of the social contract. All that was left of Catholicism, when the *philosophes* were done with it, was a moral system. Eventually the French Revolution would attempt to substitute another religion entirely, that of Reason. It did not succeed.

The French Church before the Revolution was remarkably like the English Church before Reformation. Out of twenty-six million people in France, the French Church had 130,000 priests and religious, roughly divided in half between diocesan clergy and religious. There were also 35,000 nuns. The church's fortune was in land, though this ownership was unevenly spread out. In some places, the church owned as much as one-third of the land, but in other places it owned only three to four percent. Generally, it is agreed that it owned between six and ten percent, tax free. Its responsibilities included running all of France's hospitals (2,200 at the time of the Revolution). Fourteen thousand nuns were nurses. There was no such thing as a laywoman who was a nurse. The poor were also the concern of the church. The bishops did a lot for the poor, especially during times of duress. In education there were 600 colleges (what we would call high schools), which educated 75,000 pupils. Two-thirds of these were run by secular clergy, and less than one-third by Jesuits. There were 37,000 parishes, of which 25,000 had primary schools. The Ursulines had 9,000 nuns and 350 houses. They educated children from all classes. Even practical education (bookkeeping, navigation, architecture) was in the hands of the church.

There was a large divide between the bishops and their clergy. The bishops were drawn mostly from the nobility, the priests from the lower classes. The bishops were moral, for the most part, but distant; the priests were moral, poor, and highly regarded. They were educated and were the local leaders. John McManners wrote, "Frenchmen tended to anti-clericalism, but they liked the local clergy they knew and retained a respect for their old schoolmasters."[3] There were very few cases of serious scandal, either among the bishops or the clergy, but the city priests were greatly affected by Rationalism. Country priests were less philosophical, and more bent on the ideals of reform and equality. The religious orders were in decline, especially those founded in the Middle Ages, and most of the work was done by sixteenth-century orders such as the Jesuits and Capuchins. Some abbeys like Cîteaux and Cluny had become decadent, but most of the decadence involved comfort rather than vice.

The Catholic laity was pretty much what it always was. Some people were indifferent to the church, some hostile, and others fervent. Levels of observance cannot be categorized geographically, but seem to be partly a result of ethnic factors and the quality of preaching, and stronger than Enlightenment sympathizers would like everyone to believe. As Simon Schama points out in his brilliant history of the French Revolution, the idea that France was becoming rapidly secularized "fails to take account of just how deeply rooted the hold of Christian belief was in very large areas of the country." He continues, "Of all the failures of the French Revolution, none would be so inevitable and so dismal as the campaign of 'dechristianization.'"[4]

Gallicanism—the notion that the French Church was independent from Rome—had four main tenets:

1. Complete independence of the French king from control by Rome in matters temporal. This even extended to the religious realm, to a degree:
   —Papal bulls could not be published without the king's consent.
   —The king could appoint bishops and abbots of great monasteries.

2. The superiority of general councils over the authority of the pope.

3. The inviolability of the rights and customs of the French Church.

4. The consent of the universal church to validate papal judgments on faith and morals.

The great obstacle to all of this, the Jesuits, had been suppressed in 1773. To show how important all of this was to the French Revolution, one of the first things the Revolution was to do was to take control of the church. In fact, it eventually took the pope captive.

The French Revolution

No event has been more important in the modern world than the French Revolution. It has influenced the church and was influenced by the church. It was partly *brought about* by the church. The Jacobins got their name because they gathered in the churchyard of St. Jacques, the Dominican church in Paris. The lower clergy, in fact, seemed quite well disposed toward a revolution. They got more than they bargained for.

In 1749, after the War of Austrian Succession, the French government needed money desperately. The Controller General tried to impose a five percent tax on everyone. The *parlements* (county governments) and the church opposed him, and he lost. Between 1763 and 1774 there followed a prolonged and intense feud over similar tax proposals. These ended when Louis XIV died in 1774. But a third crisis—the American Revolution—brought about the final crisis. It affected the French in two ways: a) it showed them that a revolution could be successful; b) it bankrupted them. Minor adjustments would no longer work. The Estates General (French Parliament) had to be called for the first time since 1614. It had the power to levy a tax which would maintain the government. But it had not been called for 175 years for a reason. Just as popes were wary of calling councils, kings were wary of calling their parliaments together. One never knew what they would do if they got together.

The king called for the Estates General on 5 May 1789 for new taxes. There were three Estates: the First Estate—the

clergy, the Second Estate—the nobility, and the Third Estate—
the lower classes. At the elections, of 296 clerics elected to the
First Estate, 208 were parish priests, most of whom were allied
to the middle classes in welcoming the Revolution. Forty-six
were bishops.

Progress of Revolution

Very quickly, matters went beyond the king's control. On 13
June 1789, three priests joined the Third Estate. Four days later,
deputies from both the First and Third Estates proclaimed a
National Assembly. On 19 June, the First Estate (clergy) voted to
join the Third Estate. In doing so, the clergy voluntarily gave up
centuries of privileges, including tithes and exemption from taxes.
But these privileges did not mean much to the lower clergy, anyway. Between 20 and 23 June, the king ordered the Estates
General to disperse, and he was ignored. Having got them
together, it would now prove impossible to get them to go home.
Finally on 27 June the king conceded and ordered the first two
Estates to join the Third. Many nobles thought this ended the
revolution.

This National Assembly suddenly found itself in an ambiguous position: While it emphasized individual liberty and religious
freedom, it also emphasized the omnipotence of the state in
enforcing these freedoms, leading to threats against the church if
it refused to cooperate with reform. Much like the Protestant
churches of the sixteenth century, who wanted to overthrow the
tyranny of Rome, but found themselves substituting the tyranny
of the city council or state, so too in France, the revolutionary
ideologues substituted one tyranny (Rome) for another (their
own). The clergy was also in an awkward position: It attacked
privilege, but at the same time opposed the toleration of non-
Catholic religions.

On 14 July the king dismissed a popular priest and ordered
soldiers to Versailles. The mob went berserk and captured the
Bastille, a Parisian prison that was a symbol of oppression,
although at the time it was already marked for demolition and
housed only four forgers, two lunatics, and one dissipated noble-

man. It also contained 250 barrels of gunpowder, transferred there in the previous weeks, and this may have been what the crowd was really after. There was nothing symbolic about the attack, however, and nearly one hundred Parisians died, while several prison authorities lost their heads after being captured. The king lost all control over the proceedings. On 23 August the Assembly passed the Declaration of the Rights of Man, which essentially meant religious toleration.

The church would now become a target of the Revolution. The church had money, at least property, and the revolutionaries needed ready cash to keep their government going and solve France's immediate financial crisis. On 2 November all church property was nationalized. We have seen this before in the English Reformation. The contemplative monks were the first to go. Just as Thomas Cromwell had made his case against the monks in order to confiscate their property, so too the Assembly targeted the monks early on. (Remember, most of the clergy at the Assembly were diocesan priests.) The monks had the most land, they dominated over the secular clergy, and they tended to appeal to Rome. But probably even more, the monasteries had been regarded by Enlightenment writers as a denial of freedom and a denial of practical benefit to society. They were not useful citizens. They were also a popular target of novelists—see especially Voltaire's *Candide*—who cited forced vocations, monks who could not leave, excessive comfort, immorality, etc. As in Reformation England, the monastic buildings were used as quarries, gold melted down at a mint, bells turned into cannons, etc. Just as in England, when visitors and accountants were sent to assess the wealth of the monasteries before their planned dissolution, so the French sent commissioners to take inventories of the properties, to guarantee that none would be sold or transferred. While some of this was practical—e.g., the elimination of the national debt— the suppression was really ideological and this is proved by what followed. On 28 October 1789, the Assembly prohibited the taking of vows in all monasteries. On 13 February 1790, religious orders that used solemn vows were suppressed. Men and women religious were treated differently: Men were sent off into a few selected monasteries without regard for their different orders or rules, or they were pensioned off. Many men left: The Benedictines, Dominicans, and Canons of St. Genevieve lost heavily. The Capuchins and Carthusians were remarkably faithful to their vows.

Almost all religious women wanted to stay. And because women often did charitable work, they were often spared, at least in the beginning. They could remain in their own houses and under their own rule. While some would argue that it was more difficult for a religious woman to start life over, their fidelity is impressive. The Carmelite houses in Paris made a joint declaration: "In the world, people like to say that the monasteries are full of victims, slowly consumed by regrets, but we protest before God that if there is true happiness on earth, we enjoy it, in the shelter of the sanctuary."[5] Complaints about the Revolution began to become more serious because of the Assembly's actions, but nothing would galvanize the opposition to Revolution so much as its legislation in regard to the church, called the Civil Constitution of the Clergy.

The Civil Constitution of the Clergy

Some arrangement with the Catholic Church was seen as desirable, spelling out especially the government's authority over the governance of the church. This was called the Civil Constitution of the Clergy (CCC) and was passed on 12 July 1790. It put control of the church completely into the hands of the state. Diocesan boundaries would be redrawn in order to match civil boundaries. This reduced the number of dioceses from 135 to 85. Many parishes were abolished as well (33 of 52 in Paris alone). Parishes were to have 6,000 people. Bishops and priests were to be elected by the people. Local electoral bodies, sometimes consisting of people who were openly hostile to the church, would choose and assign bishops and priests.

It is true that some administrative reform was badly needed in the French Church. Privilege breeds exceptions and vested interests and they quickly become difficult to take away unless by an outside agent. There were too many dioceses and parishes in France, and the church was slow to reduce their number. It is possible that too many clergy had salaried positions without much work to do. So the revolutionary government took upon itself the task of reducing the excess. Unfortunately, it overreached. The CCC met with serious opposition from the start because it deprived the church of its independence, such as it was, and freedom. Changes were made without the approval of the church, either through the pope or the French bishops. Many priests lost their jobs: Parishes were closed immediately, without waiting for the pastor to die or making arrangements for his care. A curé (pastor) could be appointed to a parish by a board that did not include a single cleric, in which the bishop was not represented, and no one knew anything about the parish or pastor in question.

Because opposition to the CCC was so determined, an oath was imposed on 27 November 1790—forcing any office-holding clergy to comply by 4 January. This, if anywhere, is where the Revolution went wrong. It was thought that the pope would yield. Even the French bishops thought he would accept the CCC. But he did not say anything. It was not until May 1792 that he finally condemned the CCC. It was also thought by the Assembly that the French bishops would cave in to avoid schism. Finally, it was thought the clergy would never abandon the Revolution. The Assembly was growing impatient. The auction of land was approaching, and some clerical posts had opened which the Assembly began to fill in the prescribed way. The Assembly did not want to appear to be too dependent on Rome, waiting around for the pope to make up his mind. Any priest employed by the state had to take the oath or lose his job.

Civil war broke out, and the opposition of the church became focused. Schism followed. The clergy divided into those who took the oath ("juring" or constitutional priests) and those who refused to take the oath ("nonjuring" priests). Only 7 of 160 bishops (Adrian Dansette calls these seven "the dregs of the episcopate") took this oath. Only one-third of the clergy in the Assembly signed it, while about half of the clergy in general took it. Archbishop Boisgelin tried to salvage the explosive situation and issued the *Exposition des Princepes sur la Constitution Civile*. In this document he moderately summarized the arguments against the CCC and requested that the Assembly should suspend enforcing its decrees until the pope had spoken. His point was that it was neither permissible nor constitutional to reform the church without consulting the church, and that the pope should give his approval and remove any canonical difficulties to the CCC. The archbishop then sent the *Exposition* to Pius VI with a request that he would dispense from canonical objections to the CCC. This is regarded by some historians as the first Ultramontane act in modern church history.*

But the fever rose—the Revolution had gained a momentum of its own and was not to be stopped or slowed by the pope. The CCC was widely ignored, and the king's two elderly aunts headed off to Rome for their annual Holy Week trip in February 1791. This caused more of a stir than one might think—it represented the monarchy, flouting the obvious intent of the new law, by going to attend papal ceremonies. The two aunts were stopped by the police, and a serious debate ensued in the Assembly: Should not people be allowed the freedom to travel where they liked? Isn't this what the Revolution was all about: Liberty? The radicals said no, and Simon Schama writes that this decision "was indeed *the* turning point of the French Revolution—the moment at which, less than two years after the opening of the Estates-General, it licensed itself as a police state."[6] The king attempted to flee in June 1791 and was caught. In September 1791 a more radical Legislative Assembly took over and sought to wipe out all resistance. After a revolutionary was killed in Avignon, more than sixty Catholics were killed either in the town's prisons or on the streets. The Assembly then imposed a further oath on all clergy, and the awkward peace that had existed—permitting nonjurors to say Mass in some places—was gone.

The Girondins came to power in March 1792 and hoped to strengthen their own power and weaken that of the king by declaring war on Austria in April. News arrived in Paris in early September 1792 that Verdun had fallen to the enemy, and cries for vengeance reached fever pitch. The clergy were immediately suspect because they were increasingly vocal against the direction the Revolution was taking. The pope did not help the plight of the

---

* Ultramontanism is explained on p. 281.

clergy by sending an exiled French abbé to Austria as an envoy, a man who was known to be an opponent of the Assembly, and thereby announced (everyone assumed) that the pope and his church were the political allies of nations making war against France. Accusations of treason flew everywhere. On 10 August 1792, all remaining religious orders were suppressed, all remaining nonjuring priests were banished, and even juring priests could be banished if six people asked to have them deported. The "constitutional clergy" steadily declined from 28,000 priests who signed the oath to about 8,000.

Amidst this mass hysteria, the September Massacres took place, beginning when twenty-four priests, who were being transported to prison, were stopped by a mob. In an hour and a half, nineteen of them were hacked to pieces. In four days the death toll was at 1400 people, more than 225 of whom were priests and bishops—about half as many victims, in fact, as were claimed by 300 years of the Spanish Inquisition! About 30,000 priests fled, most ending up in the Papal States (4,000), Switzerland (5,000), or in England (8,000). The French won victories at Valmy and Jemappes in late September, victories which guaranteed that the Revolution would continue with renewed fury.

The king was executed in January 1793, and the Reign of Terror began a few months later, lasting from September 1793 to July 1794. Seventeen thousand death sentences were handed down and 10,000 people died in jails. Horror stories abound. In November 1793, ninety priests interred at Nantes were told they were being transferred to the other side of the Loire in order to process their liberation. Prison wardens took them, bound two-by-two, onto an old barge, which was taken out to the middle of the river. Cries were heard coming from the river, then silence. The wardens had gotten into boats and rowed away, shortly after removing plugs below the water line of the barge.[7] Those priests not lucky enough to flee or who were not massacred were put on prison ships to be exiled to Guiana. The British blockaded the French ports in order to prevent this, which only resulted in the priests dying on board amid horrible conditions. Five hundred priests were crammed onto one ship which had room for 250. In less than a year, three-fourths of them were dead. Furious resistance broke out in the Vendée and neighboring areas in March 1793, after smoldering since the CCC. By the fall of 1794, the worst was over. Apologists for the Revolution have claimed that the irrational violence was a result of revolutionary "fervor" or "excess," an unnecessary and unfortunate appendage to the principles of the Revolution. But the violence resembled too closely the iconoclasm of the Reformation, which Eamon Duffy called the "sacrament" of the Reformation. Simon Schama notes:

> The [Reign of] Terror was merely 1789 with a higher body count. From the first year it was apparent that violence was not just an unfortunate side effect from which enlightened Patriots could selectively avert their eyes; it was the Revolution's source of collective energy....From the very beginning—from the summer 1789—violence was the motor of the Revolution.[8]

Napoleon

Napoleon watched all of this from a distance. He had learned the importance of appeasing the church while fighting against the Austrians in Italy in 1795 and 1796, by which time he realized that the leaders in Paris were his rivals and he began to plot to take control of the government. In a succession of victories in Italy, he refused to occupy Rome or dismiss the papal government and replace it with a French government, as his leaders were calling on him to do. He knew he would have to deal with this pope later on, and his support could be of some use. While Napoleon was in Egypt in February 1798, a French army entered Rome, and carried Pope Pius VI north, first to Siena, then Florence. The Austrians attempted to free him, and consequently the French decided to take the pope to Paris. He was eighty years old. He got as far as Valence and died there in August 1798. In March 1800, the Benedictine bishop of Imola (Chiaramonti) was elected and took the name Pius VII. He was fifty-eight years old.

In the meantime, Napoleon had successfully carried out a coup d'état (10 Nov 1799), making him first consul of France. In January 1800 he had subdued the Vendée by the simple expedient of allowing Catholic priests to restore the faith there. He soon realized how easy this was, and sought to extend this toleration to the whole country—not for religious reasons, but for political reasons. Napoleon recognized religion as a necessary component of a state, but one that must be controlled by the state. He was willing to recognize the freedom of the church only if he were to be the guardian.

The Concordat

Napoleon saw the need for an agreement with Rome, and began negotiations for a concordat. The new pope, Pius VII, was not unwilling to talk. He had certain republican sympathies, and saw no bar to the coexistence of a Catholic Church and a republican government. After eight months of haggling (and twenty-six drafts) between Pius VII and Napoleon, and between Cardinal Consalvi and Talleyrand (their respective ministers), the Concordat was signed on 15 July 1801.[9]

Napoleon did not intend to serve religion, but to use it. The pope was expected to recognize the work of the Revolution and its principles—the secular character of the state and the freedom of religion. In regard to persons and property, the church's fortune and property were not to be returned. Those Frenchmen who owned church property were to be recognized as owning a legitimate title. The church was to become an instrument of government. Napoleon would nominate bishops, the pope would approve them, and the bishops would appoint parish priests. All clergy would be paid a salary by the state and the practice of worship would be under police control. The advantages to the French government are obvious. But the church benefited as well. Revolutionary cults would be abandoned, as well as "constitutional" worship. The pope was recognized as having the right of canonical institution of bishops, and the clergy would be materially provided for. The pope was concerned that a statement of principles be made, even if those principles were unworkable for the moment. They were not to be abandoned, even though they might not be recognized. The church would maintain its right to own property, to form religious orders, and to regulate its own affairs.

Negotiations dragged on, with rapid progress made on some points (church property) and almost no progress on others. Napoleon had temper tantrums and threatened to become a Calvinist and recognize the constitutional church again. Pius VII, with "gentle inflexibility," refused to budge. The night of the signing was a bit dramatic. Consalvi had worked out a compromise—allowing worship to be controlled by civil authorities, and promising that married priests would have their excommunications lifted, but obtaining a promise that the consuls (state officials) would make a profession of the Catholic faith. Three hours before the time fixed for signing, Consalvi was shown a final draft which had left out the provision on the consuls submitting to a profession of faith. The negotiations went on until the next afternoon, then Joseph Bonaparte showed the final draft to his brother, who reacted badly, saying, "I want my text or it is all over." Consalvi refused to give in, but finally worked out an agreement on the 15th.

Napoleon would add the "Organic Articles," the practical applications of the Concordat, which Rome never agreed to. The Articles attempted to put the French Church into a straitjacket—bishops could not go to synods or councils, ordain priests, and leave their dioceses, without the permission of the state. Papal bulls or envoys could not come to France without state permission. Holy days, special prayers, and celebrations could not be celebrated unless the state agreed.

The Effects of the French Revolution and the Concordat

The church had never before experienced such a catastrophe as the French Revolution. In some ways, it was a completion of the Reformation, but with a new twist. The state, which previously was either clearly for or against the continuation of the Catholic Church, was now neither. The state preferred that the Catholic Church would go away, but since it would not, some accommodation had to be made. This accommodation would not only radically change the church in France, it would affect the papacy to its core. The French Church, because of the

Revolution, simply (and practically overnight) ceased to be Gallican—with all its privileges and independence. The French Church could no longer cooperate with a government which now treated it as a department of state. Its only court of appeal was Rome. Priests also, under the bishop's thumb, could appeal only to Rome. Catholicism was restored in France, but it would have a very new look. It was the look of Ultramontanism.

Napoleon would do some foolish things toward the end of his reign. In 1809, he captured and imprisoned the pope, who was delighted to be back in a Benedictine-style cell and away from the Roman curia.[10] From then on, the pope's authority became less encumbered by political obligations and would be measured more by his spiritual force. This was a real revolution. In 1809, Napoleon even invented a dubious Saint Napoleon for his birthday—August 15. When the feast arrived, the first since the pope had been removed, only one church in Rome—the French church of St. Louis—sang a *Tè Deum*, and even there French troops had to force a choir and organist to perform.

The Aftermath of Revolution

Despite the catastrophe of the French Revolution and the disillusionment of many revolutionaries, certain of its ideas persisted. The more extreme manifestations were in opposition to the monarchy, organized religion, and sometimes God himself. Closely related to this was the philosophy of Liberalism, whereby divine revelation (i.e., the Bible) is regarded as invalid as a source of information, religion as sentiment, truth as relative, and all creeds as of equal value. Nationalism and a greater confidence in science flowed from this. The Catholic Church's reaction took two forms, that of *Liberal Catholicism* and *Ultramontanism*. The two reactions did not begin as mutually opposed to each other, as early Liberal Catholics put confidence in the pope, but with time the two would go their separate and quite different ways.

Liberal Catholicism

Liberal Catholicism was an attempt to salvage the "healthy core" of the Revolution. Liberal Catholics thought that the Revolution contained some good ideals which had been obscured by extremists. These ideals, they thought, could be recovered and serve to bring the church into the modern world. Thus Liberal Catholics sought to reconcile such things as the freedoms of religion, press, assembly, and speech, with Catholicism.

In France, Liberal Catholics suspected that one of the reasons the French Revolution became so violent was because of the great gulf between modern thought and the teaching of the church, especially on political matters. Could not the church make some accommodation to modern realities: religious diversity, the press, and scientific discovery? Their program read like the American Bill of Rights: freedom of religion, assembly, press; the free education of all; extension of the suffrage. These Liberal Catholics felt that the church would not be harmed by these ideals at all, but would benefit from them. The foremost Liberal Catholic in France was Lamennais, a complicated thinker who attempted to combine the notions of freedom and theocracy. In doing so he attracted the opposition of Liberals and Ultramontanists alike. He gained the following of Montalambert and the Dominican Lacordaire and began a journal called *L'Avenir*. So confident was he in the pope's support that he went to Rome to explain his program in more detail. He was treated very rudely by the pope—the exact details of the interview were only released in 1984. The pope not only refused to speak about any of the issues Lamennais had come to talk about, preferring to ask only about mutual friends, but he then proceeded to condemn Lamennais in two documents: *Mirari Vos* in 1832 (the year of the visit) and *Singulari Nos* in 1834.

In the former decree, the pope condemned the Liberal Catholic program in general, especially its support for freedom of the press, conscience, and freedom to revolt. The pope was nervous about revolution and had condemned two revolts in 1830, even though Catholics in both cases were revolting against obvious oppression. The Belgians won their independence from the

Netherlands, despite the pope, on a program of freedom of worship, opinion, and education. The Polish also ignored the pope, but were defeated by the Russians. The pope was himself the ruler of a theocratic state and feared that any revolution that toppled a legitimate government, even if carried out by Catholics, would provide Italian revolutionaries with the justification to do the same to him. He also feared that the application of such freedoms as press, opinion, and religion would be incompatible with his spiritual authority. The pope generally opposed movements in other countries that showed signs of causing trouble in his own. But many political liberals went untouched. Daniel O'Connell, Ireland's Great Liberator, was never condemned, even though he said, "I'll take my religion from Rome and my politics from Ireland." Americans went untouched as well, mainly because America was still an overwhelmingly Protestant country and was not deemed by the pope to be worth his time. The second decree, *Singulari Nos,* condemned Lamennais in particular. Lamennais eventually left the priesthood and was excommunicated, while Montalambert and Lacordaire submitted to Rome and followed other pursuits.[11]

In Germany, Liberal Catholicism was more theological than political. It can best be seen as an attempt to fill the vacuum left by the disappearance of eighteenth-century Scholasticism, and to investigate what of modern research could be used for the service of religion. A surprising number of scholars came into the church as a result. In response to Hegel's and Schleiermacher's attack on the church, Johann Adam Möhler wrote *Symbolik* in 1832. Schleiermacher had taught that religion was a feeling of absolute dependence and that dogmas were unimportant. Möhler, a historian, responded by showing how Christ lived on in his church through history. Dogmas do not change; they develop. New vocabularies, new thought forms, and changing circumstances all contribute to this "development of doctrine." Other important names in this Catholic response were Michael Sailer and Friedrich Schlegel. Catholic faculties were founded at Berlin (1810) and Tübingen (1817) as well as at Mainz and Munich.

Modernism

Liberal Catholicism ran afoul of the official church on the issue of the temporal power of the pope (i.e., his reign over the Papal States) and his infallibility. Ignaz von Döllinger, a German historian, tried to demonstrate through history that popes had not always made correct theological decisions. He was eventually excommunicated and was never reconciled to the church. Such threats to the church's teaching were not welcome at a time when the very existence of the Papal States was in jeopardy.

But Liberal Catholics pushed the limits of the church's tolerance in other areas as well. In the field of Scripture, scholars adopted what is known as the "critical method," a scientific study of the texts. This led several Catholic scholars to question the historicity of certain books and the reliability of the Bible for scientific information. Did God create the world in six days? Was there, for example, really an Adam and Eve? Did Moses write the first five books of the Bible, David the Psalms? How were the Gospel accounts written—was there some borrowing between authors, and were there multiple authors of one book? Was the Bible literally true? Was the world older than 4004 BC, as Cardinal Cullen of Ireland believed? Some scholars, like the French priest Alfred Loisy, proclaimed that their scholarship had led them to the conclusion that Jesus Christ was not God. In dogmatic theology there arose an inclination to subordinate doctrine to practice. Following Maurice Blondel's philosophy of action, some Catholic scholars saw the essence of Christianity in life (praxis) rather than in an intellectual system or creed. Hegel's philosophy of "process" also led some scholars to conclude that dogmas were changeable and had no final content. In historical theology the *process* of history became more important than any factual events. Whether Christ founded a church, instituted a Mass, or died and rose from the dead, was unimportant relative to how these events were experienced at the present time. What was important to some of these historical theologians was not that Christ had founded a church, but that a saving church had developed which brought people into contact with supernatural reality. What mattered were not the facts behind the institution of sacraments, but how they affected one in the present. This became the position of the Lutheran scholar Rudolf Bultmann and underpins liberation theology to this day.

The problem with all of this is that it was a jumble. The combination of errors became known as "Modernism," but Modernism is not so easily defined. Some Modernists were unorthodox in some areas, but not in others. The Jesuit George Tyrrell always remained very devoted to the doctrine of the Eucharist, but was condemned for his teaching on hell, among other things. His predicament was highlighted by a Eucharistic Congress, held in London in 1908. When Cardinal Gasquet, who was carrying the Eucharist, learned that Tyrrell was in the church where the Congress would take place, he stopped the procession. Either Tyrrell would leave the building (his excommunication carried with it the stricture that no Catholic could be in the same room with him!), or the procession would find somewhere else to go.

Some very sound conclusions were reached by some Modernists, but at the same time as some very questionable ones. Pope Leo XIII (1878–1903) had encouraged learning but was losing patience with theologians who were becoming heterodox. Unfortunately, theologians fell increasingly under a cloud and could be disciplined by a nervous Rome. Père Duchèsne, a French Catholic historian, was suspended from the Institut Catholique in Paris for two years because he taught that there was no evidence that Mary Magdalene ever lived in France. French Dominicans, who began the Ecole Biblique in Jerusalem in 1890, were suspect and were not permitted to grant academic degrees until the 1980s. Fr. Francis Duffy was told to end his new and promising *New York Review*. He would later achieve fame in World War I as the chaplain to the New York 69th Division as Fighting Father Duffy. Editors of Catholic journals were monitored closely. Wilfrid Ward, the editor of Britain's *Dublin Review*, was typical of those caught in the middle. He wanted a free exchange of ideas, but also needed to ensure the orthodoxy of his journal. That he kept the *Dublin Review* in print was a testimony to his diplomatic skill.

Pius X disliked Modernists right from the beginning of his tenure as pope and wrote the decree *Lamentabili* and the encyclical *Pascendi* (both in 1907) condemning Modernism. In *Lamentabili* he stated that scholarly devices could not be put above, nor separated from, the teaching authority (magisterium) of the church, that human knowledge is subject to the authority of the church, that the church can demand internal consent, and that dogma comes from on high. Dogma is not merely a recommendation for living. Truth is immutable and dogma is its expression. Finally, under the aegis of dogma, the pope reasserted the importance of the truth that Christ is God. In *Pascendi* Pius X muddied the waters by contending that Modernism was a clear, well-thought-out, unified body of heresy. It began a widespread and almost embarrassing intimidation of scholars. One organization (*Sodalitium pianum*— the "Quiet Sodality") was set up as a secret society to root out Modernists. Baron von Hügel was told by one professor of Scripture that "Rome is swarming with spies." Even the Roman *trattorie* had spies, and secret names were used. The next pope, Benedict XV, condemned this sodality in his encyclical *Ad Beatissimi*. An anti-Modernist oath was required of seminary professors from 1910 until 1967.

Ultramontanism

The second reaction to the French Revolution was Ultramontanism, a looking "over the mountains (i.e., Alps)" to Rome for direction and support. It was led by many disillusioned ex-revolutionaries. The first step toward Ultramontanism was the turning of French Catholics to Rome. The desperate situation they found themselves in, combined with the virtual impossibility of continuing the Gallican Church, gave them no choice. The next step was the restoration of the Society of Jesus in 1814. It had been suppressed in 1773 by the pope under pressure from the governments of France, Spain, and Portugal. The Jesuits, always strong supporters of the pope, were viewed by these governments as too powerful and too independent of their control.[12] Now, because governments had declared their independence from the pope, the pope was also freer to act. This was an unexpected benefit of the Revolution.

Two important books were written after the French Revolution providing an intellectual and cultural foundation for

Ultramontanists. In 1802 the Vicomte de Chateaubriand wrote *The Genius of Christianity*, in which he argued that Christianity had been the main fountain of art and civilization in Europe. In 1819 Joseph DeMaistre wrote *Du Pape* which argued that the only true basis of a civilized society lay in authority—a temporal authority vested in human kings, and spiritual authority vested in the papacy.

The Romantic Movement also helped to enhance the pope's prestige. Reacting to the sterility of the Enlightenment, authors and musicians began to look to the Middle Ages for inspiration and to recover what had been lost through Revolution. Walter Scott began a series of romantic novels about medieval times, of which *Ivanhoe* is the best known. Church architecture began to revert to Gothic forms, and thus a Gothic revival was born. In England, Gilbert Scott and Augustus Welby Pugin, as brilliant as he was eccentric, were the great advocates of Gothic architecture. Not only did Pugin build Gothic churches (and assist in the design of the Houses of Parliament), but he wrote books claiming that Gothic was the high point of architectural history just as Scholasticism was the high point of theological understanding. It was no coincidence, he noted, that the two—Gothic architecture and Scholasticism—developed at exactly the same time.

Pius IX

The election of Pius IX in 1846 was important in the development of Ultramontanism. He was young, handsome, charming, and witty, and he made some decisions early in his reign which gave liberals the wrong idea that he was one of them. He declared a general amnesty, freeing nearly a thousand political prisoners. Lay people were chosen to be part of a cabinet to run the Papal States more efficiently, and as a committee to run his newly established press. He lit the streets of Rome with gas and proposed the building of a railroad near the Vatican. (The previous pope thought railroads were sinful.) There was even talk of making the pope the head of a united Italy.

But trouble was afoot which would cause the liberals (revolutionaries) to turn against him. Ever since 1815 the Austrians had ruled the northeast part of Italy and this occupation was increasingly resented. The pope was asked to lend his small papal army to help the northern Italians oust the Austrians. He refused to do so, saying "I cannot bless warfare." In 1848 Austria soundly defeated the Italians and the pope was accused of being responsible by his inaction. In the same year, Rossi, his prime minister and friend, was assassinated on his way to the chancery. Pius IX fled to the Quirinal Palace and from there escaped in disguise to Gaeta, south of Naples. He was never the same. He called on European powers to restore him, and the French took over Rome and brought the pope back in 1850. His opposition to the revolutionaries hardened as Cavour came to power in the northern kingdom of Piedmont and legislation there was directed against Catholics and the church.

Pius IX has been accused recently of obstructing the formation of the modern Italian State, but in reality he was trying to protect the Papal States from being simply stolen from the church. But even more was thought to be at stake at the time. Journals from the mid-1800s are filled with debates about the necessity of the pope's having some autonomous country or jurisdiction from which to speak freely. It was commonly thought that a papacy deprived of such political autonomy would likewise be deprived of spiritual authority. This is what the pope was really trying to preserve. When the revolutionaries finally conquered all the property of the Papal States, including Rome itself in 1870, the pope remained in his apartments as a "Prisoner of the Vatican." This awkward situation continued until 1929, when Pope Pius XI and Mussolini signed the Lateran Treaty, recognizing Vatican City as an independent country.

The "Syllabus of Errors"

In 1864, ten years after he defined the dogma of the Immaculate Conception, Pius wrote the *Syllabus of Errors*, possibly one of the most misunderstood documents in the history of the Church. In it he attempted to erect a barrier against Liberalism. The *Syllabus* had been suggested by the Bishop of Perugia, who would later succeed Pius as Leo XIII. It was a list of eighty propositions condemning modern errors, but it culminated with the seemingly outrageous statement that it was an error to hold that "the Roman Pontiff can and should reconcile himself with, and accommodate himself to progress, liberalism, and modern civilization." The European press thought the pope had lost his mind and proved that the church was hopelessly out of touch. Americans simply did not know what he was talking about. But Italians knew exactly what he meant. In the middle of the century liberal Italian governments had passed laws stating that monasteries, convents, the sacramental view of marriage, and belief in religious education were out of date and out of touch with progress, liberalism, and modern civilization. The pope had already condemned these laws (convents were to be suppressed) in 1861, so the *Syllabus* was nothing new. But the pope overstepped by thinking the entire world would know what he intended.

The problems with the *Syllabus* were many. For one thing, it seemed to attack the freedoms of speech, religion, press, and the separation of church and state—so hallowed in the United States and among republicans generally. In addition, the document was too complicated for popular consumption. Attached to each condemnation, which were merely statements drawn from previous encyclicals since the time of the French Revolution, was a reference number alluding to the original document. But what reader was going to look up the original context? Proposition 77 is a good example. It states, "It is an error to say it is no longer expedient that the Catholic religion should be established to the exclusion of all others." When untangled, this seemed to be saying that the Catholic religion should be the official religion of every country, and anyone who thought differently was in error. But the statement is drawn from a papal document that concerned Spain, which had proposed disestablishing the church. The pope was expressing his shock that Catholic Spain, of all places, would do such a thing. By adding it to the *Syllabus*, the pope made a local problem into a universal problem. Also, doctrinal errors (e.g., denying the divinity of Christ) were mixed in freely with political "errors," such as the freedom of the press. It used vocabulary which made sense in one country, but looked hopelessly outdated in others.

Thus, the *Syllabus* was problematic for defenders of the papacy. It was more than embarrassing. It not only confused the bishops, but it played right into the hands of the church's critics, who saw it as a confirmation of all their fears. The Bishop of Orleans, Felix Dupanloup, saved the day by offering an explanation for the *Syllabus*. First, he said, the propositions needed to be put in context, and no one was doing this. Secondly, according to Dupanloup, what was being condemned was not the actual situation, such as freedom of religion in the Bill of Rights of the United States, but the notion that freedom of religion was an *ideal*—effectively allowing people to believe things that are not true. Thus, freedom of press, which theoretically allows a newspaper to spread misinformation and untruths, is not *necessarily* a good thing. Freedom of speech, which allows people to spread lies and slanders and even pornography, is not an absolute good to be sought. *Truth* is the good to be sought. Dupanloup was thanked in writing by the vast majority of bishops, for whom he had provided a tool to answer the deluge of protests.

Pius IX's problems were not over. His beatification in 2000 by John Paul II has brought back to the surface the story of the kidnapping of Edgardo Mortara. Mortara was a six-year-old Jewish boy who was secretly baptized by a Catholic nurse when he was an infant and seemed on the point of death. When she revealed that she had done this, an over-zealous Dominican sought to have the boy removed from his Jewish home and placed in the protective custody of a Catholic home. This was done amid howls of protest from the family and the international community. Pius IX was involved only because he was appealed to, and failed to take any action by returning the child to the family. The boy went on to become a Catholic priest and died in 1940, never embittered by the experience. Until this famous "kidnapping," Pius's treatment of the Roman Jews seemed almost miraculous to them. He ordered all public insults against them, most frequently heard during the *Carnevale*, to cease. Sermons to convert them to Christianity—in place since the construction of the ghetto in the 1550s—were ordered stopped. And the ghetto walls were torn down in 1848 on Pius's order. One must also contextualize Mortara's "kidnapping." At the very time the six-year-old

Edgardo was taken from his family, slave children in the supposedly enlightened United States had no rights and were frequently bought and sold without reference to their parents. Furthermore, laws in the American colonies prior to the Bill of Rights had permitted states to gain custody of children if the Protestant party of a mixed marriage died.

But Pius was beleaguered on many fronts and viewed any concession in regard to the Mortara matter to be weakness. On any issue where he could fight and win, he was going to dig in his heels. In some ways, this obstinacy was his Achilles' heel. At times, against all common sense, or sensitivity to popular reaction, he forged ahead and printed a *Syllabus of Errors*, or declined to intervene in the Mortara case, or sought a definition of infallibility. He was not perfect. Saints are not canonized because they are perfect. He must also be judged against the background of revolutionary Italy, where every Catholic institution and belief was being threatened with ridicule and extermination. Almost single-handedly, he managed to preserve them. Flawed as he might be seen today, he was a martyr for the faith. That is why he has been beatified.

Popular Devotions

Several post-Revolution apparitions of the Blessed Mother also focused attention ultimately on the pope. In 1830 Catherine Labouré had a vision of Mary bestowing the Miraculous Medal. The Blessed Mother appeared again at LaSalette in Savoy in 1846 and then again to Bernadette Soubirous in Lourdes in 1858 proclaiming, "I am the Immaculate Conception," a doctrine the pope had defined in 1854. Devotion to the Sacred Heart also made tremendous gains. The image of the Sacred Heart had been used as the symbol of resistance to the French Revolution in the civil war in the Vendée. Several large churches devoted to the Sacred Heart would be built following the Revolution, among them the church of Sacre Coeur in Paris. The Sacred Heart was made a feast of the church in 1856. These devotions aided the cause of the papacy because they focused the popular mind on an alternative to revolution and irreligion.

Vatican Council I (1869–70)

Most cardinals were in favor of a general council. One had not been called since Trent, 300 years before. Councils, Parliaments, or Estates General, were risky things to summon because they were unpredictable. But councils could also serve as a catalyst for projects long neglected. A number of issues in the 1850s and 1860s demanded widespread discussion, such as a unified position on Liberalism, a defense of papal authority vis-à-vis the disappearance of the Papal States, a reform of the breviary and liturgy, and the codifying of canon law. A definition on papal infallibility was not initially seen as a major topic, but it soon became one.

The papal nuncio to France wrote an article about infallibility in the conservative newspaper *Civiltà Cattolica*, published by Italian Jesuits. The article was a trial balloon and it drew the attention of the German historian Döllinger, who denounced the temporal power of the pope and the notion of infallibility. Twenty German bishops assembled for their annual meeting at Fulda asked the pope not to define infallibility because such a definition would be "inopportune." Catholic writers and bishops took sides with the majority favoring a definition (the "infallibilists") and the minority opposing a *definition*, though not necessarily the *notion* of infallibility (the "inopportunists").

Advocates on both sides could be excessive. Some infallibilists wanted the *Syllabus of Errors* to be upgraded to the level of an infallible statement. William George Ward, the editor of the British Catholic *Dublin Review* at the time, made the now-famous statement that he would like nothing better than a new infallible statement on his breakfast table every morning with his London *Times* and bacon and eggs. The inopportunists were nervous that a "definition" would tie the church's hands, and would prove embarrassing if it went too far. One problem faced the First Vatican Council from the start: secrecy. There was an almost absurd imposition of secrecy, even in the planning of the council. Almost no information was provided by the curia, so newspapers sought out insignificant people, and jumped to conclusions.[13] There was a proliferation of lies, leaks, and misrepresentations right from the start. The inopportunists were the most talkative.

Lord Acton went to Rome himself to monitor the sessions and was a tremendous source of misinformation. Owing to circumstances—the abrupt closing of the council and the onset of World War I—real accounts and documents of the council did not emerge until more than fifty years after it concluded!

Nearly 700 clergy took part. A Commission on Faith was formed which did not include any representative from the minority party. This was an injustice, and so an "opposition" party of some 200 members was formed. This helped to modify future statements and decisions. The agenda proceeded simultaneously: issues of doctrine, the revision of canon law (including items on religious orders, missions, and liturgical rites), as well as the reform of the breviary and catechism. The main issue was "De Fide Cattolica." It passed on 24 April 1870, and became *Dei Filius*. It condemned pantheism, it asserted that revelation was valid and that the church was the guardian of the content of faith, and that there was an intimate relation between faith and reason.

But infallibility was in the air. In March 1870 it was announced that it would be discussed. On 18 July 1870, it passed 533 to 2 during a tremendous thunderstorm—which both parties claimed as a divine comment on the vote—and became known as *Pastor Aeternus*. Almost all of the inopportunists had gone home before the vote, except Bishop Fitzgerald of Little Rock, Arkansas, and one other who wanted to make sure that the vote was not unanimous. In the end, both parties had to settle for a very reduced position. Four conditions were spelled out in the final definition.

1. The pope must speak as supreme pastor and teacher of all Christians. This is what is meant by speaking *ex cathedra*. It means that the pope is not infallible as a private theologian or as Bishop of Rome.

2. He must act in virtue of his supreme apostolic authority as the successor of Peter.

3. He must teach in the area of faith or morals.

4. He must propose the defined doctrine as something to be held by the universal church.

Canon law added one more condition: "No doctrine is understood to be infallibly defined unless it is clearly established as such."

So what, in the end, had been accomplished by the definition of infallibility? The more extreme infallibilists were disappointed because it did not go far enough. Inopportunists sidestepped the definition and, instead of arguing whether a statement was infallible or not, now argued whether it was *ex cathedra* or not. In fact, such a properly infallible statement has been proclaimed only once—in 1950—when Pius XII declared the Assumption of Mary to be a doctrine of the church.

The First Vatican Council ended in chaos. War broke out between France and Prussia. French troops, who had protected Rome and the pope from Italian revolutionaries, were pulled out and sent to France. The revolutionaries, who had been waiting for such an eventuality, poured into the city, and the council ended. All of the remaining business—the revision of canon law, the reform of the breviary and catechism, and legislation on the missions—was tabled.

The Catholic Church in the United States

The English colonies were uniformly opposed to the existence of Roman Catholicism. Even Maryland, which had begun in a spirit of toleration and passed the first laws of religious toleration, had been taken over by people who now declared Catholicism to be illegal. By the time of the American Revolution, every colony except Pennsylvania had laws prohibiting Catholics from voting, running for and holding political office, attending religious services, as well as other disabilities. Massachusetts had laws forbidding all Irish and priests to enter the colony. Priests were to be expelled on a first offense, and executed on a second. Christmas was abolished as a public holiday in 1659 because of the disgraceful conduct of younger colonists, who were flaunting the plain will of God by celebrating and making merry on the Lord's birthday.[14] Roughly speaking, whatever happened in Britain and Ireland in regard to Catholics, happened in the American colonies. Most of it was bad.

Pre-Revolution Anti-Catholicism

Catholics appeared in appreciable numbers in only three colonies: New York, Pennsylvania, and Maryland. They numbered about 25,000. In New York and Philadelphia, Catholics totaled one out of every two hundred people. In Maryland, they were one in ten. They did not emigrate to the colonies in any numbers because the laws against them were the same as pertained in Britain and Ireland. Maryland offered them their only real chance, but even Maryland was a risk. There are numerous places on the borders of Maryland (in West Virginia and Pennsylvania) where Catholic priests fled and were hidden during periods of intense persecution. By 1700, only in Rhode Island could a Roman Catholic enjoy full civil rights, but Rhode Island was never a haven for Catholics, and later, penalties were applied even there.

The objection to Catholics was that they could not hold allegiance to two different sovereigns—one, the king of England, and the other, the pope. Samuel Adams wrote in 1768 in the Boston *Gazeteer*, "I did verily believe, as I still do, that much more is to be dreaded from the growth of popery in America, than from the Stamp Act or any other acts destructive of civil rights." John Adams wrote to Jefferson, "Can a free government possibly exist with the Roman Catholic religion?"[15] Even by the end of the Revolution, seven states (Massachusetts, New Hampshire, New Jersey, Connecticut, North Carolina, South Carolina, and Georgia) specified that office-holders must be Protestant. Other states inflicted other liabilities against Catholics in their constitutions, which only began to be removed in the early 1800s. Connecticut still regarded Congregationalism as the official religion of the state until 1818.

Three factors broke down this ignorance of Roman Catholicism: Catholic patriotism, French aid, and the Bill of Rights.

Charles Carroll of Maryland was one of the richest men in the colonies, some claim even richer than George Washington himself, and he was unbending in his opposition to the king of England and his representative, the governor of Maryland. He was the only Catholic signer of the Declaration of Independence.[16] When the Revolution began, he was asked by the Continental Congress to accompany a diplomatic mission to French-speaking Canada, in the company of Benjamin Franklin and Samuel Chase, and to enlist the aid of the French Canadians against the British. Carroll took with him his nephew, the Jesuit priest John Carroll, who would later become the first Catholic bishop of the United States. The mission was a failure. The French Canadians were as suspicious of the Americans as they were of the British, and thought better of plunging into another war. They had just lost one war in 1760 and were not anxious to repeat the experience. However, the Carrolls so impressed Franklin and Adams that Catholic patriotism was no longer a question. These men were as committed as anyone to the Revolution.[17]

Another reason anti-Catholicism dissipated during the Revolution was the fact of French military aid. The French, being Catholics for the most part, made victory possible, and it would have been ungrateful to continue to be mean-spirited. But also, the very fact of fighting together brought these two countries closer. That Lafayette and Washington became friends is almost symbolic of this decline of prejudice. Washington, on hearing that a "Pope Day" celebration—an American equivalent of the virulently anti-Catholic Guy Fawkes Day in England—was to take place at Valley Forge, issued an edict expressing his disappointment. Not only did the Pope Day celebration not take place at Valley Forge, it never happened again anywhere, such was the influence of George Washington.

Finally, the Bill of Rights helped to cement this decline in anti-Catholicism. Some historians have argued that freedom of religion was granted out of ideological optimism and a spirit of toleration. Others have argued that religious freedom was granted only because of practical necessity. Because no one religion dominated throughout the colonies, and thus no religion stood out as the obvious choice for an "official" or state religion, the best solution was to declare all religions free to worship. Despite the Bill of Rights, Episcopalians still insist on calling their church in Washington, D.C., "the National Cathedral."[18] This is not to say that anti-Catholicism ended with the Bill of Rights; local governments could continue to legislate against Catholics. In Boston in 1795, the Bishop Fenwick purchased three acres of land for a cemetery on Bunker Hill next to a Protestant cemetery. He was told that the health regulations of the city prevented the burial of Roman Catholics, though they did allow the burial of Protestants. The various battles over trusteeism were complicated by city and state governments wishing to curtail the power of Catholic bishops. Anti-Catholicism did not end with the Bill of Rights; it simply entered a new phase.

Immigration and Nativism

As immigration to the United States from Europe increased in the 1830s, the nature of anti-Catholicism changed. Previously, it had been directed by Englishmen against their fellow Englishmen. Now the immigrant, the "foreigner," would bring added problems. Immigrants, especially non-English-speaking immigrants, were regarded as different, clannish, and ignorant. Immigrants tended to cluster in neighborhoods, print their own language newspapers, and patronize their own shops. Even the Irish, who could speak English, were labeled as uneducated drunken brawlers. The fact that the English had prevented them by law from attending school does not seem to have qualified the stereotype. Most importantly, the immigrants posed an economic threat to the "natives" already in the United States. Willing to work long hours in subhuman conditions for cheap wages, they could put other people out of work or could be used as a bargaining weapon to keep wages low. As a result, anti-Catholicism became allied with anti-immigration and took two forms: anti-Catholic literature and secret societies.

Anti-Catholic Literature

In the 1830s a cottage industry of anti-Catholic literature developed, funded in part by the inventor of the telegraph, Samuel Morse. The best known of these works was *The Awful Disclosures of Maria Monk* (1836), written by a woman in Canada who had supposedly escaped from a convent. *Maria Monk* told lurid tales in which priests entered convents of women through tunnels, impregnated the nuns, and threw the baptized babies down holes cut in the floor. Three hundred thousand copies were sold in a week. Catholics reacted in various ways. Most bishops wanted to start their own newspapers, to disseminate news of their dioceses, and generally give the faithful an alternative to the popular and sensational press. The first such Catholic newspaper was begun in Charleston, South Carolina. Other Catholics were more direct. A certain Catholic priest from the diocese of Philadelphia, John Hughes, took on the journal, *The Protestant*, in a rather unorthodox way. He contributed several articles denouncing Catholic outrages under the pseudonym of "Cranmer." The outrages committed supposedly by Catholics were ridiculous, but believable to the journal's public, which then learned that all of the articles had been written as a joke by a Catholic priest. Howls of protest went up, charging Hughes with "Jesuitry," but the Protestant press, which trafficked in such anti-Catholic propaganda, was discredited. Fr. Hughes later became the archbishop of New York City where he was known as "Dagger John."

The populace could be easily led by anti-Catholic propaganda. In the most famous of reactions to media coverage, a large convent in Charlestown, Massachusetts, was searched by the town magistrates and, when nothing suspicious was found, burned to the ground by the townspeople. In other episodes, an Orange society attempted to recreate the annual march through the Catholic neighborhood of Belfast, by marching through the Catholic neighborhood of Philadelphia. Stories are told of a cannon being positioned by Irish Catholics and fired directly into the parade. In any event, thirty homes and two Catholic churches were burnt in Philadelphia in May 1844, and fourteen people killed there in July of the same year. In Louisville, Kentucky, twenty people were killed in similar anti-Catholic rioting in 1855. When the Philadelphia violence threatened to spread to New York City, Bishop Hughes called out the Irish to surround the Catholic churches and publicly announced that one Protestant church would be burned down for every Catholic one. This ended the violence in New York before it began.

Secret Societies

Another form taken by anti-Catholicism was that of secret societies. The two most notorious among them were the Know-Nothings and, after the Civil War, the Ku Klux Klan. The Know-Nothings made so many political advances that they hoped to win the presidency in 1856. The Massachusetts legislature consisted of one Whig and 256 members of the Know-Nothing party, who earned the moniker by claiming to "know nothing" whenever asked about their program. They also, fortunately, did not know very much about enacting legislation. They were nativist, which meant opposing anybody who was not a "native," i.e., a white, Anglo-Saxon Protestant. They failed to win substantial seats in the national House and Senate and were eventually discredited by their secrecy. They also split over the issue of slavery—finding it contradictory to oppose slavery and legislate against blacks at the same time. The Klan, on the other hand, operated mostly through terror.

The church reacted by being suspicious of secret societies generally and forbidding Catholics to join them. This became problematic after the Civil War as several secret societies (and men's clubs were all secret to some harmless extent) were founded, especially the veterans' organization known as the Grand Army of the Republic. General William Rosecrans, a Catholic (his brother was the bishop of Columbus) who often kept his staff up long into the night arguing about theology, was the head of the organization. Most of these groups were neutral on the subject of religion, but the official church regarded their rites as substitute religion. A genuine crisis occurred toward the end of the nineteenth century when the first labor union, the Knights of Labor, was formed and attracted many Catholics. Rome's inclination was to condemn membership in the union, which was secret out of necessity—industry was such at the time that it would have ruthlessly stamped out any union activity it detected—until Cardinal Gibbons, the archbishop of Baltimore, intervened and wrote to Rome requesting that he be allowed to monitor the activities of the Knights of Labor and decide on its acceptability. The American Catholic historian John Tracy Ellis regarded this letter as the most important document in American Catholic history. Rome trusted Gibbons—he had recently been vocal in supporting the definition of infallibility—and granted his request. Thus, the working man in the United States was saved for Catholicism.

Anti-Catholicism since 1920

Obvious anti-Catholicism has flared up since 1920 in several different ways. Politically, the election of Catholic candidates, especially national candidates, has been questioned because of their obedience to a "foreign prince," the pope. When Al Smith ran as the Democratic candidate for president of the United States in 1928, he lost the election mainly because he was Roman Catholic. Losing the election was fortuitous, since Herbert Hoover won, and he has been blamed for the Great Depression ever since. The election campaign of John Kennedy in 1960 also provides insights into the ways of American prejudice. He was constantly asked by the respectable media what he would do if the pope were to tell him to follow a certain policy which would be harmful to the interests of the United States.[19] Since then, the abortion debate has alienated candidates from the Democratic Party, long a bastion of immigrant and Catholic votes. William Casey, a recent Democratic governor of Pennsylvania and a pro-life advocate, was denied permission to speak at the convention that nominated Bill Clinton for president. His ostracization from the Democratic Party has been indicative of the problems faced when Catholicism meets politics. Even more recently, practicing Catholics who have been nominated for federal judgeships have been attacked for their "extreme views" on abortion.

The news media has been increasingly ignorant and misrepresentative of Catholicism in its reporting. The opportunity to "hype" every issue and occasion, especially if it can be construed in a way detrimental to the church (e.g., the pope, the local bishop), is rarely lost. Hollywood has been worse. Complicated issues such as the New Testament, the Inquisition, the Crusades, and the church's role in Nazi Germany have been oversimplified, slanted, and otherwise treated unfairly. Movies based on historical personages, such as Savonarola, Queen Elizabeth, and Martin Luther, have been ludicrously inaccurate. Controversial subjects such as the reality of abortion are virtually ignored by the media; the once popular claim of the Vietnam War reporting, that the public has a "right to know," has suspiciously disappeared from the abortion debate. While lurid footage of combat and casualties became a part of the nightly news, no such coverage is granted to the carnage of abortion. Catholic ethnic groups such as the Irish and Italians are frequently caricatured in a bad light. Clergy and religious are looked on as pious idiots at best, as in Fr. Mulcahy of the television series MASH. Ken Burns, in his award-winning Civil War series, failed even to *mention* the existence of Catholic nuns among the nursing corps—they comprised at least one-half and possibly as much as two-thirds of the nurses who took part in the Civil War—certainly a fact worth noting. When confronted with this glaring omission, he responded lamely, "I couldn't do everything."

The recent sex abuse scandal has produced an enormous editorial literature pathetic in its ignorance of the nature and extent of the problem, of the workings of the church to solve the problem, and grossly naïve in its own proposed "solutions." Peter Steinfels, certainly no defender of the bishops, wrote a balanced and thoughtful article in the London *Tablet*, where he claimed that media reports have been seriously simplistic and one-sided.[20]

Anti-Catholicism is probably the greatest prejudice exhibited over time in the United States. It was manifest in the colonies before there were any slaves. And it still stubbornly manifests itself, long after the slaves are gone.[21]

Patterns of Immigration

Between 1820 and 1880 most of the immigration to the United States came from Western Europe and was due to the instability of governments and ensuing revolutions, especially those of 1830 and 1848, and the Potato Famine, in which 725,000 Irish died of starvation while the landlords were exporting grain and beef. However, after 1880, when the majority of immigrants entered the United States, they came from eastern Europe as a result of poverty, lack of opportunity, and the looming threat of war. It has been estimated that since 1820 roughly one-third of the immigrants to the United States have been Roman Catholic.

Patterns of immigration affected the Catholic Church profoundly. In the early 1800s, owing to the French Revolution, French Catholics sought asylum in the United States. In the 1830s, owing to revolution in Germany, waves of German Catholics came to the United States, to find an Anglo-American hierarchy in place. In the 1840s, the Irish suffered through the Potato Famine, the worst peace-time disaster in history (next to the Black Death), and sought refuge in the United States and Australia. The Slavs and Italians later found the Irish entrenched as the leadership of the American Church. Each succeeding group found another group of Catholics in place, often as bishops, and needed to stake a claim to some autonomy. This led to *trusteeism*, whereby the laity of a parish took control of the finances, appointments, and general running of the parish. Bishops fought this, realizing that such an arrangement took away all control of the diocese from the bishop and was a sure road to schismatic churches. City and state governments began by siding with the trustees because it annoyed the bishops and seemed to weaken the church. Eventually, they realized that more trouble was to be had from lay trustees than from bishops, and passed laws making the bishop the ultimate owner of all church property in a diocese. But schismatic churches did appear. There is still a Polish National Church, which has just recently reconciled with Rome, but the splintering that greatly affected Orthodox churches in the United States was avoided to a large degree in the Roman Catholic Church. Some trouble was averted by allowing "succoral parishes" to exist—national parishes within a larger parish not of the same nationality.

Because they tended to cluster in "ethnic neighborhoods," immigrants found their parish church the center of neighborhood activity—liturgical, educational, and social. Normally, a parish school would be constructed first, staffed by religious sisters, then a church building and rectory would be added. Some of these neighborhoods and ethnic parishes still exist in large cities, but most have disappeared in the flight to the suburbs following

Frances Xavier Cabrini (1850–1917) was born in northern Italy and, in 1880, founded the Missionary Sisters of the Sacred Heart of Jesus. In 1889 she emigrated to America with her sisters to care for the Italian immigrants to New York, overcoming many obstacles (including opposition from the clergy) to found schools, hospitals, and orphanages. An outstanding educator, she worked hard to integrate immigrants into mainstream American life. In 1946 she became the first American citizen to be canonized a saint.

World War II. Most recently, Catholic immigrants have come to the United States from Spanish-speaking countries of Central and South America and from Asia—especially Vietnam, Korea, and the Philippines—and have repeated the patterns of clustering in neighborhoods and founding ethnic parishes or (at least) offering Sunday Masses in their native languages.

Immigration can now be looked on as providing a vibrancy and richness to Catholicism in America, but it was not without its difficulties. Rivalries between Catholics of different nationalities could be bitter. While neighborhoods with different nationalities tended to live peacefully next to each other, ethnic groups vied for ecclesiastical power. Germans had to fight hard to have their own appointed as bishops and were successful in Milwaukee and, to a lesser extent, Cleveland. Compromises could be inventive, as in some dioceses where Germans and Irish alternated as bishops. Italians and Slavs found it nearly impossible to break into the Irish-German pattern, although African-American and Hispanic appointments to the episcopate have been proportionately very high.

African-American Catholics

The experience of African-American Catholics is both very different from that of the Catholic immigrants and very much the same. The main differences are that Africans did not come to this continent freely—they came as slaves—and they did not come as Catholics. Thus, they did not have an army of religious women and men to support them after they arrived here. There was a smattering of Spanish and French-speaking blacks in North America prior to the foundation of the United States. Blacks were also lured to Spanish Florida on the condition that they become Roman Catholic on arrival. For the most part, black slaves became Catholics through their owners. In some cases their owners were Catholic religious orders. They would attend religious services with their owners or be given permission to have their own services. Catholic missionary involvement with slaves was suspect by the state. Attempts by Catholic religious orders to educate the slaves—specifically to teach them to read—were regarded as disloyal to the state and subversive. Most of these attempts, even in the postwar South, were met with violence.

Gradually, African-Americans began to form their own religious orders, often with the encouragement of the local bishop. The first order of black religious women in the United States was founded in Baltimore in 1829, and other orders would follow. Like their European counterparts, these women's orders often flourished or foundered on the decision of their bishops. Generally speaking, religious orders based on color did not survive as long as their ethnic cousins, because there was no supporting country from which to draw additional reinforcements, though they served to further the cause of the church for a time. Eventually, African-Americans joined traditional religious orders. Some of these orders, such as the Josephites, made it their special mission to evangelize, care for, and recruit African-American Catholics. Other orders were not interested or were heavily dominated by one ethnic group. Yet Catholic blacks, as was the case with Catholic religious women, tended to advance through church structures much faster than their counterparts in the secular world. Just as Catholic nuns were the first women presidents

Henriette Delille (1812–1862), a free woman of African heritage born in New Orleans, rejected a prosperous and secure life to serve the poor and oppressed. Under Henriette's leadership an order of black nuns known as the Sisters of the Holy Family was founded and dedicated to the education and aid of slave children. The sisters also built schools, orphanages, and homes for the aged.

of colleges and hospitals in the United States, likewise the first black president of the Jesuit-run Georgetown University took office in 1874. His brother became the first African-American bishop in the United States a year later.

Black parishes, just as their ethnic counterparts, were founded and flourished, not to move African-Americans out of the way, but to give them a place where they could worship together with pride. With time this meant the foundation of gospel choirs the rival of any Protestant church. This was as much an ethnic development as a racial one. As European ethnic groups struggled to establish their identity and place in a new world, often to the exclusion of other white ethnic groups, so blacks struggled, though without a supporting cast from the "old country." Their greatest handicap was not prejudice, but the absence of religious men and women from a supporting country. Most parishes and religious orders were "ethnically driven," dominated by the immigrants of one country, and did not discriminate so much because of race as because of ethnicity.

Social Catholicism

In the early nineteenth century the Industrial Revolution appeared in Europe. The invention of the steam engine led to the factory system of producing goods and mass production. This eventually caused great shifts of populations from farms to cities and led to inhuman living and working conditions. During the Enlightenment Adam Smith wrote *The Wealth of Nations,* in which he argued that free trade would produce world peace and would better the condition of the worker by opening new markets. He did not realize that free trade *depends on* peace, and that workers could be more easily exploited, as well as more easily made wealthier, under a system of broad markets and large companies. One reaction was that of Karl Marx, who wrote his *Communist Manifesto* in 1848. In both cases, the writers were more than economic theorists; they were interested in improving the moral lot of the average worker.

But Marx introduced an ominous note, at least as far as the church was concerned. He thought religion was part of the economic problem and needed, ultimately, to be eliminated. Initially

Katharine Drexel (1858–1955), though born into a wealthy and socially prominent Philadelphia family, was deeply influenced by her parents' concern for the needs of others. Devoting her life and her fortune to establishing schools and missions for Native American and black children, she founded the Sisters of the Blessed Sacrament for the work of caring for and evangelizing the "poorest of the poor." She was canonized in October 2000.

he saw religion, especially organized religion, as a sign that things were bad. Religion, for Marx, was a refuge for people who are desperate, helpless, and have nowhere else to go. Furthermore, Marx thought that religion provided an irrational explanation for life's hardships, and then provided people with an equally irrational and false hope that all will be made well in some sort of utopian afterlife. Marx believed, along with the philosopher Hegel, that life consisted of a series of opposites that are alienated from each other. Natural man can be made unnatural. The human being can be alienated from nature, his neighbors, even himself. Labor is the key because it can hold all of these things in harmony. But when done for the sake of the market, labor is alienating because ultimately it is not done for the sake of those doing the work, the *proletariat*. It is being done, rather, for the owners, the *bourgeoisie*.

Alienation occurs because the worker must produce a surplus in order to support the owner, and thus Marx regarded the worker as being exploited. The surplus leads to consumerism and more exploitation. This class struggle is the essence of Marxism (or communism) and only the "Revolution" will correct this.[22] Religion arises from this alienation (and does not create it) by preaching acceptance of the situation. In fact, religion has its own forms of alienation, when it stresses the overcoming of our natures: the suppressing of our passions; making war between the spirit and the flesh, conscience and wickedness, virtue and vice. Religion blesses the acceptance of rich and poor, slave and free, and preaches that evil is a result of sin and that strife in this "vale of tears" is our condition.

Marx was, in some ways, a logical extreme of the Enlightenment. Arguments have been put forth defending Marx by saying that he was only opposed to *organized* religion and that his quarrel was with churches and not religion as such. But it seems that Marxism was, and is, essentially antireligious for several reasons:

1) *It is materialistic.* This means that the only reality that can be known and measured is material reality. It believes, as a result of this, that the only things that exist are material. Solutions to life's questions are, therefore, material things.

2) *It is atheistic.* To believe in God is, for Marxists, to agree to be a slave. Lenin said that religion is "bad spiritual vodka in which

the slaves of capitalism drown their human existence."
Religion puts its faith in God rather than in the Revolution
and thus only gets in the way.

3) *It is totalitarian.* Communism's first great experiment, in Russia,
began idealistically as the Mensheviks tried to usher in a legal,
parliamentary state to take the place of the czars. This lasted one
year until the Bolsheviks, who wanted revolution at all costs,
took over. They set the pattern for future communist countries,
where the state had supreme control of the life of the individual
from birth to death. The economics, education, justice, morality, religious belief, and even travel of every individual of a communist country were completely controlled by the state.

Furthermore, communism's assault on the church has been
consistent. It is too convenient to say that the church was closely
identified with the political party overthrown by the communists.
It was (and is), in fact, the church's protection of individual conscience that threatened the communist program in most cases.

The Church's Response to the Industrial Revolution

The first countries to be affected by the Industrial
Revolution were Great Britain and the United States, and neither
was predominantly Catholic, so the Catholic Church did not see
the problems of this industrialization as soon as it might, nor did
it respond as soon as it should.[23] One of the first churchmen to see
difficulties was Wilhelm von Ketteler, bishop of Mainz, Germany,
from 1850 to 1877, who addressed the problem of the factory
worker. He called for profit-sharing, reasonable working hours,
sufficient rest days, factory inspection, and regulation of female
and child labor. He criticized both the tendencies of the socialists
to be totalitarian and of the industrialists to be exploitative. Yet
the church, from the beginning, seemed to be more wary of the
socialists because their program, in contrast to that of the capitalists, called for a systematic elimination of religion. In 1864 Pius
IX denounced the "delusion" of socialism which held up the state
instead of Divine Providence as the driving force of society, for
the pagan character of economic liberalism, and for the exclusion
of moral considerations from capital-labor negotiations.

Dorothy Day (1897–1980), a radical journalist and convert to Catholicism, and Peter Maurin (1877–1949), a French scholar, founded the Catholic Worker movement in 1933 in New York. Dorothy and Peter worked tirelessly for peace and social justice through nonviolence. Their legacy survives in *The Catholic Worker* newspaper and the many Catholic Worker communities worldwide. The cause for Dorothy's canonization was opened in March 2000.

In 1872, Cardinal Manning backed the farmers of Britain in a labor dispute, marking the first time a bishop had openly sided with labor in a dispute. In 1889 he took the lead in forming an arbitration committee in resolving the London Dock Strike. He was eighty-two years old at the time, and his sympathies were clearly with the workers. In 1886 Cardinal Gibbons of Baltimore saved the United States' first labor union, the Knights of Labor, from a Roman condemnation. Pope Leo XIII was the most active pope in speaking out on labor issues. In 1878 he condemned communism as "this fatal pest which attacks the marrow of human society and may destroy it." In 1891 he wrote the ground-breaking encyclical *Rerum Novarum*, which spelled out the rights of the worker both against the communists and the capitalists. At this time, the age of the industrial barons (Rockefeller, Carnegie, Frick, Mellon, Rothschild, Krupp) was in full swing. Leo XIII condemned socialism, but also insisted on a just wage, wage-settlements by free agreement, and the integrity of the family. Private property, he added, was a natural right and served as a means by which other rights could be protected.

Leo XIII's encyclical had a significant influence in two areas: the formation of Christian trade unions as well as the formation of Christian Democratic parties. The Christian trade unions began as clubs, usually led by priests, but by the late 1870s they were turning into real unions as we know them today. Movements sprang up in Germany, France, Belgium, and the United States. The Knights of Labor was the first labor union in the United States. It enjoyed great success in the 1880s when it was led by the Catholic Terence Powderly and had about 700,000 members. Part of the success of these unions was that they refused to get bogged down in mere anti-socialism. Instead, they developed a positive program, calling for collaboration between employer and worker, and recognizing the individuality of the worker rather than his subordination to the state or some vague "revolution."

Christian Democratic political parties grew out of these unions. In Germany the Christian Democratic Center Party was influential after the Kulturkampf of the 1870s, in which the Chancellor Bismarck attempted to destroy the Catholic Church in his newly united Germany. The Center Party became a watchdog for violations against Catholics and individual rights, and between 1918 and 1933 elected eight of fourteen chancellors, while holding 12 to 13 percent of the national vote. It dissolved amid

Pope Leo XIII (1810–1903) brought a breath of modernity into a church recovering from the long reign of the beleaguered Pius IX. He promoted study of the Bible and wrote the first of the church's great social encyclicals, *Rerum Novarum,* thereby encouraging Catholic work for social justice.

pressure from the Nazis, who eventually abolished all rival political parties, and internal feuding. Its original purpose in being founded—as a defense against the hostile government—seemed to have dissipated and the party split along ideological and geographic lines.[24] In Italy the *Partito Popolare*, led by the Catholic priest Don Luigi Sturzo, was a considerable force until Pius XI withdrew his support. It was never able to overcome the popularity and mob tactics of Mussolini.

Despite the success of these Christian unions and political parties, Rome was nervous about too much power being in the hands of the laity, who could represent the church but not fall under Rome's supervision. Added to this was the threat of socialism and communism, which were greater threats to the church than fascism. Labor unions, which preached a modified socialism, were considered by Rome to be naïvely sleeping with the enemy. Thus Rome did not mourn their passing. However, after the Second World War, as in Germany, the *Partito Popolare* returned in Italy as the Christian Democratic Party and has recently resumed its original name. Christian Democratic parties have surfaced in South America with a leftward tendency, favoring radical land and educational reforms, but have been relatively ineffective to date owing to the ruling political parties and the hesitation of Rome over their politics. A real insight into the power these Christian labor unions and political parties wielded might be gained from an examination of the impact of the Solidarity movement in Poland which, with the blessing of Pope John Paul II and the leadership of Lech Walesa, managed to assist greatly in the toppling of European communism and the Soviet Union.

The Condemnation of Communism

As socialism and communism took visible shape in several countries, the church grew increasingly wary of their obvious anti-Catholicism. Pope Leo XIII did not merely condemn socialism in *Rerum Novarum*, he set forth a comprehensive social program, holding up the family as the basic unit of society and claiming that private property was a natural right. Furthermore, he called for a just wage to be settled by free agreement. In 1937

Pope Pius XI wrote the encyclical *Divini Redemptoris*, which condemned communism systematically, saying that no agreement, not even tactical agreement, was permissible between Christianity and communism, which was based on a false concept of man, the world, and life. Bishops, priests, and religious in all communist countries have spoken out against the evils of communism and have paid the price. Most spectacular was the involvement of Pope John Paul II in bringing communism down, first as a bishop in Poland and then as pope. Such was the Soviet Union's unease at his activity, that its secret police arranged an assassination in 1981. It very nearly succeeded. In 1991, the Soviet Union fell apart.

The Revival of the Missions (1800–2000)

1815 really marks the revival of the church's missionary efforts. In that year *Propaganda Fide*, the Vatican commission overseeing mission countries, was reorganized and revived. France would prove to be the principal agent of missionary revival. Already under Napoleon, the Foreign Mission Society was restored, the Holy Spirit Seminary opened, and the Vincentians founded—all with an eye toward missionary activity. But once the Revolution was finally over, and Napoleon gone from the scene (his final defeat in the Battle of Waterloo was in 1814), the energy of the French Church knew no bounds. The spiritual life of French Catholicism revived, partly out of relief that the persecution of the church was over, and partly because of the urging of Chateaubriand for Catholics to do more.

Growth of Missionary Religious Orders and Mission Societies

Several religious orders were founded in the early nineteenth century with missionary work in mind. Many of them concentrated their efforts in certain parts of the world. The Congregation of the Sacred Heart of Jesus and Mary was established as early as 1800. Its headquarters was on the Rue Picpos in Paris, and so it received the more manageable name of the "Picpos Fathers." Its principal area of ministry was in the Hawaiian

Islands. The Society of Mary (Marists) served in Australia and New Zealand. The Oblates of Mary Immaculate, founded in 1916 by Charles de Mazenod, served in the Canadian Pacific and Yukon areas. The Congregation of the Immaculate Heart of Mary (Missionhurst) was founded in 1862 in order to serve in China. The Congregation of the Holy Ghost (now known as Spiritans) concentrated on Africa. The White Fathers and White Sisters were found in northern Africa. As Americans began looking beyond their own borders for evangelization opportunities, Maryknoll was founded in 1911. Established religious orders (and eventually dioceses) also joined in the mission effort, often designating a proportion of their members to mission countries.

In the beginning, mission activity often followed the routes of explorers. There were several famous expeditions in the mid–nineteenth century, when central Asia and sub-Saharan Africa were explored by Europeans. Missionaries accompanied these explorations. The *Dublin Review*, Britain's premier Catholic journal, included notes on recent explorations in the back of each issue. Mission societies also published letters from missionaries. By far, the most important of these mission societies was the Society for the Propagation of the Faith, founded in 1822 by a factory worker named Telicot. Its *Nouvelles des Missions* is still published today under the name "Annals of the Propagation of the Faith."

The growth of the missions was rapid. In 1850 there were two vicariates (a form of a diocese dependent on another) south of the Sahara Desert. By 1900 there were sixty-one. Unfortunately the grab for converts accompanied a grab for colonies. Most of the mission groups of the nineteenth century were associated with the parent country, and thus could be identified with the colonizer. Asians were particularly suspicious of foreign activity. As early as 1833 in Indochina, the notorious Minh Mang was hostile to Christians and ordered all Christians to abandon their beliefs. By way of emphasis, he had Bishop Diaz beheaded. The Spanish and French invaded and stayed until 1954. This brought about a revival of the mission, but it also clearly identified the missionaries with the invaders. The same process occurred in China between the 1830s and 1860s, and again in the Boxer Rebellion of 1900.

Mission Directions after 1900

In the early 1900s, two things began to happen: The colonies began breaking up, and the church began to encourage the formation of indigenous (native) clergy and religious. The latter was not an obvious direction to take. Europeans felt superior, and were unwilling to hand over responsibility to natives. One priest wrote to Propaganda in 1847:

> On the necessity in the abstract for an indigenous clergy, there is fairly general agreement; but when it comes to the point, no one is willing to put the policy into practice, and the reason nearly always given is that the people of this country are so devoid of intelligence and so weak in character that they are incapable of conceiving the grandeur and dignity of the priesthood and of fulfilling its demands.[25]

Another problem facing religious orders in the mission field is that they were reared in a certain theological and spiritual tradition that was very much based on an individualistic notion of salvation and private devotion. There was little regard given to building a "church" or community. In such a scheme of things, a native clergy could serve, at best, as reinforcements.

A final problem was that mission territories were carved up and given to the exclusive ministry of particular religious orders. While this had its practical advantages—the ministry enjoyed a definite unity of purpose, consistency in administration, and pride in achievement—the downside was that missions were regarded as the private responsibility and property of one religious order. The local clergy were looked on as auxiliaries.

Pope Benedict XV (1914–22), until recently a very neglected pope, was not called "the Pope of the Missions" for nothing. In 1919 he wrote an encyclical, *Maximum Illud*, which called for an indigenous clergy. This had been called for previously by Propaganda and several popes, but Benedict XV was insistent:

> For since the Church of God is Catholic, and cannot be a stranger in any nation or tribe, it is proper that out of every people should be drawn sacred ministers to be teachers of the Divine Law and leaders in the way of salvation for their own

countrymen to follow. Hence, wherever there exists a sufficient number of indigenous clergy, well-instructed and worthy of their holy vocation, it may justly be said that the
missionaries have successfully completed their work, and that
the Church has been thoroughly well-founded....Remember
that you have to make citizens not of any country upon earth,
but of the heavenly country.[26]

Pope Pius XI underlined this in 1926 by urging the foundation of local seminaries: "Why should the native clergy be prevented from governing its own people? What are the missions for,
except to establish the church on firm and regular foundations?"
With these principles firmly in place, a great change began to take
place. The first non-European bishop in India was ordained in
1923. Six Chinese bishops were ordained in 1926, the first since
the seventeenth century. In 1927, the first Japanese bishop was
ordained. By 1941, all of the bishops in Japan were Japanese.

Mission policy today insists on three things: 1) That local
clergy and religious be fostered; 2) That local customs be
respected; and 3) That nationalism be avoided. The normal pattern which came of this policy was for a religious order or diocesan clergy to move into a certain assigned area and begin to
evangelize. This is done by preaching and the building of schools
and hospitals. After time, candidates for the priesthood and religious life are accepted and trained. After some more time, these
priests and religious will have their own regular bishops and superiors. This process takes about thirty-five years. It has been very
successful, and has resulted in a quiet revolution in the make-up
of the number of bishops. In 1870, when the First Vatican Council
ended, all of the bishops at the council were either European or
had parents who were born in Europe. In less than one hundred
years, at the opening of the Second Vatican Council in 1962, only
one-third of the bishops were European.

War and Dictatorship

The church in the twentieth century was faced with many
new challenges. Foremost among these were two global wars and

several powerful dictatorships, beginning with the Communist Revolution in 1917.

World War I

Pope Pius X died one month after World War I began in August 1914. It is said he died of a broken heart at not being able to prevent the outbreak of hostilities. His successor, Benedict XV, had been secretary to Cardinal Rampolla (Leo XIII's Secretary of State) and was made Archbishop of Bologna by Pius X in order to get rid of him. Benedict XV was unpopular during his lifetime and is only now being appreciated. He was against the war from the start and spoke against violations of human rights on both sides. Within two months of the beginning of the war, he was openly demanding peace negotiations. Throughout the war he remained neutral, a fact which made him unpopular with both sides. The Germans called him the *Franzosenpapst*, the French Pope, while the English called him the "Boche Pope."

In addition to calling for warring parties to come to the negotiating table, Benedict XV also sought help for war victims, successfully calling for the repatriation of civilians who were displaced and POWs who had been injured in battle. He spent his entire personal fortune as well as the ordinary revenue of the Holy See on relief, which consisted of gifts of money, food, clothing, and medicine. The Vatican became a clearinghouse for tracing and exchanging prisoners, searching for missing persons, returning the remains of those killed in action. As much as the warring countries did not like his neutrality, they courted his favor. Even England sent a temporary ambassador to the Vatican. The upshot of this was a dramatic increase in the Vatican's diplomatic activity. In 1914, The Vatican had diplomatic relations with seventeen countries; by 1922 it had diplomatic relations with twenty-seven countries; by 1939 there were thirty-nine nuncios (often of the rank of ambassador) and twenty-three apostolic delegates (representatives).

Tragically, efforts to broker a peace came to nothing. The Axis powers thought that, with the withdrawal of Russia from the war in 1917, a victory was possible before the Americans committed any troops. The Allies were cautious, and saw a negotiated peace as throwing away a victory, and wanted to wait until the Americans arrived. Even worse, the Holy See was banned from participating in the Peace Conference held at Versailles, and was powerless to prevent the ruthless terms of the Armistice.

Russia

Revolution came to Russia in 1917 and Benedict XV made gestures of friendship from the start by establishing relief missions to feed and clothe those affected by the war and revolution. The Vatican even accepted the terms that there was to be no proselytizing or public display of religion. Even so, an antireligious program developed immediately. In 1918 the separation of church and state was declared, followed by decrees abolishing the post of religion teacher, subjecting all sermons to state censorship, confiscating all sacred vessels and icons, and banning all religious youth groups. In 1921 there had been 963 Catholic (as opposed to Orthodox) priests in the territory of Russia (which included Poland, the Baltic states, and the Ukraine). By 1932 there were 300, and one-third of them were in prison. Stalin came to power in 1924 and attempted to eliminate the Catholic Church. Pope Pius XI, by way of protest, held a service in Rome in 1930 that mingled elements of Latin and Slavonic chant, invoking a litany of Russian saints, and singing a *De Profundis* in memory of the victims of communism. This antagonistic state of affairs would worsen with the end of World War II, when Russia gained control of several Eastern European countries, from the Baltic Sea south to the Balkan Peninsula. Churches were closed or turned to other uses, bishops and priests were imprisoned, the faithful intimidated from practicing the faith in any form.[27] World shock attended the savage beating and execution of a Polish priest, Jerzy Popieluszko, in 1984. Matters would improve only with the collapse of the Soviet Union in 1991.

Mussolini and Fascism

When Pius XI was elected in 1922, his first goal was improving relations with the Italian government. Despite Italian resentment at the pope's interference in World War I, relations were warming. Benedict XV had lifted the papal ban on Catholic rulers visiting the king of Italy. Catholics could now become involved in politics both by voting and running for office without the threat of excommunication. When Benedict XV died, the Italian government officially mourned his passing.

Fascism was gaining in strength. In 1922 Benito Mussolini was asked by the king of Italy to form a government. Socialism loomed as the most immediate and greatest threat, and Mussolini's Fascists were looked on as the only way to prevent the Socialists from assuming power. Mussolini was anticlerical—calling priests "black microbes who are as fatal to mankind as tuberculosis germs"—and thought he could replace Catholicism with a religion of "strength and courage," but soon realized (like Napoleon) that he could not overcome the church. All things considered, the church had suffered far less under the Fascists than their Socialist counterparts, and was somewhat relieved when he took over.

A solution to the "Roman question" was desired by both church and state. In 1929 the Lateran Treaty was signed, in which the Vatican recognized the king of Italy and ceded all its territorial claims to the Papal States; Italy in turn made Vatican City into an independent state and compensated the church for the loss of the Papal States. Other concessions were important. The new Vatican state was not only guaranteed an independent government (with free access of diplomats and communications), but was allowed to have its own police force, civil service, postage, coinage, railway station, newspaper, and radio station. Papal churches and buildings outside Vatican City were given extraterritorial immunity usually reserved for foreign embassies. This would prove crucial for the protection of several thousand Jews in World War II.

Mexico and South America

The persecution of the church in South American countries followed a similar pattern. As the yoke of Spain was cast off by these fledgling countries, the church was similarly targeted by revolutionaries who identified it with the ruling class and were eager to plunder its property. Mexico by far provides the most violent example of this problem. Prior to World War I, the Mexican dictator Carranza initiated a persecution of the church which included expelling a great number of priests and religious, torturing some and hounding bishops through the desert, profaning sacred objects and consecrated hosts. With the advent of communism, foreign priests were expelled and religious orders suppressed. In 1920 Carranza's successor, an Indian named Obregon, was worse—blowing up shrines (including Guadalupe) and episcopal residences. In 1924 the new president, Calles, did everything he could to eradicate Catholicism—arresting, expelling, or executing priests and distinguished Catholic laymen; dismissing religious from hospital work; insisting on lectures in schools on atheism. In 1925 an apostate priest was allowed to establish a national church, featuring a bizarre use of maize wafers and agave juice. This was not popular. Only two priests joined him and services inevitably ended in mob scenes.

The most famous hero of the time was the Jesuit priest Miguel Pro, who was pursued by the police for a year before being caught and executed in 1927. His final words were *Viva Cristo Rey*, "Long Live Christ the King." All told, about 5,300 people are said to have been executed by Calles. Resistance to his policies stiffened. Pilgrimages to Guadalupe persisted. Catholics were elected in labor unions and often had Mass celebrated in factories. By the beginning of World War II, the government was less imbued with old-style Marxism and lessened the harassment. Even so, when Pope John Paul II came to Mexico in 1979, a law had to be passed allowing him to wear his cassock in public. But it was the people of Mexico who did not let the faith be driven out. Their Catholicism is very public, and today large and impressive pilgrimages still go off to various shrines.

Spain

Catholicism in Spain had fallen on hard times since the French Revolution, which provoked a nationalization of church property in the early 1800s and the expulsion of religious orders.

In the early 1900s, matters became more violent as a bloodless coup in 1923 became so radicalized that, in 1931 anticlerical leftists assumed control. May 1931 saw the looting and burning of major Catholic buildings, from the Jesuit residence in Madrid and its adjoining 90,000-volume library, to churches in Valencia, Malaga, and Cordobà. In 1936 a Catholic member of the government's council read a list of outrages committed in the previous four months: 169 churches and convents were burned down, 257 damaged by fire or looted, 269 people had been killed and 1879 wounded. Priests and religious were hunted down, the cardinal-primate expelled, and church property nationalized once again. Loyalty to Communist Russia was to be proclaimed, the army disbanded. Spain was on the verge of civil war as right-wing associations (most notably the Falange, also called Nationalists or Fascists) formed to fight back. Resistance centered around Francisco Franco, who had been head of the military academy until he had been exiled to the Canary Islands, where he could be carefully watched and kept away from any trouble that might develop. Unfortunately for the communists (otherwise known as Republicans), Franco was rescued and reunited with his troops in North Africa.

Thus the Spanish Civil War began in 1936. The communists sought the help of Russia, and also received aid from socialists in France, England, and the United States. The Fascists looked to Hitler and Mussolini for help. Franco tried portraying himself as the protector of the church, which did not have much choice. The communists had laid waste the church, executing twelve bishops and almost 8,000 priests, monks, and nuns. Thirty months later, in 1938, Franco was victorious and was recognized by the Holy See, while he in turn restored the church's existence. The pattern of anticlericalism, established by the French Revolution, dogged the church in almost every twentieth-century revolution—in Russia, Mexico, Italy, Spain, and later in Cuba and China—but was often warded off by local resistance or by the signing of concordats. The biggest challenge to the church was yet to come.

Nazi Germany and the Catholic Church

In the 1870s Otto von Bismarck, the Iron Chancellor, attempted successfully to unify Germany's many provinces into a single nation. Feeling that Roman Catholics were a threat to that unity—and were allies of his enemies Austria, France, and Poland—he targeted them with his *Kulturkampf*. In the period between 1871 and 1875, the Catholic education system was dismantled and brought under the control of the state, the Jesuits and eventually all religious orders were expelled, and the German ambassador to the Vatican recalled.

Bismarck underestimated the opposition of the church. Two bishops were imprisoned, which had the effect of making martyrs of them, and the *Kulturkampf* eventually failed by 1879. It even provoked a Catholic revival. By the late 1920s, Catholic organizations were flourishing; the Catholic Youth Organization in Germany boasted 1.5 million members. The Catholic press and publications were strong and aided a Catholic intellectual revival. While there were 16,000 ministers for forty million Protestants, there were 20,000 Catholic priests for the twenty million Roman Catholics in Germany. The Center Party, the Catholic political party, consistently drew 12 to 13 percent of the national vote and had an influence beyond its numbers. Between 1918 and 1933, the Center Party held the chancellorship eight out of fourteen times.

But, as a result of the *Kulturkampf* and Bismarck's stigmatizing of German Catholics as unpatriotic, they had an inferiority complex. Wanting to prove they could be good Germans, Catholics compensated with superheated patriotism. Bishop Bares of Hildesheim said, in an address to the Catholic youth of Berlin: "We are patriotic to the core, German through and through, prepared to make every sacrifice for *Volk* and Fatherland."[28]

Some Catholics wanted to influence Nazism, to appreciate its "healthy core." In 1920 a small group of Catholics founded the Catholic League for Patriotic Politics, which tried to reconcile Catholicism and right-wing radicals. They opposed Marxism, communism, Jews, and Freemasons. Fr. Joseph Roth contributed to its newspaper; he specialized in anti-Semitic tirades. For his efforts, he was made an official in Hitler's Ministry of

Ecclesiastical Affairs. Abbot Albanus Schachleiter, former head of the Benedictine monastery in Prague, also supported Hitler early on. In 1933, another group, *Kreuz und Adler* ("Cross and Eagle"), was formed, attempting to help form the new Reich.

The cohesion of the Center Party began to unravel. For one thing, its reason for coming into existence—the attacks of Bismarck and the prejudices of German Protestants—had begun to fade from memory. Long a bulwark against both left- and right-wing extremism, Center Party members began to look on themselves as redundant, since the Nazis were obviously opposed to the left and had not yet begun to show their true colors. Membership in the Nazi party became more attractive, either because of policy positions or through intimidation, and this combined with internal feuding to bring about the collapse of the Center Party.

Its policy of compromise with the Nazis under Msgr. Kaas proved its undoing. Kaas had sent Hitler birthday greetings on 20 April 1933, which read: "For today's birthday sincere good wishes and the assurance of unflinching cooperation in the great enterprise of creating a Germany internally united, enjoying social peace, and externally free."[29] Kaas typified the Center Party's wishful thinking about Nazi intentions and a fear of having its patriotism questioned. The party eventually showed a desire to give up its own existence if Catholic interests could be guaranteed.

Rome was also nervous about Catholic political parties. They seemed to give laymen too much power in representing Catholic interests without the church's guiding hand. So to the pope, the Center Party, like Don Sturzo's *Partito Popolari* in Italy, was expendable. The Center Party was going to go, anyway, one way or another. On 28 June 1933, Josef Goebbels demanded the dissolution of the Bavarian People's Party and Center Party, and they succumbed on 4 July and 5 July, respectively.

The Rise of German Nationalism

The worldwide economic collapse of 1929 brought the Nazis new gains in the Reichstag. By September 1930, they had nine times the parliamentary members they had in 1928. They had 20 percent of all the seats, but their gains were smallest in Catholic constituencies, and Hitler wanted to further limit the opposition of the Catholic Church to his program. Hitler thought that Bismarck had made a big mistake in starting a *Kulturkampf*, because it made martyrs of the clergy. He thought it was better to ridicule the clergy. Whatever his diplomatic statements and postures, Hitler's scorn for Christianity remained as strong as ever. He said in 1933: "One is either a German or a Christian. You cannot be both."[30]

Catholic opposition was considerable. Even as late as the July 1933 elections, the ten voting districts most hostile to Hitler (except Berlin) were Catholic. Derek Holmes commented, "There is no doubt that the Catholic districts resisted the lure of National Socialism far better than the Protestant ones."[31] One reason for this resistance was the suspicion on the part of the younger Catholic bishops. They had not experienced the *Kulturkampf* and tended to be both more wary of National Socialism and more outspoken against it. The older bishops, fearing a repetition of the *Kulturkampf*, were either supportive of National Socialism or were willing to compromise.

In 1930 Cardinal Bertram of Breslau condemned the Nazi glorification of the Nordic race, its contempt of divine revelation, and its program of "positive Christianity," a reinterpretation of the Scriptures in which the Old Testament would be eliminated as well as embarrassing passages from the New Testament. Bertram also condemned destructive forms of nationalism, of which he thought National Socialism was one.

Also in 1930, a local priest in Mainz named Weber had preached against the Nazis, saying that Catholics were forbidden to be Nazis, that Nazis could not attend funerals and church functions in group formation, and that Catholics who agreed with the Nazi party's teachings were barred from the sacraments. When Dr. Mayer, the Vicar-General of Mainz, was asked by the Nazi's district office about this, he explained that Catholics were not permitted to join the Nazi party and that Fr. Weber was acting under instructions from the chancery. He added several caveats of his own, namely that the Nazis' desire to subordinate Christian moral law to the "ethical and moral sense of the Germanic people" was unacceptable, that the religious policies of National Socialism contradicted Catholic Christianity, and, finally, that his bishop supported him.

Bavarian bishops forbade priests from taking any part in the Nazi movement. They forbade Nazi parading into Mass. The bishops of Cologne issued a similar, but more restrained statement. Three bishops in Paderborn said membership in the Nazi party was not permitted, for "entirely religious" reasons. They pointed out that the Nazi program was not merely political, but proposed a worldview which involved an attitude toward religion, and made demands on religion.

But the German bishops were not united. In 1931 the older bishops prevailed at the bishops' annual conference at Fulda. Many bishops felt that the Nazis could be converted from their "positive Christianity" and prove to be helpful in the fight against left-wing radicalism. Hermann Göring had just visited Rome and assured the Vatican of Nazi disapproval of anti-Catholicism among its members. Some members of the Nazi party had resigned because it was not anti-Catholic enough. In all of this, the Nazis realized that the German bishops were not unified, so they stressed the threat from the left.

Some Catholics saw hope in this. Bishop Schreiber of Berlin said Catholics in his diocese could become members of the Nazi party. In 1933, Archbishop Gröber, while deploring the slanderous attacks made on the church by the Nazis (especially the removal of Catholics from government posts), became a "promoting member" of the SS. He thought the stories of atrocities on the Jews were the work of enemy propagandists. (So did American Jews at the time, for that matter.) He became known as the "Brown Bishop," so named because of the "brownshirts," the symbol of Hitler's followers.

The German Catholic people were, for the most part, swinging toward Nazism and made some sort of agreement between the church and the Nazis a necessity. After the Fulda (Catholic bishops') Conference of 1933, the trend was toward cooperation with the Nazis, even enthusiasm for the Nazis. On 25 June 1933, the annual Catholic Congress *(Katholikentag)* met in Berlin. It was attended by 45,000 people. The papal nuncio attended and was ushered in by soldiers waving swastika flags. Vicar-General Steinmann, taking the place of Bishop Schreiber of Berlin, told a meeting of several thousand Catholic youths: "What we all have longed and striven for has become reality: We have one Reich and one leader and this leader we follow faithfully and conscientiously.... For us this is not a question of personality. We know that he who stands at the head is given us by God as our leader."[32]

Bishop Gröber said that he gave "his complete and whole-hearted support to the new government and the new Reich."[33] German intellectuals, the biggest names being Karl Adam, Joseph Lortz, and Michael Schmaus, defended the Reich. Both Germany and the Catholic Church, Lortz reasoned, were opposed to Bolshevism, liberalism, relativism, atheism, and public immorality. Adam, much to his later embarrassment, said that Nazism and Catholicism belonged to each other as nature to grace.

One priest, a Fr. Senn of Freiburg, went too far in this regard and wrote a pro-Nazi pamphlet which said that Hitler and "the wonderful movement for the liberation of Germany created by him" were "instruments of divine providence." He had not submitted this for approval, and was suspended by his bishop. He was reinstated only after apologizing and denouncing the anti-Catholic elements of National Socialism.

By 1933, the bishops were worried that Catholics would leave the church in droves if they were not permitted to join the party. The Nazis had begun a policy of encouraging party members to infiltrate churches in order to subvert them. It was hoped a formal recognition or agreement would end this. Besides, the Nazis were leaving the interests of Catholics largely alone, so it is easy to understand the church's willingness to go along.

Things happened very quickly in 1933. At the end of January, Hitler was appointed chancellor by von Hindenburg. A month later, the Reichstag burned, a fire set by the Nazis and blamed on a mentally disabled Jewish man. The panic following the fire enabled Hitler to obtain a "Decree for the Protection of People and State," and to step up repressive measures against political opponents. A week later, elections saw the Nazis gain a sizable plurality, but no majority. Later in March, Hitler promised peace between church and state. Shortly after, the bishops agreed to allow Catholics to join the Nazi party. Nazi members could now attend services in uniform and be admitted to the sacraments. The statement of the bishops constituted a formal recognition of Nazism and of Catholic membership in the party, which gave the Nazis a certain respectability.

The Concordat—20 July 1933

Both sides wanted an agreement. A number of issues—such as Germany's financial subsidies to the church, the legal status of the clergy, the appointment of bishops, recognition of religious schools—all had to be ironed out.

Hitler was primarily interested in a public relations coup; an agreement with the Vatican would further legitimize his party in the eyes of the world. But he also had issues which he wanted to settle. He wanted to avoid the realignment of diocesan boundaries in the Saar, Danzig, and Upper Silesian districts—areas taken from the Germans after World War I—because this would have strengthened French and Polish claims to these areas and would have made any repossession more complicated. Hitler also wanted military chaplains to have exempt status, thus forming a military diocese over which he, and not the local bishops, would have more control.

Intimidation of political parties opposed to the Nazis began in earnest in June 1933. Between 22 and 29 June, the Social Democratic Party had been outlawed, the Democrats disbanded themselves, and the German Nationalists saw their leader resign from office and the party dissolve. Hitler next set his sights on the Catholic Church. Nearly one hundred priests were arrested within a few weeks, a meeting of the Catholic Journeymen was broken up by force, and the Congress of Christian Trade Unions was dissolved on 24 June. This sent the message that some agreement with the church would be helpful. Negotiations had begun in 1919, but the Holy See had to be content with local concordats with Bavaria (1924), Prussia (1929), and Baden (1932). As in its negotiations with the Fascists in Italy, the church did not think Hitler's régime would last very long, and an agreement would be helpful in the future, when a less agreeable régime could take power.

Terms of the Concordat

ART. 1—Guaranteed the freedom of profession and public practice of the Catholic religion and the right of the church to manage her own affairs.

ART. 3—Reaffirmed diplomatic representation with a papal nuncio in Berlin, and a German ambassador at the Holy See.

ART. 4—Guaranteed full freedom of communication for the Holy See with the German clergy, and for bishops with their faithful.

ART. 5–10—Concerned with legal status of clergy.
  a) Clergy were assured exemption from jury duty.
  b) The secret of the confessional was assured.
  c) Ecclesiastical appointments would be made by the church.
  d) Parishes, sees, and religious orders were publicly recognized.

ART. 14—Appointment of bishops was subject to government veto for "political reasons." (This right had appeared in several previous concordats.) Only German citizens could become priests.

ART. 15—Guaranteed religious orders freedom to carry on pastoral, educational, and charitable work.

ART. 16—New bishops were required to take an oath of loyalty; their clergy had to do the same. They were to prevent anything that might be detrimental to the Reich.

ART. 17—Guaranteed the property of the church, continuation of state subsidies. (These were, amazingly, paid to the end!)

ART. 19–25—Catholic education system guaranteed. Theological faculties would continue at state-run schools, the church had the right to establish seminaries, Catholics also had the right to teach religion in public schools, the church had the right of veto over appointment of religion teachers, and the continuation of confessional schools and establishment of new ones was guaranteed. These latter two were considered great victories by the church.

ART. 26—Gave priests the right to marry people in church before the civil ceremony in case of great moral emergency. (This was used by a few daring priests to circumvent racial laws which prohibited a civil marriage.)

ART. 27—Gave the Nazis their wish for an exempt military chaplaincy. Army bishops would be chosen by the mutual consent of Holy See and Reich. Local bishops had to approve one of their priests being made chaplain.

ART. 28—Guaranteed the church the right of pastoral care in state-run hospitals, prisons, etc. (This provision was soon violated when the government refused to allow Catholic services in concentration camps).

ART. 30—A special prayer would be said at the end of every High Mass for the welfare of the German Reich and its people.

ART. 31—Guaranteed the existence of Catholic organizations which were "devoted exclusively to religious, cultural, and charitable purposes." Any organizations which had social or professional purposes would be protected by mutual consent of church and state.

ART. 32—The clergy were to be excluded from politics. (This was one of Hitler's main aims in agreeing to a concordat. Interestingly enough, priests were still allowed to be members of the Nazi party.)

An additional, secret provision stated that seminarians and priests were exempt from any universal military training, except in times of mobilization. Even then, most of the diocesan clergy would be exempt, while others were to be used in noncombatant roles.

Significance of the Concordat

The Concordat received mixed reviews. The Prussian Minister of Education, Science, and Culture felt that the Concordat gave away too much to the church. But Hitler did not care about the fine print; he had no intention of keeping the pact (or most of it), anyway. Hitler felt Catholicism was defunct and a great idea which had outlived its usefulness. Still, he feared it enough not to take it head-on. When Bishop von Galen harangued the Nazis Sunday after Sunday from his cathedral in Münster, Hitler decided not to punish him, telling Josef Goebbels that the bishop would be taken care of after the war. Von Galen was arrested once, in fact, but the public freed him on his way to jail and he was never touched again.

As a result of the Concordat, Hitler's prestige increased substantially around the world. He wanted to seem a reasonable man. Five days earlier he had signed the Four Powers Pact with France, Britain, and Italy, so who were they to complain?

From the Catholic side, Rome knew that Hitler (like Napoleon) would attempt to ignore articles of the Concordat which were inconvenient to the Nazis, but Rome also preferred to have a legal document spelling out its rights. Such a document was to be a useful tool for the church, providing it with a legal basis for protest. In fact, so pragmatic was the Concordat that, in 1957, the West German Federal Constitutional Court upheld its validity. This is also true of the Concordat with Mussolini, which still stands today with only minor modifications. The church had to be careful not to protest too loudly or too frequently. Too loud a protest could lose all.

Violations of the Concordat

The Concordat was immediately and frequently broken: The three favorite targets were Catholic labor unions, the Catholic Youth movement, and the Catholic press. One Catholic weekly was appalled: "We are convinced that Hitler represents the incarnation of evil."[34]

One tactic used by the Nazis was to forbid dual membership in a state organization and a church organization. This was used to get rid of Catholic labor unions and the Catholic Youth movement. Even before the Concordat was signed, Cardinal Faulhaber, who would prove to be a heroic opponent of the Nazis, was pressured by the Nazis to ask for the resignation of the head of Catholic Action in Munich, Emil Muhler, who was outspoken against the Nazis. He had spread reports of atrocities at Dachau. In November Muhler was arrested. In August 1933, the Catholic Teachers' Association dissolved itself.

Despite Cardinal Faulhaber's protests, which consisted of a series of three Advent sermons in 1933 in which he was very critical of the Nazi violations of individual rights, the persecution continued. In June 1934, the President of Catholic Action (Erich Klausener) and the President of the Sporting Association of German Catholics (Adalbert Probst), were shot and killed and their bodies, in violation of Catholic teaching at the time, were cremated and the ashes sent to the families. In July 1934, the Austrian Catholic Chancellor (Engelbert Dollfuss) was executed as part of an abortive putsch. Friedrich Beck, a Catholic professor at Munich, was killed "accidentally." Fritz Gerlich, editor of the largest Catholic newspaper in Germany, was found dead in prison. In 1935 the episcopal palaces of Wurzburg, Rottenburg, and Mainz were ransacked. The assault on the church was thorough. The German press attacked the church; priests were imprisoned or exiled, and parents who sent their children to Catholic schools were asked for "explanations." Between 1933 and 1937, parents who sent their children to Catholic schools in Munich fell from 65 percent to 3 percent. Six hundred teaching sisters were told to find civilian employment.

Youth groups did not escape. In 1935 all youth groups, except Hitler Youth, were forbidden to play organized sports, wear uniforms, and march in parades. By the end of 1936, only Hitler Youth was allowed to exist. Often, ordinances against the Catholic Youth movement were accompanied by propaganda associating Catholic Youth with communism and disloyalty. In 1937, one Catholic newspaper in Münster was ordered by the government to print an article describing a secondary schoolboy in Catholic Youth as guilty of sexual offences. Bishop von Galen refused to comply. The newspaper was shut down until it would comply; it did not, and three months later the Gestapo shut it down for good. In 1937 the Catholic Young Men's Association was suppressed in four dioceses. Bishop Von Galen denounced this, saying it was a "perverse and wanton insult to German Catholics." Cardinal Faulhaber protested in 1938 when the same thing happened in Bavaria.

The first assault on the Catholic press began in the 1933 election, after the Reichstag fire. Some Catholic dailies were forbidden to publish. In October 1933 a "Law Concerning Editors" was passed. Editors now had to meet a number of qualifications including being "Aryan." Anything weakening the Reich was to be kept out of the papers. Everything fell under Goebbels' Propaganda Ministry. This effectively destroyed the independence of the Catholic newspapers. In one case, a newspaper had to print articles defending the compulsory sterilization law without including the warnings of the bishops. There were two ways to go for Catholic papers: comply and get along as best they could, or cease publication. But even compliance was not without its problems. In 1935, no paper was allowed to print articles having to do with religion. The Nazis defended this by claiming that, since they now protected the church, the church did not need a press. From 1935 on, there was no daily Catholic press. There had been 400 daily Catholic papers in Germany in 1933!

However, the bishops still had their weeklies, and they fought on longer. Periodicals also survived longer. Between the two, there were 416 such journals, reaching more than 11 million people. In 1935, the weeklies were forbidden to touch on politics. In 1936, the journal of the Catholic Youth Movement was suppressed. Approval of editors came from the Propaganda Ministry, and was often withheld. Only one diocesan paper was allowed per diocese, and between 1938 and 1939 most of these ceased. The few papers that stayed alive paid dearly for their existence, complying fully and willingly with the Nazis. Once the war began, the Catholic press that remained never questioned the war. Catholics were confused by these papers, thinking them the official teaching of the church. In 1941, all Catholic weeklies and journals which remained were ordered shut down (part of this was from a lack of paper). In 1934 there were 435 Catholic periodicals in Germany. By 1943 there were only seven.

Popes and the Nazis

Pius XI's greatest coup was in writing the encyclical *Mit Brennender Sorge* ("With Burning Desire") in 1936, and having it distributed secretly and ingeniously by an army of motorcyclists, and read from every pulpit on Palm Sunday before the Nazis obtained a single copy. It stated (in German and not in the traditional Latin) that the Concordat with the Nazis was agreed to despite serious misgivings about Nazi integrity. It then went on to condemn the persecution of the church, the neopaganism of the Nazi ideology—especially its theory of racial superiority—and Hitler himself, calling him "a mad prophet possessed of repulsive arrogance." But perhaps Pius XI's most memorable protest against anti-Semitism came just before his death, when he told a group of pilgrims in 1938:

> Mark well that in the Catholic Mass, Abraham is our Patriarch and forefather. Anti-Semitism is incompatible with the lofty thought which that fact expresses. It is a movement with which we Christians can have nothing to do. No, no, I say to you it is impossible for a Christian to take part in anti-Semitism. It is inadmissible. Through Christ and in Christ we are the spiritual progeny of Abraham. Spiritually, we are all Semites.[35]

The Nazis promptly called him "the Chief Rabbi of the Christian World."

Pius XII (1939–57)

Eugenio Pacelli was an able diplomat when elected to be pope in 1939 (Pius XI wanted him to be pope).[36] He had been a papal nuncio for thirteen years, mostly in Germany. He was the first Secretary of State to be elected since 1775 and the first Roman to be elected since 1721. Italy and Germany were both opposed to his election due to his opposition to their regimes. Germany was the only major power not to send a representative to his coronation. As a result, a question arose as to whether the Vatican should break diplomatic ties at such a deliberate slight. Pius XII, along with the German bishops, decided that a break would only hinder communications between the pope and the German bishops, and that the Nazis would demand even more concessions if relations were to be restored.

Even before war broke out, the first conflict came in the Sudetenland where almost all of the three million Sudeten Germans were Roman Catholic. Pius XII felt that the annexation was using them. He proposed a peace conference, unsuccessfully, and asked Mussolini to do all he could to restrain Hitler's territorial plans. The Germans kept telling him about their strength, and the Italians had territorial plans of their own. When war finally broke out, his first encyclical, *Summi Pontificatus*, clearly condemned both Germany and Russia for gobbling up countries, but it lacked the force and urgency that had characterized Benedict's and Pius XI's censures. Pius XII seemed to be too intellectual and too general. Encyclicals tend to put forth universal principles and let the local constituencies see to their more immediate application. Still, the encyclical was pointed enough to lead the German leaders to ban its publication.

In 1940, Dr. Josef Muller approached the pope and told him of a coup being planned by German generals to depose Hitler. They wished to make contact with Great Britain in the hopes that Britain would limit its military activities and offer reasonable peace terms after the coup succeeded. This plan, which used the services of several Vatican officials (including the pope's personal secretary, the German Jesuit Robert Leiber), failed because of the German successes in France and because the British were skeptical and refused to discuss anything until Hitler was removed.

When Denmark and Norway were invaded in April 1940 and Belgium, Holland, and Luxembourg in May, the pope responded by sending telegrams of sympathy to their rulers. The Allies regarded these as inadequate and short of a condemnation of aggression. One reason he held back a little in these telegrams is that he wanted to keep Mussolini out of the war, but Mussolini took the message personally and said that the pope had incited "the Catholic King of the Belgians to cause the blood of his people to flow, in order to help the Jews, the Freemasons, and the bankers of the City of London."

If the pope initially hesitated to condemn the Nazis explicitly, part of the reason was that he did not trust the Allied powers to conclude a just peace. Their terms after World War I were a primary cause of the present war. But by May 1940, the pope had lost his confidence that the Allies could win a war, and realized that the Holy See must learn to live in a world dominated by Nazism and Fascism. He asked Britain to consider terms of peace, which it refused to do. When Italy entered the war, the pope said nothing, but some bishops declared that obedience to the state during wartime was a commandment from God. By 1943, however, Italy's taste for war had soured, and more and more Italian priests became disillusioned.

Resistance to the Nazis during the War

Catholic resistance initially took the form of self-defense rather than an ideological opposition to Nazism. It protested against attacks on the church, rather than the Nazi program or the pursuit of the war. Efforts were initially concentrated on defending Catholics, rather than all victims. Catholic resistance, however, was stronger than that of any other institution. The universities, courts, and trade unions (the most powerful in the world) hardly said a word about the direction in which Hitler was taking the nation.

Local Catholic opposition could be strong. In Dachau, there is a bulletin board that gives the statistics on the *Priester-Block* or priests' barracks. Of 2,700 ministers imprisoned there of all faiths, 2,600 were Roman Catholic priests. Two thousand priests were put to death there. Of 10,000 priests in Poland, 3,700 were imprisoned, and 2,700 executed.[37] The Dean of St. Hedwig's Cathedral in Berlin denounced an anti-Semitic pamphlet from the pulpit, and ordered all the churches in his diocese to have it read:

> An inflammatory pamphlet anonymously attacking the Jews is being disseminated among the houses of Berlin. It declares that any German who, because of allegedly false sentimentality, aids the Jews in any way, be it only through a friendly

gesture, is guilty of betraying his people. Do not allow yourselves to be confused by this un-Christian attitude, but act
according to the strict commandment of Jesus Christ: Thou
shalt love thy neighbor as thyself.[38]

That and several other acts (reading prayers aloud for the
Jews, saying, "I have only one Führer, Jesus Christ") were enough
to get him imprisoned. He died in 1943 on his way to Dachau.

Granted, there were some who supported the Nazis: Bishop
Rarkowski called Hitler "the shining example of a true warrior,
the first and most valiant soldier of the Greater German Reich."
In 1940 Cardinal Bertram sent Hitler a letter of congratulations
on his birthday, and there was some talk that the papal nuncio
(Orsenigo) was too accommodating. Possibly the most shameless
document was a pastoral letter issued by the Slovak bishops in
1942. It read:

> The greatest tragedy of the Jewish nation lies in the fact of
> not having recognized the Redeemer and of having prepared
> a terrible and ignominious death for him on the cross....Also
> in our eyes the influence of the Jews has been pernicious. In
> a short time they have taken control of almost all the eco-
> nomic and financial life of the country to the detriment of
> our people. Not only economically, but also in the cultural
> and moral spheres, they have harmed our people. The
> church cannot be opposed, therefore, if the state with legal
> regulations hinders the dangerous influence of the Jews.[39]

These sentiments, fortunately, are the exceptions rather than
the rule. There are genuine heroes all over the place. In fact, as
Clive James points out, the reason that the general population did
not rise against Hitler was because "you had to be a hero to do
so."[40] Among the heroes was Fr. Rupert Mayer, a decorated WWI
veteran, who at first embraced the Nazis in the 1920s, then began
preaching against them despite several periods in prison. His confessional in Munich was decorated with flowers during his
absences. He survived the war by a few months. Further, Fr.
Bernard Lichtenberg, after the burning of the synagogues on
Kristalnacht (1938), began closing his evening services with a

prayer for the Jews. When he protested the deportations, he was put on a train himself—to Dachau.

Bishop von Galen of Münster was probably the most outspoken member of the hierarchy. After the murders of Klausener, Probst, and Dollfuss, he proposed that membership in the party be banned once again. He preached every Sunday against the Nazis, saying on one occasion: "We will do our duty out of love for our German Fatherland. Our soldiers will fight and die for Germany—but not for those men who bring shame upon the German name before God."[41] He frequently condemned the Nazi practices of euthanasia, imprisonment without trial, confiscation of property, and concentration camps. He also used the annual Corpus Christi procession to denounce the Nazis for whole afternoons. Münster was 90 percent Catholic at the time and the whole diocese so revered him that the Nazis were actually afraid to execute him. Goebbels was afraid to lose the whole population in what was a very industrial part of the Reich. A statue of von Galen now stands in the plaza outside his cathedral. He survived the war by a few months.

In Holland Bishop de Jong issued a pastoral letter denouncing the Nazis for their treatment of the Jews. As a result, ninety-two converts were rounded up (including Edith Stein), deported, and murdered. The brutality of the retaliation made an enormous impression on Pius XII.

Roman churches and religious houses provided shelter for some 5,000 Jews (more than half the Jews in Rome) including several dozen in the Vatican itself. A Capuchin friar, Pierre Benoît, took care of 400 Polish Jews who had arrived in Rome in September of 1943, and 500 French Jews. He was given a gold medal by the Italian Jewish Union at the end of the war.

In Assisi, Fr. Rufino Niccacci was ordered by his bishop to help a group of 300 Jewish refugees to escape in 1943, after Italy had gotten out of the war. The running of Italy was now in the hands of the Gestapo. In an interesting twist, the Wehrmacht Commander (Valentin Mueller), who had already informed the bishop about the impending arrival of the Gestapo and that he (Mueller) knew there were hundreds of Jewish refugees living in Assisi, managed to get rid of the SS by claiming he had received an "order" to have Assisi declared an open city—a letter in fact written by one of Niccacci's aides. The Jews were hidden in religious houses in the area, taught Gregorian chant and dressed in Franciscan habits, then sent on day trips to Switzerland. When this ploy was discovered (too late) and Niccacci arrested, he was told by the Commander of the SS that "the Catholic clergy is our enemy; we have shot 3,000 priests in Europe so far."

In Italy 30,000 Jews were saved. The Chief Rabbi of Rome became a Catholic in 1945 and took the name Eugenio, the pope's first name. A former Israeli consul in Italy claimed:

> The Catholic Church saved more Jewish lives during the war than all the other churches, religious institutions, and rescue organizations put together. Its record stands in startling contrast to the achievements of the International Red Cross and the Western Democracies....The Holy See, the Nuncios and the entire Catholic Church, saved some 400,000 Jews from certain death.[42]

Bishop Angelo Roncalli, the nuncio in Turkey but soon to be elected Pope John XXIII, forged baptismal certificates for hundreds of Jewish children and had them sent out of the country.

There will never be a complete record of local Catholic efforts to help the Jews during the Holocaust. Hiding Jews from arrest was punishable by execution and yet was done to a heroic extent by families, schools, and religious houses. Anne Frank's protectors, for example, were Roman Catholic. The teachers at the high school that was the subject of the award-winning film *Au Revoir Les Enfants*, where Jewish schoolboys were hidden from the Nazis, were Benedictine monks.

Conclusion

Pius XII was better able than Benedict XV to have an effect on world war. He was more the diplomat and knew the importance of waiting. Pius was more independent from the government of Italy. He had more nuncios and delegates throughout the world. He could play a role as mediator only if he maintained strict neutrality. There is even new evidence that the Japanese made peace overtures through him, because he was the only one in the west trusted by the emperor Tojo to conclude a just peace.

There are several questions surrounding the influence of Pope Pius XII. A lot of ink has been spilled since the mid-1960s and the appearance of the play *The Deputy*, about whether Pius XII knew more and could have done more to stop Nazi atrocities against the Jews. The answer to this is not simple and demands an understanding of how the Catholic Church works. Three things have to be kept in mind:

1. The Catholic Church is not the monolithic, politically controlling device that some in the media assume it is. Catholics do not think alike and politicians, certainly American politicians, make the mistake of thinking there is a "Catholic vote." There is no such thing. There may be an immigrant vote, or an ethnic (i.e., Italian or Irish) vote, but people do not think politically as Catholics. Had the pope told the German people to oppose Hitler, they would probably not have. It was simply too dangerous.

2. The Catholic Church cannot enforce policy. The pope has often said that a particular position is policy—on birth control, for example—or local conferences of bishops have said that this is policy—on capital punishment, for example—and many Catholics have said that this is not something they agree with. The German bishops realized that a policy forbidding membership in the Nazi party in 1933 would be largely ignored, and so did not insist on it.

3. Resistance to the Nazis was very risky. Pius XII had learned from the de Jong affair that encyclicals only put people in peril. He suspected that his verbal protests would have no influence on the offending powers, but would only endanger Catholics more. Hitler's lust for revenge went far beyond the Jews. He killed all the gypsies and homosexuals he could find. He let 2.5 million Russian POWs perish (mostly by deprivation). As a Dominican priest who was a seminarian at the time in Cologne told me, "We had the distinct feeling that we [i.e., Catholics] were next." As Clive James states, "Sooner or later, [Hitler] would have got around to everybody."[43]

Part of the criticism of Pius XII is that he seemed to be very explicit about some things, such as the bombing of the San Lorenzo neighborhood of Rome, and virtually silent on others, such as the deportation of 1,000 Jews from Rome. Yet new evidence reveals that he acted swiftly and strongly when he heard of the deportation, warning the German commander privately (through his Secretary of State) that any further deportations would force him to go public, no matter what the consequences were for him or the Vatican. There were no more deportations.

Pius XII may have made errors of judgment, but he did not do so because he was anti-Semitic or because he liked Nazis. He chose to condemn or affirm things in general and allow local hierarchies to do what they could. Should he have justified his conscience in the eyes of the world, or thought about saving those Jews he could save? The ones who were saved were very glad he thought about them and not about posterity.

Post–World War II Catholicism

After World War II the church found itself faced with different challenges and opportunities. Dictatorships in the Soviet Union and China cost the church dearly. In the Soviet Union, Josef Stalin forced the Orthodox Church into increasingly humiliating compromises (government censorship of sermons, literature, even music, and control over buildings and building materials) in order to maintain its existence. In the Ukraine the Uniate church (in communion with Rome) did not cooperate and suffered terrible losses as a result. Roman Catholics throughout the Soviet Union saw their churches desecrated, seminaries and Catholic schools closed, and the practice of the faith generally driven underground.[44]

Promising missionary efforts in China came to a standstill in 1949 as the communist Mao Tse-tung assumed power and missionaries were imprisoned, deported, or executed. A schismatic Chinese Catholic Church was substituted, controlled totally by the government. In Vietnam communist revolts in the north forced Catholics first to the south and then, as the Vietnam War spread south, large numbers of Catholic Vietnamese fled to Canada and the United States.[45]

But missionary efforts in other parts of the world met with more success. Africa and the Indian subcontinent saw great gains for the church, shown by the building of schools, hospitals, and clinics, and the spread of parish churches, monasteries, and chaplaincies. Vocations have increased dramatically in these areas.

In the 1950s attention was given to restoring the liturgy, especially the Holy Week liturgies, to their more ancient forms. Research had uncovered several ancient documents in the late 1800s that justified a considerable reform. The Easter Vigil was restored to its proper place in the evening prior to Easter Sunday.[46] Vocations rose in Western Europe and North America, fueled by the returning soldiers and their heightened sense of religious values.

The Second Vatican Council

Without question, the greatest ecclesiastical event of the postwar period was the Second Vatican Council (1962–65). The First Vatican Council had ended chaotically in 1870 and left much business unfinished. As time went on and two world wars intervened, a continuation of the council seemed more and more remote. And, in fact, the Second Vatican Council was a different animal altogether from its predecessor.

Pope John XXIII had been elected in October 1958 at the age of seventy-seven. Less than ninety days later he announced to a small group of seventeen cardinals, gathered in the church of St. Paul's Outside the Walls in Rome, that he had decided to convoke a general council for the universal church. The reaction was not encouraging. Of the cardinals who were asked to respond to the pope's invitation, only twenty-five responded by April, ten of whom responded in a purely formal manner. Thirty-eight did not respond at all. Cardinal Spellman of New York said that any such council was "destined for certain failure."[47] Spellman did not like the new pope to begin with, and on his election was heard to say, "He's no pope; he should be selling bananas." Cardinal Montini, who would be elected to be the next pope, said the proposed

The Second Vatican Council (1962–1965), the great ecumenical council called by Pope John XXIII and continued by Pope Paul VI, brought about wide-reaching reforms in virtually every area of church life, including liturgy, religious freedom, and conceptions of how the church is constituted both in itself and in relation to the rest of the world.

council would "open up a hornet's nest."[48] The Italian bishops waited to hear from the pope before they acted.

But several conferences of bishops (West Germany, Canada, and Poland) made suggestions and set up preconciliar committees. A board of the Catholic Conference for Ecumenical Affairs wrote a "note" that both warned against making new dogmatic definitions, especially about the Blessed Mother, and suggested a recognition of biblical and patristic theologies, as well as an emphasis on baptism and *communio*. The Orthodox Churches were interested in a council as a means to reunion with Rome, while Protestant Churches were both excited about the possibilities of dialogue with Rome, but nervous that a) any Orthodox-Catholic negotiation would relegate Protestants to a secondary place and b) the Romans would dominate ecumenical work in the future.

For many months it was uncertain what John XXIII had in mind. Previous councils had addressed contemporary errors or schisms and had pronounced on faith and morals. But he did not seem to have this in mind. His talk of "opening windows" made the curia nervous. They either hoped that the idea of a council would go away, or took steps to minimize the "damage" such a council could bring.

Preparations for the council took longer than the council itself. During a preparatory phase, opinions were elicited from bishops and theologians all over the world, and planning commissions were established. Then another preparatory phase saw the drawing up of schemata to be proposed to the assembly. Ninety percent of these schemata were never considered by the Council. Confusion surfaced in these preparatory phases because of John XXIII's vagueness about the goals of a council. The curial heads of Vatican congregations led the various preparatory commissions and tried to control the direction of the Council, the kind of maneuvering which proved to be highly unpopular with the bishops. When the Council finally convened on 11 October 1962, one of the first things the assembled bishops did was to elect their own commission members to take the place of the curial officials. This signaled a serious difference between the bishops and the curia. The first session ended on 8 December.

In June 1963 John XXIII died and was replaced by Paul VI, who pledged to continue the Council. The second session ran from late September to early December 1963. During this session, the collegiality of bishops was emphasized, a permanent diaconate instated, and the *Constitution on the Sacred Liturgy* passed. The third session (September–November 1964) saw the passing of the *Constitution on the Church*, as well as *Decree on Ecumenism* and *Decree on the Eastern Churches*.[49] Paul VI concluded this session by going against the Council's wishes and declaring Mary the "Mother of the Church." The fourth and final session (September–December 1965) saw the passing of *Decrees on Priestly Formation, Non-Christian Religions*, the *Apostolate of the Laity*, the *Church in the Modern World*, and the *Declaration on Religious Freedom*. Paul VI also called for a synod of bishops to follow the Council. Postconciliar commissions were set up to implement decisions made by the Council. Thus a new missal (divided into *Sacramentary* and *Lectionary*) and a new breviary were produced in 1970 and 1971, respectively. These would be translated from the Latin into vernacular languages quickly and not always accurately.

Liturgical battles were common during the late 1960s and 1970s. Because of the vagueness of the Council, and even of some of its decisions, theologians ran with things a little further than the council fathers would have liked. Experimentation in liturgy, much of it carried out with little catechesis and no supervision from bishops, caused serious divisions among laity and clergy alike. At times, the outrageous became commonplace as when priests wore vestments imprinted with a photo of Woodstock Nation, or said Mass, as in one case occurring at a major U.S. seminary, on Halloween, dressed as a nun. One priest in Virginia drove down the center aisle of his church in a Volkswagen on Palm Sunday and declared that, if Christ had come to Jerusalem today, this is how it would be done.

Some of the liturgical changes brought about in the aftermath of Vatican II emphasized the meal or communitarian nature of the Mass. Wooden tables substituted, in many places, for altars; the priest now faced the congregation, and people stood instead of knelt to receive the Blessed Sacrament. Oftentimes, people gathered around the altar for the celebration of Mass, and "home Masses" became popular. Church architecture stressed the Mass or community at the expense of the reserved sacrament, which was relegated to a side altar or a separate room. Liturgical music stressed communal singing. The English-speaking Catholic world was fortunate to have a rich tradition of Anglican and Lutheran hymns on which to draw, but other countries (Italy among them) still have a long way to go before establishing a tradition of sacred song in the vernacular. As the church went into the last decade of the twentieth century, many of these liturgical conflicts settled down. Church architecture became more traditional. The American bishops issued a document reining in some of the more irresponsible experiments and demanded that the tabernacle be visible upon entrance into the church.

Vocations to the priesthood and religious life declined after Vatican II. Various reasons have been proposed. Among the internal reasons are the rigidity of church structures, the insistence on celibacy, the denial of ordination to women; among the external reasons could be cited the trend of society away from lifelong commitment, increasing secularization, an emphasis on material advancement, feminism, etc. Those religious orders hardest hit were men's orders founded in the nineteenth century with a mission focus, and large teaching orders of women, which had been the backbone of Catholic education. Religious clothing and community life were discarded in favor of "professionalism," but with that came a loss of identity and purpose.

On the other hand, lay activity increased or adapted to new challenges. While Holy Name Societies and Altar and Rosary Societies, so vital to parish life in the pre–Vatican II years, waned, other groups emerged, such as Cursillo, the charismatic movement, Marriage Encounter, and Opus Dei to take their place.

John Paul II and Beyond

There is no question that the last pope of the twentieth century and the first of the twenty-first has had a huge impact on the church. He produced three revolutions: in the communist world, in his program of canonization, and in his travels.

In the communist world, his ties to the labor union, Solidarity, and his immense influence on the east definitely helped to topple the communist empire. There is a history yet to be written about his special relationship with President Ronald Reagan in this endeavor.

He also brought about a revolution over how saints are canonized, not only streamlining the saint-making process, but introducing a new category of saints (martyrs for charity), and updating the list of saints, making them more relevant. Between 1234 and 1983, fewer than 300 saints had been canonized. In 1988 alone, John Paul canonized 124, 114 of whom were the Martyrs of Vietnam. By October 2002, he had canonized 464 saints, and would beatify Mother Teresa of Calcutta a year later.

His traveling and connecting with different parts of the world is unprecedented among popes. The immense gatherings of the Catholic faithful everywhere he has gone—with special mention of his Mass on the Mall in Washington D.C., his trips to the Philippines and Mexico, which drew crowds the size of which no one in history has been able to bring together, and his final trip to Poland, not to mention his particular attention to World Youth Days and the outpouring of support shown on all his visits—will no doubt endear him in the memory of the world for years, if not centuries, to come. This was an extraordinary pope and one recognized by the unprecedented international outpouring of feeling at his funeral in April 2005. His successor, Joseph Ratzinger, took the name Benedict XVI, undoubtedly as a tribute to the little-known but highly effective Benedict XV (1914–1922), who was known as the "Pope of the Missions." He inherits a Church that is truly worldwide, facing new challenges with the confidence of its durability through the ages.

The End of the Sixth Age

If Christopher Dawson's theory of Six Ages of the Church is correct, two conclusions might be drawn. One is that we do not know when, exactly, this Sixth Age is going to end. Past experience would suggest that we have another hundred years to go.

The second conclusion is that, no matter when or how it ends, the church will somehow survive and develop. Horace Walpole, in 1769, wanted to go to Rome to witness, as he wrote to a friend, "the election of the last pope." In looking over the ups and downs of the church from its beginning, one thing should be very clear: The church will emerge active and challenging to a new world. We could not do better than cite the twentieth-century English writer, G. K. Chesterton, who noted that, in all the centuries of the church's life, and all of the predictions that the church was going to the dogs, "it was always the dog that died."

Recommended Readings

(B) Ray Allen Billington, *The Protestant Crusade*, 1800–1860 (New York, 1938). An account of anti-Catholicism in the USA from its founding to the Civil War.

(B) Owen Chadwick, *Catholicism and History: The Opening of the Vatican Archives* (New York, 1978). A delightful short book, which reads like a detective novel.

(A) Walter Ciszek, *With God in Russia* (New York, 1964). A riveting account of what life was like under Stalin for this heroic Jesuit priest and his fellow Christians.

(B) Cyprian Davis, *The History of Black Catholics in the United States* (New York, 1990). The best account of the Catholic African-American experience in the United States.

(B) John Tracy Ellis, *American Catholicism* (Chicago, 1969) and *Catholics in Colonial America* (Baltimore, 1965). Both written by the dean of American Catholic history.

(C) Peter Gay, *The Enlightenment* (New York, 1966–69). A masterful and sympathetic account of the Enlightenment.

(B) James Hennessy, *American Catholics* (New York, 1981). An updating of Ellis's *American Catholicism*.

(B) Derek Holmes, *More Roman than Rome* (London, 1978), *The Triumph of the Holy See* (London, 1978), and *The Papacy in the Modern World* (New York, 1981). A readable trilogy, unfortunately marred by printers' errors. The first two books are about the

Catholic Church in England in the 1800s, and the last about the European scene of the first half of the twentieth century.

(B) Clive James, "Blaming the Germans," *New Yorker* (April 22, 1996), pp. 44–50.

(B) Philip Jenkins, *The New Anti-Catholicism: The Last Acceptable Prejudice* (New York, 2003). This is a thorough documentation of anti-Catholicism as it is currently practiced in the United States.

(B) John McManners, *The French Revolution and the Church* (London, 1969). A masterful short summary.

(B) George Weigel, *Witness to Hope: The Biography of Pope John Paul II* (New York, 1999). By far the most thorough biography of John Paul II to date.

AUDIO-VISUALS:

The Assisi Connection, a feature-length movie about the efforts of the Franciscans to smuggle Jewish refugees to Switzerland in World War II.

Au Revoir Les Enfants, an award-winning film about a French Catholic high school and Catholic religious order that sheltered Jewish children during World War II. The director was a student at the high school at the time.

Inside the Vatican, National Geographic, 1999. Narrated by Martin Sheen, this is one of the most interesting specials ever done on the workings of the Vatican.

A Man Named John, a one-hour account about Pope John XXIII (when he was the papal legate to Bulgaria) and how he managed to smuggle several hundred Jewish children out of the country. Starring Raymond Burr.

The Red and the Black, a feature-length movie about the efforts of an Irish priest in the Vatican to help downed Allied airmen to safety. Starring Gregory Peck, Christopher Plummer, and John Gielgud.

Saving Grace, a documentary about the survival of Christianity under the Communists in Czechoslovakia, made by independent film-maker Ken Gumbert, OP, and available through him at Providence College, Providence RI 02918.

Notes

1. Dawson, *Progress and Religion*, p. 154.

2. See Joseph Ellis's superb *Founding Brothers: The Revolutionary Generation* (New York, 2000) for a discussion of the dilemma American Rationalists found themselves in over the slavery issue.

3. John McManners, *The French Revolution and the Church* (London, 1969), p. 13.

4. Simon Schama, *Citizens: A Chronicle of the French Revolution* (New York, 1989), pp. 349–50.

5. McManners, p 33.

6. Schama, *Citizens*, p. 541. The italics are Schama's. As thorough as his monumental book is, Schama gives surprisingly little space to the CCC and its implications.

7. Adrien Dansette, *Religious History of Modern France* (Freiburg, 1961) I, pp. 74–75.

8. Schama, *Citizens*, pp. 447, 859.

9. Talleyrand, the founder of the Constitutional Church, was a defrocked bishop who had taken the oath and married. He is one of history's great survivors.

10. Popes would not leave Italy again until Paul VI in the 1960s!

11. Lacordaire helped to restore the Dominican Order in France.

12. The English bishops were not exactly favorable to the Jesuits, either, and did not allow them to return to England until 1829.

13. Even as late as Vatican Council II, in the early 1960s, the curia did not have a press desk or a press secretary to answer the media's questions. The Americans finally set one up themselves, staffed by *periti* (experts).

14. Ray Allen Billington, *The Protestant Crusade, 1800–1860* (New York, 1938), p. 8.

15. Billington, p. 30.

16. He was also the last surviving signer.

17. See James Hennesey, *American Catholics* (New York, 1981), for an excellent summary of Catholic involvement in the Revolution.

18. Anglicans faced a dilemma in the American Revolution since the head of their church was the king of England. They opted for a new form of ecclesiastical government run by the bishops of the USA, hence the names "Episcopal" and "Episcopalian."

19. As late as 1985, the newly appointed head of the New York Public Library, the former President of Georgetown University and a Jesuit, was asked by the *New York Times* what he would do if the pope ordered him to do something detrimental to the New York Public Library.

20. Peter Steinfels, "Abused by the Media," the London *Tablet*, 14 September 2002, pp. 9–11.

21. See Philip Jenkins, *The New Anti-Catholicism: The Last Acceptable Prejudice* (New York, 2003).

22. Real Marxists, in fact, do not seek the betterment of workers' rights and working conditions because such improvements will only delay the Revolution.

23. Marx, who was living in London when he wrote the *Communist Manifesto*, thought that the Revolution would begin in industrialized Britain, instead of Russia.

24. The Center Party was revived after the Second World War to become the Christian Democratic Party led by Konrad Adenauer (1949–63).

25. In Derek Holmes, *The Papacy in the Modern World, 1914–1978* (New York, 1981), p. 22.

26. In Holmes, *Papacy in the Modern World*, pp. 23–24.

27. See Walter Ciszek's *With God in Russia* (New York, 1964).

28. Guenter Lewy, *The Catholic Church and Nazi Germany* (New York, 1965), p.16.

29. Lewy, p.47.

30. Ibid., p. 26.

31. Holmes, *Papacy in the Modern World*, p. 102.

32. Lewy, 104–105.

33. Ibid., 107.

34. Lewy, p. 21.

35. In Holmes, *Papacy in the Modern World*, p. 116.

36. Pius XII was elected on the third ballot of the 1st day of the conclave (1939) and crowned in the Lateran on 2 March.

37. Also in Poland, 1,200 nuns were imprisoned, 3,800 displaced, 350 executed.

38. In Holmes, *Papacy in the Modern World*, pp. 143–145.

39. In Jonathan Lewis, "Pius XII and the Jews: The Myths and the Facts," *The Tablet* (25 February 1995), pp. 251–252. The pope protested directly to the government about the expulsion of the Slovak Jews (see Holmes, *Papacy in the Modern World*, pp. 159–160).

40. Clive James, "Blaming the Germans," *New Yorker* (April 22, 1996), p. 48.

41. In Lewy, p. 311.

42. Holmes, p. 158.

43. Clive James, p. 50.

44. See Walter Ciszek's classic *With God in Russia* and Boris Gudziak's *Crisis and Reform*.

45. See Dr. Tom Dooley's three great books: *Deliver Us from Evil, The Edge of Tomorrow*, and *The Night They Burned the Mountain* (New York, 1960), and his autobiography, *Doctor Tom Dooley: My Story* (New York, 1962).

46. See Josef Jungmann's *The Early Liturgy* (Notre Dame, 1959).

47. Joseph Komonchak, English ed., *History of Vatican II* (Maryknoll, 1995), p. 19.

48. Ibid.

49. *Constitutions* (either Pastoral or Dogmatic) are addressed to the entire church and are the most formal and solemn of conciliar statements. *Decrees* are directed to specific groups (e.g., bishops), and *Declarations* are nondefinitive statements of the position of the church on specific issues of the time.

CHRONOLOGICAL LIST
OF THE POPES

Peter	d. 64
Linus	66–78
Anacletus	79–91
Clement	91–101
Evaristus	101–109
Alexander I	109–116
Sixtus I	116–125
Telesphorus	125–136
Hyginus	138–142
Pius I	142–155
Anicetus	155–166
Soter	166–174
Eleutherius	174–189
Victor I	189–198
Zephyrinus	198–217
Callistus I	217–222
Urban I	222–230
Pontian	230–235
Anterus	235–236
Fabian	236–250
Cornelius	251–253
Lucius I	253–254
Stephen I	254–257
Sixtus II	257–258
Dionysius	260–268
Felix I	269–274
Eutychian	275–283
Gaius	283–296
Marcellinus	296–304
Marcellus	306–308
Eusebius	310
Miltiades	311–314
Silvester I	314–335

Mark	336
Julius I	337–352
Liberius	352–366
Damasus I	366–384
Siricius	384–399
Anastasius I	399–401
Innocent I	401–417
Zosimus	417–418
Boniface I	418–422
Celestine I	422–432
Sixtus III	432–440
Leo I ("the Great")	440–461
Hilarus	461–468
Simplicius	468–483
Felix II	483–492
Gelasius I	492–496
Anastasius II	496–498
Symmachus	498–514
Hormisdas	514–523
John I	523–526
Felix III	526–530
Boniface II	530–532
John II	533–535
Agapitus	535–536
Silverius	536–537
Vigilius	537–555
Pelagius I	556–561
John III	561–574
Benedict I	575–579
Pelagius II	579–590
Gregory I ("the Great")	590–604
Sabinian	604–606
Boniface III	607
Boniface IV	608–615
Adeodatus I	615–618
Boniface V	619–625
Honorius I	625–638
Severinus	640
John IV	640–642
Theodore I	642–649
Martin I	649–653

Eugene I	654–657
Vitalian	657–672
Adeodatus II	672–676
Donus	676–678
Agatho	678–681
Leo II	682–683
Benedict II	684–685
John V	685–686
Conon	686–687
Sergius I	687–701
John VI	701–705
John VII	705–707
Sissinius	708
Constantine	708–715
Gregory II	715–731
Gregory III	731–741
Zacharias	741–752
Stephen II	752–757
Paul I	757–767
Stephen III	768–772
Hadrian I	772–795
Leo III	795–816
Stephen IV	816–817
Paschal I	817–824
Eugene II	824–827
Valentine	827
Gregory IV	827–844
Sergius II	844–847
Leo IV	847–855
Benedict III	855–858
Nicholas I	858–867
Hadrian II	867–872
John VIII	872–882
Marinus I	882–884
Hadrian III	884–885
Stephen V	885–891
Formosus	891–896
Boniface VI	896
Stephen VI	896–897
Romanus	897
Theodore II	897

John IX	898–900
Benedict IV	900–903
Leo V	903–904
Sergius III	904–911
Anastasius III	911–913
Lando	913–914
John X	914–928
Leo VI	928
Stephen VII	928–931
John XI	931–935
Leo VII	936–939
Stephen VIII	939–942
Marinus II	942–946
Agapitus II	946–955
John XII	955–964
Leo VIII	963–965
Benedict V	964
John XIII	965–972
Benedict VI	973–974
Boniface VII	974–983
John XIV	983–984
John XV	985–996
Gregory V	996–999
Silvester II	999–1003
John XVII	1003
John XVIII	1003–1009
Sergius IV	1009–1012
Benedict VIII	1012–1024
John XIX	1024–1032
Benedict IX	1032–1044, 1045, 1047–1048
Silvester III	1045
Gregory VI	1045–1046
Clement II	1046–1047
Damasus II	1048
Leo IX	1049–1054
Victor II	1055–1057
Stephen IX	1057–1058
Nicholas II	1058–1061
Alexander II	1061–1073
Gregory VII	1073–1085
Victor III	1086–1087

Urban II	1088–1099
Paschal II	1099–1118
Gelasius II	1118–1119
Callistus II	1119–1124
Honorius II	1124–1130
Innocent II	1130–1143
Celestine II	1143–1144
Lucius II	1144–1145
Eugene III	1145–1153
Anastasius IV	1153–1154
Hadrian IV	1154–1159
Alexander III	1159–1181
Lucius III	1181–1185
Urban III	1185–1187
Gregory VIII	1187
Clement III	1187–1191
Celestine III	1191–1198
Innocent III	1198–1216
Honorius III	1216–1227
Gregory IX	1227–1241
Celestine IV	1241
Innocent IV	1243–1254
Alexander IV	1254–1261
Urban IV	1261–1264
Clement IV	1265–1268
Gregory X	1271–1276
Innocent V	1276
Hadrian V	1276
John XXI	1276–1277
Nicholas III	1277–1280
Martin IV	1281–1285
Honorius IV	1285–1287
Nicholas IV	1288–1292
Celestine V	1294
Boniface VIII	1294–1303
Benedict XI	1303–1304
Clement V	1305–1314
John XXII	1316–1334
Benedict XII	1334–1342
Clement VI	1342–1352
Innocent VI	1352–1362

Urban V	1362–1370
Gregory XI	1370–1378
Urban VI	1378–1389
Boniface IX	1389–1404
Innocent VII	1404–1406
Gregory XII	1406–1415
Martin V	1417–1431
Eugene IV	1431–1447
Nicholas V	1447–1455
Callistus III	1455–1458
Pius II	1458–1464
Paul II	1464–1471
Sixtus IV	1471–1484
Innocent VIII	1484–1492
Alexander VI	1492–1503
Pius III	1503
Julius II	1503–1513
Leo X	1513–1521
Hadrian VI	1522–1523
Clement VII	1523–1534
Paul III	1534–1549
Julius III	1550–1555
Marcellus II	1555
Paul IV	1555–1559
Pius IV	1559–1565
Pius V	1566–1572
Gregory XIII	1572–1585
Sixtus V	1585–1590
Urban VII	1590
Gregory XIV	1590–1591
Innocent IX	1591
Clement VIII	1592–1605
Leo XI	1605
Paul V	1605–1621
Gregory XV	1621–1623
Urban VIII	1623–1644
Innocent X	1644–1655
Alexander VII	1655–1667
Clement IX	1667–1669
Clement X	1670–1676
Innocent XI	1676–1689

Alexander VIII	1689–1691
Innocent XII	1691–1700
Clement XI	1700–1721
Innocent XIII	1721–1724
Benedict XIII	1724–1730
Clement XII	1730–1740
Benedict XIV	1740–1758
Clement XIII	1758–1769
Clement XIV	1769–1774
Pius VI	1775–1799
Pius VII	1800–1823
Leo XII	1823–1829
Pius VIII	1829–1830
Gregory XVI	1831–1846
Pius IX	1846–1878
Leo XIII	1878–1903
Pius X	1903–1914
Benedict XV	1914–1922
Pius XI	1922–1939
Pius XII	1939–1958
John XXIII	1958–1963
Paul VI	1963–1978
John Paul I	1978
John Paul II	1978–2005
Benedict XVI	2005–present

A SELECT BIBLIOGRAPHY

Reference Works

You should have the starred books at home!

Butler's Lives of the Saints, 4 vols. New York, 1956. This four-volume work is still wonderful to read.

The New Catholic Encyclopedia. New York, 1967. This widely respected work should be the starting-point for any question you might have about theology, church history, liturgy, or biography.

* *Oxford Dictionary of the Christian Church*, ed. F. L. Cross and E. A. Livingstone. New York, 1974. A one-volume reference, with a heavy emphasis on Anglicanism, but superbly written.

* *Oxford Dictionary of the Popes*, ed. J. N. D. Kelly. New York, 1986. Every pope is in here, including the legendary Pope Joan!

* *Oxford Dictionary of the Saints*, ed. David Farmer. New York, 1987. A superb resource.

* *The Religions of Man* by Huston Smith. Probably the best one-volume summary of the religions of the world.

Books and Articles

Ackroyd, Peter. *The Life of Sir Thomas More*. New York, 1998.

Augustine of Hippo. *The Confessions of Saint Augustine*. Nashville, 1983.

Barraclough, Geoffrey. *The Medieval Papacy*. New York, 1968.

Bellitto, Christopher. *The General Councils*. Mahwah, NJ, 2002.

Benson, Robert Hugh. *By What Authority*. New York, 1910.

———. *Come Rack! Come Rope!* New York, 1913.

———. *The King's Achievement*. London, 1904.

———. *The Queen's Tragedy*. London, 1906.

Billington, Ray Allen. *The Protestant Crusade, 1800–1860*. New York, 1938.

Brown, Peter. *Augustine of Hippo*. Los Angeles, 1967.

———. *The Cult of the Saints*. Chicago, 1982.

Brown, Raymond. *The Birth of the Messiah*. Garden City, 1977.

———. "Hermeneutics," in *Jerome Biblical Commentary*. Englewood Cliffs, 1968.

353

Butterfield, Herbert. *Christianity and European Civilization*. London, 1951.

Cameron, Euan. *The European Reformation*. New York, 1991.

Chadwick, Henry. *Early Christian Thought and the Classical Tradition*. London, 1966.

———. *The Early Church*. Grand Rapids, 1968.

Chadwick, Owen. *Britain and the Vatican during the Second World War*. New York, 1986.

———. *Catholicism and History: the Opening of the Vatican Archives*. New York, 1978.

———. *The Popes and European Revolution*. Oxford, 1981.

———. *The Reformation*. Baltimore, 1968.

———. *The Victorian Church* (2 vols.). New York, 1966–70.

Chautard, Jean Baptiste. *The Soul of the Apostolate*. Garden City, 1961.

Chenu, Henri. *An Introduction to the Summa*.

Chesterton, G. K. *Orthodoxy*. New York, 1909.

———. *Saint Francis of Assisi*. New York, 1924.

———. *Saint Thomas Aquinas*. New York, 1933.

Ciszek, Walter. *With God in Russia*. New York, 1964.

Clark, Kenneth. *Civilisation*. New York, 1970.

Congar, Yves. *After Nine Hundred Years*. New York, 1959.

Dalrymple, William. *From the Holy Mountain*. New York, 1996.

Daniel-Rops, Henri. *Cathedral and Crusade*. London, 1957.

———. *The Church in the Dark Ages*. New York, 1959.

Danielou, Jean. *The Bible and the Liturgy*. Notre Dame, 1956.

———, *Primitive Christian Symbols*. London, 1964.

Dansette, Adrian. *Religious History of Modern France*. Freiburg, 1961.

Davis, Cyprian. *The History of Black Catholics in the United States*. New York, 1990.

Dawson, Christopher. *The Dividing of Christendom*. New York, 1965.

———. *The Formation of Christendom*. New York, 1967.

———. *The Making of Europe*. New York, 1945.

———. *Medieval Essays*. Garden City, 1959.

———. *Progress and Religion*. New York, 1938.

Dickens, A. G. *The English Reformation*. University Park, PA, 1991.

———. *Reformation and Society in Sixteenth Century Europe*. London, 1966.

Duffy, Eamon. *The Stripping of the Altars*. New Haven, 1992.

———. *The Voices of Morebath: Reformation and Rebellion in an English Village*. New Haven, 2001.

Ellis, John Tracy. *American Catholicism*. Chicago, 1969.

————. *Catholics in Colonial America*. Baltimore, 1965.

Ellis, Joseph. *Founding Brothers: The Revolutionary Generation*. New York, 2000.

Fraser, Antonia. *Faith and Treason*. New York, 1996.

————. *Mary Queen of Scots*. New York, 1969.

Gasquet, Aidan. *Henry VIII and the Dissolution of the English Monasteries*. London, 1888–89.

Gay, Peter. *The Enlightenment*. New York, 1966–69.

Granfield, Patrick. *The Limits of the Papacy*. New York, 1987.

Grundmann, Herbert. *Religious Movements in the Middle Ages*. Notre Dame, 1995.

Hennessy, James. *American Catholics*. New York, 1981.

Holmes, Derek. *More Roman than Rome*. London, 1978.

————. *The Papacy in the Modern World, 1914–1978*. New York, 1981.

————. *The Triumph of the Holy See*. London, 1978.

Huizinga, Johan. *Erasmus and the Age of Reformation*. New York, 1957.

Janson, H. W., ed. *History of Art*. New York, 1995.

Jarrett, Bede. *The Life of St. Dominic*. London, 1934.

Jedin, Herbert and John Dolan, eds. *History of the Church*. New York, 1980–81.

Jenkins, Philip. *The New Anti-Catholicism: The Last Acceptable Prejudice*. New York, 2003.

Johnson, Paul. *A History of Christianity*. New York, 1976.

Jones, Edwin. *The English Nation: The Great Myth*. Thrupp, England, 1998.

Jungmann, Josef. *Christian Prayer through the Centuries*. New York, 1978.

————. *The Early Liturgy*. Notre Dame, 1959.

Jurgens, William. *The Faith of the Early Fathers*. Collegeville, 1970.

Kamen, Henry. *The Spanish Inquisition: a Historical Revision*. New Haven, 1998.

Kelly, J. N. D. *Early Christian Doctrines*. New York, 1960.

Kirby, Dianne, ed. *Religion and the Cold War*. New York, 2003.

Knowles, David. *Christian Monasticism*. New York, 1972.

————. *The Religious Orders in England*, 3 vol. Cambridge, 1948–59.

Komonchak, Joseph, ed. *History of Vatican II*. Maryknoll, 1995.

Lewis, C. S. *Miracles*. New York, 1947.

Lewy, Guenter. *The Catholic Church and Nazi Germany*. New York, 1965.

MacCulloch, Diarmaid. *The Reformation: A History*. Oxford, 2004.

————. *Thomas Cranmer: a Life*. New Haven, 1996.

McManners, John. *The French Revolution and the Church*. London, 1969.

Madden, Thomas. *A Concise History of the Crusades*. New York, 1999.

Mallett, Michael. *The Borgias.* Chicago, 1987.

Maritain, Jacques. *Three Reformers.* London, 1928.

Meeks, Wayne. *The First Urban Christians.* New Haven, 1983.

Morrill, John. *Oliver Cromwell and the English Revolution.* New York, 1990.

Neill, Stephen. *A History of Christian Missions.* New York, 1986.

O'Brien, John. *The Inquisition.* New York, 1973.

Oldenbourg, Zoë. *The Crusades.* New York, 1966.

Pastor, Ludwig von. *The History of the Popes from the Close of the Middle Ages.* St. Louis, 1898.

Pelikan, Jaroslav. *The Spirit of Eastern Christendom.* Chicago, 1974.

Peters, Edward. *Inquisition.* New York, 1988.

Rahner, Hugo. *Greek Myths and Christian Mystery.* New York, 1963.

Ramsey, Boniface. *Beginning to Read the Fathers.* Mahwah, NJ, 1985.

Runciman, Steven. *A History of the Crusades.* 3 vol. New York, 1966–68.

Sayers, Dorothy. *The Man Born to be King.* Grand Rapids, 1943.

Scarisbrick, J. J. *Henry VIII.* Berkeley, 1968.

———. *The Reformation and the English People.* Oxford, 1984.

Schama, Simon. *Citizens.* New York, 1989.

Shanley, Brian. *The Thomist Tradition.* Boston, 2002.

Sienkiewicz, Henryk. *Quo Vadis.* New York, 1960.

Tuchmann, Barbara. *A Distant Mirror: the Calamitous 14th Century.* New York, 1978.

Waddell, Helen. *The Desert Fathers.* London, 1936.

Waugh, Evelyn. *Edmund Campion.* London, 1935.

Weigel, George. *Witness to Hope: The Biography of Pope John Paul II.* New York, 1999.

Woodward, Kenneth. *Making Saints.* New York, 1990.

INDEX